U0603227

英语教师专业
素养发展丛书

语篇分析
与阅读教学

Discourse Analysis and
the Teaching of Reading

曲卫国⊙著

上海教育出版社
SHANGHAI EDUCATIONAL
PUBLISHING HOUSE

图书在版编目（CIP）数据

语篇分析与阅读教学 / 曲卫国著 . -- 上海：上海教育出版社，2025. 4. -- ISBN 978-7-5720-3453-4

Ⅰ . G633.412

中国国家版本馆 CIP 数据核字第 2025AY1532 号

策划编辑　黄　艳
责任编辑　姚玉莹
封面设计　静斓工作室

语篇分析与阅读教学

曲卫国　著

出版发行　上海教育出版社
官　　网　www.seph.com.cn
地　　址　上海市闵行区号景路 159 弄 C 座
邮　　编　201101
印　　刷　上海展强印刷有限公司
开　　本　700×1000　1/16　印张　20.5
字　　数　226 千字
版　　次　2025 年 4 月第 1 版
印　　次　2025 年 4 月第 1 次印刷
书　　号　ISBN 978-7-5720-3453-4/G・3086
定　　价　78.80 元

如发现质量问题，读者可向本社调换。　　电话：021-64373213

序

当我们在谈论语篇分析时，我们在说什么？当我们在进行阅读教学时，语篇分析能帮助我们做什么？这两个问题指向语言教育理念、语篇分析原理、语篇教学方法、阅读教学设计、教学效果评价等，是当下我国基础教育领域各学段英语教师、教研员、教材编写者所关心的问题。

有兴趣者应该阅读曲卫国教授的新著《语篇分析与阅读教学》。曲教授长期从事英语文体和话语分析研究，是国内该研究领域的巨擘。其扛鼎之作《话语文体学导论：文本分析的方法》影响广泛，意义深远，是我国外国语言文学专业研究生的必读著作。近年来，因诸多主客观原因，曲教授对我国中小学外语教育的关注不断加大，对英语课程建设、教师发展、教材编写、教学实施、教研教培的兴趣越发浓厚，主动将自己常年形成的学术思想和研究成果付诸笔端，以飨读者，为推动英语课程改革和学科建设做出了卓越的贡献。

语篇是什么？语篇分析是什么？语篇分析的对象是什么？语篇分析研究从何缘起？如何在学习西方经典的同时汲取和传承语篇构式的东方智慧？语篇分析的跨文化视角对外语教学和语言能力发展有何裨益？语篇分析理论和方法如何赋能英语阅读教学？英语教师如何运用语篇分析理论和方法改进英语阅读教学，提高学生的语篇意识、语篇认知能力和语篇建构能力？这些问题之所以成为问题，源于其理论意义和实践价值。这些问题有的属于概念认识，有的属于实践操作，答案也是各不相同。一家之言的独乐乐，还是万家灯火的众乐乐？可能问题不在于有无相同的答案，而在于能否提出问题，在于所提问题的意图、指向和情境。有些问题之所以成为没有答案的问题，或许在于问题的原题，或许在于问题的提问。

我有幸成为曲教授新著《语篇分析与阅读教学》付梓书稿的第一位读者，何其幸矣，谨以识之并致谢忱。拜读完书桌上的这叠文稿，体会颇深。《语篇分析与阅读教学》从理论和实践两个方面，并以大量的来自教材的语篇和来自教学的实例，不仅完整地回答了"当我们在谈论语篇分析时，我们在说什么？"之问，而且还深入地解读了"当我们在进行阅读教学时，语篇分析能帮助我们做什么？"之惑。《语篇分析与阅读教学》从问题的提出，到陈述、反思、批判、解构、重构，娓娓道来，引人入胜，其语篇结构、话语技巧、案例支撑，堪称谋篇方略的典范。我作为曲教授的学科同仁、30多年的同道挚友、话语研究翘楚的仰慕者，承蒙赐稿，静心拜读，不仅获得了一次登门求教的天赐良机，更获得了一次学习交流的绝佳机会。

语篇是一种有意义的语言信息单位，以自然语言为载体，基于特定语境和目的，表达思想、观点、意图、态度、立场等。语篇是语言，是想法和说法的言语表现，但语言不等同于语篇，譬如语音、语词、语法是语言，但不是语篇，而是构成语篇不可或缺的基石。索绪尔将语言划分为 Langue 和 Parole 两部分，前者是一种抽象的、系统的、社会的符号系统，即"语言"，后者指具体人根据语境、意图、态度等之所说或所写，即"言语"。乔姆斯基认为，语言可以分为 I-language 和 E-language 两种形式，前者指由人类物种共享的生物禀赋而形成的语言生成系统，即"语言能力"，后者指由语言能力和语言经验叠加形成的语言运用系统，即"语言表现"。我们讨论语篇时所讲的语言，既不是指索绪尔的 Langue，也不是指乔姆斯基的 I-language，而是接近索绪尔的 Parole 或乔姆斯基的 E-language，即具体说或写的语言。

语篇有多种表现模态，也有不同的量化长度，通常以语言文字为载体，也会涉及一些非语言因素。语篇有单模态，如口语或书面语；也有多模态，如文字、图表、图标、图像、图符、声音、画面、音频、音效、色彩、动画、视频、数码等。通常，我们所说语篇指大于句子的话语片段（utterance）或话语系列（sequence of utterance），如会话、演讲、辩论、报告、广播、讲座、文章、文告、新闻报道、文学作品、影视作品、人机交流话语系列等。基于语境、表达意义的语篇可以是只言片语，也可以是鸿篇巨制；可以是书面文章，也可以是对话演讲；可以是诗词歌谣，也可以是小说散文；可以是音频信息，也可以是视觉作品。"语境"和"主旨"是语篇的关键要素。《语篇分析与阅读教学》是语篇，我为这部著作所作序言也是语篇。语篇可以短至一个字或一个词，如出现在路口的交通警示语"停"或"让"（英语的 Stop 或 Yield），贴在建筑物进出口处的"入口"或"出口"（英语的 Entrance 或 Exit），这些语言片段既有特定意义，又有具体语境。

由于语篇有不同的呈现模态，所以我们在讨论"语篇"或"语篇分析"时，根据话题、场合和意图，可能看到和用到除了"语篇"之外的一些词，如"话语""文本"和"篇章"，以及这些词的英语对应词，如 discourse（对应"语篇"或"话语"）、utterance（对应"话语"）或 text（对应"文本"或"篇章"）。中文的"语文"是一个绝妙词，涵盖"口语"和"文字"，既包括"语篇""话语"中的"语"，也包括"文本""文章"中的"文"。从严格意义上讲，"语篇"与"话语""文本""篇章"并非互为替代的同义词,这些词之所以存在,恰恰是因为各具特定意义和用意,不可随意替代。例如"话语"和"文本",前者注重言说的相对动态性,后者则强调文述的相对恒定性;前者突出过程,后者呈现事实。流水账清单可以被视为一种文本,但通常不被认为是话语。"语篇"和"篇章"也有类似的表现特征。相对而言,语篇更具通用性,既可包含结构化的篇章,也可包含非正式的口语体。日常对话通常不属于篇章范畴,但仍然可以用作语篇分析的重要对象。我们除非因学术研究之需,通常可以采用较为通用的"语篇",用以涵盖话语和篇章。基于此,我们立足教学角度,不必在"语篇分析""话语分析""文本分析""篇章分析"的选用上过于纠结。

语篇分析是一个涉及语言学、社会学、心理学等多学科交叉的研究领域,在其发展进程中出现了一些影响深远的经典理论和一些著名学者及其代表作。1952 年,美国结构主义先驱 Harris 在著名的 *Language* 杂志上发表了"Discourse Analysis"一文,提出了超越句子边界的话语结构单位的理论,欧美学界通常把这篇论文视为现代语篇研究的开山之作。1981 年,*Text* 杂志在荷兰创刊,标志着语篇分析作为一门独立学科,有了专属的研究成果发表和交流的学术载体。1983 年,英国学者 Brown 和美国学者 Yule 合著的 *Discourse Analysis* 由剑桥大学出版社出版;同年,Longacre 所著的 *The Grammar of Discourse* 由 Plenum 出版发行。这两部专著被学界视为语篇分析的奠基之作。1985 年,荷兰语言学家 van Dijk 主编的四卷本 *Handbook of Discourse Analysis* 正式出版,标志着语篇分析作为独立的跨学科研究体系业已形成。更有意义的是,上世纪后十年目睹了语篇分析进入语言教学领域,代表性作品有 McCarthy

（1991，Cambridge）的 *Discourse Analysis for Language Teachers*，Hatch（1992，Cambridge）的 *Discourse and Language Education*，McCarthy 和 Carter（1994，Longman）合著的 *Language as Discourse: Perspectives for Language Teaching*。

我们在学习西方经典理论的同时，应该汲取东方大家智慧。关于文章的立文之本、立文之要和立文之道，我们可以翻阅诸多中华典籍。唐代文学家李翱在《答朱载言书》中主张"义深则意远，意远则理辩，理辩则气直，气直则辞盛，辞盛则文工"，强调文章应兼具文、理、义三者，义深意远为文章之本，理辩气直为文章之要，辞盛文工为文章之巧，只有将深刻的中心思想融入艺术表达之中，文章才能有灵魂，思想和艺术才能相得益彰，作品才能传之久远。清代诗论家叶燮呼应了李翱的主张，在《原诗·外篇上》明示"志高则言洁，志大则辞弘，志远则旨永"的立文之要。西晋文学家陆机在《文赋》中提出了文章创作的"精、准、深"三原则，即"立言精，居要准，警策深""立片言而居要，乃一篇之警策"。南朝梁文学理论批评家刘勰在《文心雕龙》提出了文章的贯道之法，主张"文者贯道、惟字与义"，推崇"字以训正、义以理宣"，明确"理定而后辞畅"的立文之本，主张"辞约而旨丰、事近而喻远"的写作风范。

大道至简，文章的立文之本、立文之要、立文之道，皆源于"一"。《道德经》中的"道生一，一生二，二生三，三生万物"阐明了"道"和"一"的关系，是对宇宙生成和万物演化的精美解释，对现实世界具有深刻启示。在特定的语境中，汉字"一"可以表达"天地之根基""万物之缘起"。许慎《说文解字》的第一个字是"一"，许慎对"一"的"话语分析"即"造化"："惟初太极，道立于一，造分天地，化成万物。"

立文之道，从无到有，从有到精，既有历练，更有砺炼，学有"大成"，教有"大法"。孟子学生乐正克在《礼记·学记》中是这样阐释"大成"的："九年知类通达，强立而不返，谓之大成。"倡导通晓事理、触类旁通、坚定执着的学业观。学业有成往往取决于教学得法。乐正克在《礼记·学记》中大力推荐"豫""时""孙""摩"为"教之所由兴"之"大学之法"："禁于未发之谓豫，当其可之谓时，不凌节而施之谓孙，相观而善之谓摩。此四者教之所由兴也。"君子之教在于"喻"，更在于"善喻"，无非"和""易""思"："故君子之教喻也，道而弗牵，强而弗抑，开而弗达。道而弗牵则和，强而弗抑则易，开而弗达则思。和易以思，可谓善喻矣。"韩愈在《师说》中明示"道之所存师之所存"："生乎吾前，其闻道也固先乎吾，吾从而师之；生乎吾后，其闻道也亦先乎吾，吾从而师之。"在《进学解》中倡导"各得其宜，施以成室者""俱收并蓄，待用无遗者""校短量长，惟器是适者"，将这些原则视为"匠氏之工""医师之良""宰相之方"的秘诀。

中华古训言简意赅，精辟深邃，激励今人，鞭策后学，尤其对我们这些决意浸润语篇分析、推进阅读教学的师生极具启迪意义。语篇是文化的载体，也是特定文化的产物，不同文化背景的语篇在价值观念、思维方式、语言表达等方面有着不尽一致的表现。通过分析基于不同文化背景和语境的语篇，可以引导学生了解语篇的文化特征，理解和尊重不同文化背景下的文化内涵、思维方式、语言习惯和谋篇手段，避免不必要的误解误读。我们可以对英汉语篇在谋篇方式、文体特征等方面开展对比研究，包括研究东西方民族在语篇认知和元认知方面的异同，加强英汉语篇在语言特点、结构特征、建构方式等方面的跨文化研究。

语篇分析是语言教学的前提，也是落实英语课程标准、加强阅读教学的重要环节。教师应树立语篇意识，加强语篇知识学习，学会分析语篇主旨和语境，对语篇做出准确解读、反思和评价。语篇分析以研究语言的组织结构、信息编排、使用特征等为主要任务，从语用的角度研究和描写信息传递和意图实现的语言表述结构及其普遍性规律，重点分析有目的、有意义、有语境、信息完整的话语或文本，包括语言信息的衔接、连贯、意向、可接受性、情景性、篇章性（textuality）和篇际性（intertextuality）。

　　英语课程标准提出了"语篇类型"和"语篇知识"这两个既相互关联又各具特点的概念。语篇类型指自然语言在使用过程中基于不同的语用目的、以不同的文体体裁或语体风格呈现言语信息的方式。多样性的语篇类型织成了一张自然语言的全息图，语篇作者以不同的体裁和风格表达自我、他人、社会和自然。语篇分类主要取决于目的和用途，通常可以分为口语语篇、书面语语篇、多模态语篇，也可以按连续性语篇或非连续性语篇、虚构类语篇或非虚构类语篇分类。记叙文、说明文、议论文、应用文等属连续性语篇，有着不同文体特征；图表、图示、网页、广告、漫画、插图、符号、表格等属于非连续性语篇；访谈、对话、会话等属口语类语篇，口头语体特征明显。语篇类型没有绝对的界限，语篇类型之间没有刻板的界限和僵硬的标签，分析语篇要避免绝对化。同一语篇如短篇小说，其基本语篇类型为记叙文，但不排除出现说明文、议论文、应用文等不同语篇类型的片段。语篇知识主要是关于文本的篇章结构和信息的组构方式，包括语篇宏观层面的文体特征和结构框架，微观层面的衔接和连贯。具体来说，语篇知识涉及说话人或写作人在呈现或表达意义、意图、观点、情感、态度等时所采用的衔接、连贯、转承、倒叙等信息组织方式，以及说话人或写作人为了取得或增强表达效果而采用的比较、对比、类比、夸张、举例、明喻、暗喻、隐喻等修辞手段。

书面语篇是教学内容的主要载体，是阅读教学的核心资源。书面语篇赋予阅读教学以主题、情境和内容。语篇以其特有的内在逻辑结构、文体特征和语言形式，组织相关信息，呈现主题意义。教师在研读语篇时，要把握主题意义、挖掘语篇中蕴含的育人价值、分析文体特征和语言特点及其与主题意义的关联，这些是阅读教学设计的关键。在研读语篇的过程中，教师要对语篇的主题、内容、文体结构、语言特点、作者观点等进行深入的分析和归纳，注重了解、理解和评价语篇主题、内容、意义、价值、方式、方法、语境等基本要素。例如：语篇的主题和内容是什么？语篇的深层涵义是什么？作者的观点、立场、意图、态度、价值取向是什么？语篇具有什么样的文体特征、内容结构、表述风格和语言特点？作者选择什么样的文体形式、篇章结构和修辞手段，以及为何作出这样的选择？

教师还应该了解、分析并介绍语篇作者、目标受众、写作时间、发表载体，以及特定时期的写作背景和语言特点等要素。研读语篇确实可以帮助教师多层次、多角度地分析语篇所传递的意义，依据语篇的主题意义、文体风格、语言特点和价值取向，设计合理的教学任务和活动，同时利用作者视角、写作背景和时间等信息，帮助学生深入分析、深刻理解语篇及其主题意义。教师在阅读教学中，既要深入挖掘语篇中的文化内涵和育人价值，也要积极提炼语篇中的结构化知识，建立文体特征、语言特点等与主题意义之间的关联，把语言学习、文化浸润、意义探究融为一体，实现深度学习、温度学习和效度学习。

多年来,教师习惯于教语音、词汇和语法,已形成一些固定的教学范式。但是我们不是为教语音而教语音,为教词汇而教词汇,为教语法而教语法。当然,语音、词汇和语法是语篇学习、理解、创作的基础。语篇由语音、词汇、语法构成,没有语音、词汇、语法也就没有语篇。但是语篇讲究意义,语音、词汇、语法,以及衔接、连贯、修辞等,皆服务于语篇意义的表达。语篇分析重在语篇意义的分析,语篇意义既涉及语言意义,也涉及情景意义、上下文意义、言外之意、话外之音。语篇意义的认知在很大程度上取决于对语篇主题、主体和客体的认知和元认知,例如语篇中的人物、事物、事件、事由、时间、地点、过程等要素。

总之,语篇分析基于语音、词汇、语法等语言的基础构建,重在引导学生超越语音、词汇、语法学习,进入语篇和语用学习,开展主题意义、价值取向、立论立意、篇章结构、文体语体、语言风格、修辞手段等方面的学习、分析和反思。强调从宏观层面把握语篇的主旨、意图和连贯性,引导学生能跳出局部细节,厘清语言片段和论点表述之间的逻辑关系,如因果、转折、并列等关系,以及衔接、过渡等手段。引导学生在阅读文本时通过采用略读、扫读、精读等方法,抓住主旨大意和关键信息,发展信息定位和提取能力,从整体上理解、分析、质疑、评价语篇所传达的信息。设计相关问题或话题,组织讨论与交流,分享观点和理解。指导学生基于所学语篇的行文模式,运用所学语篇知识,完成写作任务,如续写故事、改写文章、撰写读后感等,巩固对语篇的理解和掌握。设计和组织语篇学习、理解和建构的评价活动,检测和评价语篇教学的成效,以评促学、以评促教、以评促用。

数智时代已来。在这个不断迭变的数智时代，每天产生着海量的 machine-generated digital text，包括似说非说的套话、一本正经的胡说，或 AI hallucination。提示词语篇、人机聊天语篇、图生文语篇……这些新形态语篇正在挑战着经典语篇分析理论，挑战着语篇教学、解读和建构。由人工智能和人类智能协同驱动的多模态语篇不断涌现，这个加速变化和演绎的时代呼唤基于人机互动的语篇意识、语篇认知能力和语篇建构能力，呼唤立足生成式文本的语篇分析和阅读教学。

梅德明

于上海外国语大学

2025 年 3 月 18 日

前　言

一、认识的误区

教育部制定的《普通高中英语课程标准（2017 年版 2020 年修订）》（以下简称《课程标准》）要求英语课程在教学过程中要有意识地引入有关语篇的基本知识，以培养学生的语篇意识。《课程标准》提到了语篇意识的两个基本内容，一是把握各类语篇的结构特点；二是提高语篇的理解能力。我们在本书中把这两个内容理解为语篇认知（cognition）和语篇元认知（metacognition）。

有关语篇认知研究成果的应用在我国外语界有较长历史。许多外语教师很早就尝试将语篇分析的方法运用到外语阅读教学。不过我们注意到在具体运用语篇分析的过程中存在三个问题。第一个问题是许多教师在运用过程中过于强调语篇的技术分析。技术分析对研究的重要性不言而喻。然而这些分析虽然能给出有一定理论意义的解释，但对阅读教学本身的帮助并不大，因为研究的重点通常只关注与研究课题有关的语篇的某些形式特征，基于单个理论的分析容易使语篇理解碎片化，很难对语篇的整体理解提供关键性的帮助。

第二个问题与第一个问题密切相关。许多教师以为只要运用语篇分析的一些技术，阅读理解中的许多问题便会迎刃而解。他们没有意识到阅读中产生的问题更多涉及知识、文化等许多语篇外的因素。语篇理解是多层次的认知问题。对语篇技术分析的过于依赖会导致语篇解读停留在语篇的形式表层，必然会忽略语篇理解的多样性和复杂性，致使语篇理解机械化和浅层化。

第三个问题与对语篇能力（discourse competence）的认知有关。目前大多数教材对语篇能力的界定还停留在语篇认知层面，即语篇能力仅仅被解释为对具体语篇的解读能力，基本忽视了语篇元认知这个层面。语篇能力不仅涉及语篇理解，更包括对自己理解过程的反思。语篇的元认知指的就是对自己理解过程的反思。没有反思的阅读不可能真正读懂语篇，更谈不上是运用批判性思维的独立自主的阅读。

我们认为这些问题的出现至少与两个认知误区有关。第一个误区，也是最大的误区，可能与不少教师混淆了语篇研究和语篇理解之间的区别有关。作为研究，语篇分析首先有很强的问题导向。语篇分析通常会根据某一个理论框架（主要是语言学的），去选择性地观察和分析与该问题有关的语篇现象。剔除与研究问题无关的内容是研究的最基本的要求。其次，为了保证研究的可复制性（retrievability），研究通常强调可观察内容的确定性。对可复制性的强调意味着语篇研究会做最大限度的简化，以排斥各种主体因素或不能确定因素对研究过程的干扰。再者，语篇分析有许多理论流派，这些流派的理论只能在该理论框架内对特定问题有较强的解释力。最后，研究的目的是要证明或修正所应用理论的一些假设，语篇则为这些研究目的提供材料。整个语篇的理解根本不是研究关注的内容。

语篇理解是读者与语篇进行错综复杂的互动的结果。虽然这些互动是通过语篇提示（cues）触发的，但有太多的语境因素会制约读者对语篇提示的反应。不仅同一语篇提示会对不同的读者产生不同的启示，就是同一读者在不同的语境里对同样的提示也会有不同的认知。语篇理解涉及的问题因而更庞杂、更具体，过程也更复杂。

如果不区分研究与理解的区别，头绪纷繁的阅读会蜕变成千篇一律的理解复制，阅读的目的就会蜕变成某个理论假设的验证。

第二个误区与许多教师仅把语篇知识看作是单独的知识板块有关。他们以为在教学中引入语篇分析就是在教学中将课文的分析层面从句子上升到语篇。早在 1994 年，McCarthy 和 Carter 就提出，语篇这个概念的引入，会颠覆对语言教学的认知：

The moment one starts to think of language as discourse, the entire landscape changes, usually, forever. (1994: 201)

这个误区的产生可能与 discourse 的翻译有关 ①。Discourse 在学界有两种译法："话语" 和 "语篇"。"语篇" 多用来指大于句子的语言单位，通常是书面语。"话语" 则包括书面语和会话。由于阅读教学的主要内容是课文理解，因此 "语篇" 是目前在阅读教学里通用的翻译。

不过，"语篇" 这个翻译忽视了 discourse 的复杂含义。一般认为 "话语" 的译法更能体现 discourse 的多重含义，因为 discourse 不仅是一个大于句子的语言单位，它也是一个重要的社会文化概念。它的核心假设是：语言使用是社会认知活动。如果从社会认知活动的角度去理解 discourse，McCarthy 和 Carter 提到的颠覆性变化可能更容易理解。他们在解释 discourse 时，从社会认知的角度强调了 discourse 互动和语境的两大特点：

... the basic notion of discourse as engaging with language as process and meaning as negotiated and contextual. (1994: 182)

---

① 具体讨论请参阅 "第一章　语篇分析的基本知识"。

如果我们同意 McCarthy 和 Carter 的假设，在教学中引入语篇分析理论和方法，这意味着，首先，我们在阅读教学时会考虑语篇理解的复杂性，不会再把教学看成是课文的语言解释。我们的视野不会局限于课文本身，各种影响语篇认知的因素也会被纳入分析范围。其次，我们会重视学生的自主参与，强调课文理解必须由学生自主完成，而不是在教学中引导学生按照教师的视角去理解，把教师的理解看成是课文的终极理解。最后，我们会关注各种语境因素对语篇理解的动态制约。由于拥有不同认知资源的学生会对语境提示和语篇线索有不同的识别和认知，他们的理解会呈多样性。我们会把多样性理解看成是教学最重要的成果。

二、关注的问题

我们这本书里没有采用"话语"的主要原因是考虑与教育部制定的《课程标准》所用的术语保持一致。另外，为了方便教师的理解和运用，我们的分析材料大都选用高中教材中的课文，是书面语料，这与我国学术界对语篇的一般理解也相符。然而，我们的分析框架还是"话语分析"的理论框架，即强调语篇认知的社会性、主体性和语境性。

基于这样的框架，我们主要关注两个基本问题：

（1）语篇分析的方法能在语篇理解中起多大的作用？

（2）语篇分析的方法在阅读教学中究竟能起到什么样的作用？

这两个关注点也是参考了《课程标准》。该标准把提高学生的英语阅读能力和思辨能力作为教学的重要任务。

第一个关注点是语篇意识的第一个内容，属于语篇认知层面的问题。简单说来就是语篇分析的方法对回答"课文传递了什么信息？"（What is the message of the text?）这个问题有什么帮助。基于这个关注点，我们在介绍相关概念和方法时主要考虑的是将这些概念和方法引入教学能在理解课文时提供什么特别的帮助。换言之，我们考虑的是如果不了解或运用这些方法，我们的理解是否会受到影响或错失一些语篇线索？也就是说：

Do they make a difference?

第二个关注点是语篇意识里语篇理解能力问题，即语篇的元认知能力。我们在第二章会具体讨论这个问题。阅读教学的主要目的不是帮助学生理解单篇课文，回答"这篇课文传递了什么信息"这个最基本的问题，而是回答"你怎么知道这是课文要传递的信息？"（How do you know it is the message of the text?）了解自己在理解课文时所识别的语篇提示和所运用的认知资源，对制约自己理解的各种语境因素有基本的意识，这样的元认知能力是语篇理解能力的关键内容。能反思自己的推导过程就能举一反三将理解单篇课文所学到的知识推及到其他语篇的认知。语篇元认知能力在培养独立自主阅读和批判性思维能力这方面，有不可估量的作用。如果用一个简单的问题概括第二个关注点，那就是：

Are they aware of the problems in the process of interpretation?

三、基本内容

语篇分析理论流派非常多，因而概念和方法也非常多。我们选择介绍和讨论的概念基本是围绕我们的关注点。我们将重点讨论语境、视角、信息、话题、主题、词义关系、体裁、立场等问题。我们的选择主要围绕语篇理解这个问题。

语境是一个大概念，包括社会文化、情境、作者和读者等许多因素。任何语篇理解都需要我们为之构建一个具有关联性的语境。如何确定语境参数的关联性，如何从这些参数中获取相关信息等，这些是语篇理解的基本前提。

视角是语篇叙述和议论的切入点。识别视角对认识作者所选择的认知框架、所希望调动的知识资源、激活的语境，以及理解语篇的整体连贯具有关键性的作用。

语篇有不同内容的呈现，这些内容会在不同层面上构成连贯关系。我们在讨论结构的时候，主要根据语篇呈现的内容讨论语篇的**信息结构**、**话题结构**和**主题结构**。我们没有按照许多学者的做法，将"连贯"（coherence）单列，主要是因为我们考虑语篇的连贯是有层级性的，不同内容层面有不同的连贯关系。

语篇的载体是语言。语言的基本构成是词汇和语法。分析语篇语言较常见的是"衔接"（cohesion）理论。由于我们关注的是理解，而衔接理论有关语法的陈述，在我们看来更多属于一般的语法知识，对语篇深层理解的贡献有限，所以虽然我们会有较详细的语法衔接介绍，但我们的重点是放在**词义关系**上。

体裁是个古老的概念。任何分析都离不开体裁。我们对体裁的介绍主要考虑的是话语与社会认知活动的关系，关注的是不同社会认知活动对语篇的不同期待，强调不同类型的体裁对语篇构成的不同要求。

语篇理解其实涉及三个层面的内容，即：作者说些什么？作者通过说这些在传递什么信息？作者为什么要传递这样的信息？第三个问题反映的是作者的**立场**。我们的阅读教学通常主要重视前两个问题，对第三个问题似乎关注不够充分。其实任何语篇，哪怕是科学报告都会受到作者立场的影响。作者的立场决定了语篇的方方面面。识别作者立场对培养独立思考和批判性思维能力有重要的帮助。

考虑到本书主要是为中学英语教学提供参考，我们在介绍时不拘泥于一个流派，也不求面面俱到。有许多重要的概念和方法，本书并没有专门章节的介绍。为了让读者对语篇分析有相对全面的了解，本书的第一章对语篇分析的重要概念做了分类介绍。

由于本书的主要目的是将语篇分析用于阅读教学指导，我们在第二章从语篇分析的角度对阅读和阅读教学里的一些问题进行了简单的梳理。梳理的目的是想呼应 McCarthy 和 Carter 的话，希望在运用语篇分析方法教学时能摒弃灌输式的阅读教学。

除了第一和第二章，本书的每个章节基本由概说、教学和运用三个板块组成。概说这部分主要介绍和讨论相关概念和方法；教学这一部分主要考虑的是相关概念和方法在具体教学运用中要考虑的问题；运用这部分旨在展示相关概念和方法在分析课文时的具体运用。

这里特别需要强调三点。第一点，语篇理解是全方位的认知活动。我们这里将相关概念和方法单列，主要是出于写作的方便。在具体教学过程中应该尽量考虑多个方法的运用，以揭示语篇多维度的复杂含义。第二点，为了使我们所展示的分析更具体、更详细，我们对许多课文进行了全篇分析。不过，由于每一章节有每一章节的重点，因此我们的分析是不全面的。即便是相关概念和方法的运用，我们在分析时也无法做到具体而微。我们所做的分析只是基于我们的理解，做这些分析的目的主要是为了展示相关方法的实际运用。第三点，我们讨论的这些概念和方法有多种理解，因此我们的介绍也只能是参考，许多理解未必合适得当。为了更好地把握这些概念和方法，我们强烈建议大家阅读相关的参考文献。

为了紧扣与教学活动的关系，本书的语篇分析材料基本来自于上海教育出版社出版的《普通高中教科书　英语》必修第一册至第三册和选择性必修第一册至第四册。

本书的成书离不开上海教育出版社黄艳和姚玉莹两位编辑的信任和支持。本书是在她们的建议下立项的。她们在本书的写作过程中提供了许多宝贵的帮助。本书还得感谢上海外国语大学梅德明教授和上海市教师教育学院汤青老师。梅德明教授在百忙之中拨冗为本书写了立意高远的序。汤青老师慷慨允许我参加她组织的市教研活动，这些活动让我对高中英语的阅读教育有了初浅的入门了解。这里要特别感谢朱彦教授、许高编辑和我的学生朱雷博士。每次我在查阅资料遇到问题时，朱雷总有办法解决。最后一如既往地要感谢我的太太和儿子。没有他们的支持，安心写作是不可能的。

曲卫国

2025 年 1 月

目　录

第一章 语篇分析的基本知识

导引问题:

- 什么是语篇分析?
- 语篇分析有哪些基本内容?

本章提要:

语篇分析通常从四个层面分析语篇。第一个层面是**语篇本身**,包括语篇的模态、结构、体裁、连贯、衔接、主题、话题、语体等内容。第二个层面是**交际**。语篇是意图传递和接受的交际活动,这个层面的分析围绕作者和读者两个交际主体,具体涉及作者和读者的身份、立场,两个主体之间形成的主体间关系等。第三个层面是**认知**。语篇理解是认知活动,因此与认知有关的各种因素如注意力、视角、图式、推导、焦点、框架、场域等都是语篇分析的课题。第四个层面是**语境**。交际和认知活动必然会受到语篇内外的各种因素的制约。这些因素构成的语境参数以及相关信息的提取是语境分析的关注点。

一、概说

"语篇"这个术语源于英语的 discourse,不过 discourse 在引入中国时有多种译法,除了"语篇"外,还有"话语""篇章"等,如我国语篇分析的开拓者之一廖秋忠就用"篇章"来翻译 discourse：

> 篇章研究，一般称为篇章分析，是语言学研究领域中的一个比较新的领域。"篇章分析"这个术语是从英文"discourse analysis"译过来的。（1992: 181）

也有学者如黄国文认为"语篇"对应的是 text，"语篇分析"应该指的是 text analysis。不过，他在具体讨论时，对语篇和话语其实并不加以区分：

> 虽然语篇分析（text analysis）与话语分析（discourse analysis）有些区别，但本书对此不加区分，所以，我们讨论的范围包括书面语言和口头语言。（1988: 4）

尽管如此，现在学界的基本共识是：discourse 和 text 是两个有不同侧重的术语。虽然 discourse analysis 和 text linguistics 在研究内容和方法上有不少重合，但两者的理论框架以及研究范围还是有重要的区别。在我们的讨论中，"语篇"对应的是 discourse，而不是 text。我们按惯例把后者翻译成"文本"。

汉语的不同翻译使"语篇分析"和"话语分析"在学科背景上也有了一定的区别。"语篇分析"是主要以语言学理论为基础的一个研究域，而"话语分析"的学科背景要杂得多。它可以和"语篇分析"一样，以语言学为理论框架。但它也可以是一个以哲学、历史、社会学、心理学等许多其他非语言学学科为理论依据的**多学科研究域**。

就语言分析单位而言，"语篇"与"文本"的区别不大，一般都指大于句子的语言单位，即包含两个或两个以上句子的语言单位。但在语言的实际使用中，单句、甚至几个单词组成的语篇或文本也不少见，如广告语、口号、警示语等。可口可乐有一则广告，里面只有一行字：

Can't Beat The Real Thing.

大多数交通指示牌和警示语都是由词组组成：

One Way.
Keep hands off.

"语篇"与"文本"最大的区别是"语篇"指语言或其他表意形式在具体语境里的动态使用，而"文本"则是指语言或其他表意形式使用前的静态状态。我们可以这么理解两者的区别：独立成章的文字在被阅读前是文本。一旦该文本被阅读或使用了，它就成了语篇。语篇与文本的这个区别意味着语篇分析不仅关注文本本身的内容，还关注影响文本理解的各种文本外的因素。也就是说，语篇分析比文本分析涉及的内容要广得多。

简单说来，语篇分析的基本知识可以分为四大板块。第一个板块是语篇本身，即通常说的文本。这个板块包括模态、结构、体裁、连贯、衔接、主题、话题、语体等内容。第二个板块是交际板块。构建和理解语篇是意图传递和接受的交际活动，因此语篇分析离不开作者和读者这两个交际主体。作者和读者的身份、立场，以及两个主体之间形成的主体间关系（intersubjectivity）也是语篇分析的基本内容。第三个板块是认知板块。语篇理解是认知活动，因此与认知有关的各种因素，如注意力、视角、图式、推导、焦点、框架、场域等，构成分析语篇理解的认知基础。第四个板块是语境。作为交际和认知活动的语篇自然会受到语境的影响和制约。语境是个多层级的概念，包括在各个层级，如上下文、社会文化环境等影响语篇构建和认知的各种因素。

二、语篇

我们可以先从了解语篇的外部形态开始。语篇的外部形态由两大类资源组成。第一类是符号资源，语篇的符号资源构成语篇的**"模态"**（modality）。由语言单独构成的语篇是单一模态语篇，由语言与其他符号资源合成组合的语篇被称为**多模态**语篇（multimodality）。在多模态语篇里，各个模态各司其职，互动合成语篇的信息。

下面的这则广告由百事公司（Pepsi）首先推出，图片形象地演绎了广告的标题（tag line）："We wish you a scary Halloween."。可口可乐公司（Coca Cola）自然也不是等闲之辈。他们巧妙地将 Pepsi 的标题修改成 "Everybody wants to be a hero!"，使图片显示出了不同的含义。①

① https://www.brandme.com.au/blog/2014/10/coke-vs-pepsi-a-scary-halloween-ad-campaign/.

在多模态语篇里，图片不仅仅解释文字，它们往往会从另外一个角度去阐释文字的意义：

Ideal beauty 这篇课文有两个版本。两个版本配有不同的图片。一个版本[①]配了下面三幅图片以展示课文文字表达的内容：

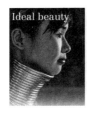

另一个版本[②]给这篇课文选择了完全不同的图片：

从文字与图片互动的角度看，不同的图片对语篇的理解会施加不同的影响。有时图片表达的意思会比文字更复杂、更丰富，如 Roads to education[③]：

---

① Jayne Wildaman et al. 2013. *Insight Intermediate Student's Book*. Oxford: Oxford University Press, 4–5.

② 邹为诚. 普通高中教科书　英语　必修第三册［M］. 上海：上海教育出版社，2021：42–43.

③ 邹为诚. 普通高中教科书　英语　必修第二册［M］. 上海：上海教育出版社，2020：23.

在这个单元主题页构成的多模态语篇里，文字只有三个：Roads to education，但图片里却有许多内容，而且这些内容的关系也非常复杂，如：

（1）作者为什么在插图里选择 tree，compass，grass，cobble path，book，sky 和 flying birds？

（2）为什么 compass，tree，grass 和 cobble path 在 book 里面，而 birds 和 sky 在 book 外面？

第二类是语篇的物质载体，也就是语篇的物质资源，专业术语是"**物态**"（materiality）。不同物态形式的语篇会对理解产生不同的影响，如读者对成书出版的语篇与以纸片形式散发的文字往往会有不同的对待；不同物态的电影和纸质小说会诱发不同的感受和认知；数字语篇与纸质语篇对阅读过程也会有不同的影响。

除了载体，文字的物理排列（typography）对我们的理解也会有作用。我们对以诗节（stanza）排列的语篇和以段落（paragraph）排列的语篇会有不同的期待。一篇题为 A Riddle 的语篇，如果以下面的形式排列，我们可能猜出谜底后就期待语篇认知结束了：

There is one that has a head without an eye, and there's one that has an eye without a head. You may find the answer if you try; and when all is said, half the answer hangs upon a thread. (pin and needle)

如果我们看到这篇语篇是以诗节的形式排列时，我们的解读不会以猜出谜底结束：

A Riddle

By Christina Rossetti

There is one that has a head without an eye,

And there's one that has an eye without a head.

You may find the answer if you try;

And when all is said,

Half the answer hangs upon a thread.

语篇的段落（paragraphing）是另外一个影响我们对语篇脉络的梳理的因素。我们通常会以作者划分的段落作为语篇脉络切分的主要依据。除非我们质疑作者的能力，一般说来，我们不会对作者的段落切分提出异议。如：

Lagos, Nigeria — Yaba market is busy, hot and dusty. People are looking around the second-hand shops, picking through piles of old clothes, and they're all searching for deals. The market is flooded with cheap clothes from America and Europe, and they usually sell out fairly quickly. "These clothes make people's dreams come true," says Abeke, a shop owner. "Everyone wears them. When they put them on, you can't tell the difference between the rich and the poor." At the front of Abeke's store is a cotton T-shirt with the words "Get Real". It's picked up by a young guy who looks at it carefully. He tries it on and smiles — it fits him and it looks good. It's a simple T-shirt, but it has a long story.

这是课文 The story of a T-shirt[1] 的第一段。不过，这一段文字是

---

[1] 邹为诚.普通高中教科书 英语 必修第三册［M］.上海：上海教育出版社，2021：24.

否有其他的排列可能呢？如：

Lagos, Nigeria — Yaba market is busy, hot and dusty. People are looking around the second-hand shops, picking through piles of old clothes, and they're all searching for deals. The market is flooded with cheap clothes from America and Europe, and they usually sell cut fairly quickly.

"These clothes make people's dreams come true," says Abeke, a shop owner. "Everyone wears them. When they put them on, you can't tell the difference between the rich and the poor." At the front of Abeke's store is a cotton T-shirt with the words "Get Real". It's picked up by a young guy who looks at it carefully. He tries it on and smiles — it fits him and it looks good. It's a simple T-shirt, but it has a long story.

或者：

Lagos, Nigeria — Yaba market is busy, hot and dusty. People are looking around the second-hand shops, picking through piles of old clothes, and they're all searching for deals. The market is flooded with cheap clothes from America and Europe, and they usually sell out fairly quickly.

"These clothes make people's dreams come true," says Abeke, a shop owner. "Everyone wears them. When they put them on, you can't tell the difference between the rich and the poor."

At the front of Abeke's store is a cotton T-shirt with the words "Get Real". It's picked up by a young guy who looks at it carefully. He tries it on and smiles — it fits him and it looks good. It's a simple T-shirt, but it has a long story.

改变文字的段落分配会影响我们的理解吗？
语篇除了形态的区别以外，还分为不同的类型，即**"体裁"**

（genre）。语篇分析对体裁的定义与传统修辞学、文学批评等有重要的区别。传统修辞学等的定义一般以语篇或文本的结构特征为主要依据，而语篇分析则以社会认知活动类型为体裁分类的基础。语篇因活动类型不同而分类标准多样化，如按社会活动分类，有政治语篇、外交语篇等；按知识体系分类，有学术语篇、文学语篇、历史语篇等；按语篇结构类型分，有叙事语篇、信息或说明类语篇、议论类语篇等。

语篇结构（discourse structure）是个多层次的概念。语篇的结构可以分成两个大类：外在结构（external structure）和内部结构（internal structure）。外在结构主要指可以直接观察到的语篇外部形式，如模态、物态等。内部结构则指语篇内各种成分组成的形式，如**话题**（topic）结构、**主题**（theme）结构和**信息**（information）结构等。

话题是语篇叙述或议论的内容，即语篇是关于什么的？（aboutness）。主题指的是作者通过叙述或议论话题所要传递的意图。话题与主题的区别可以通过下面两个问题体现出来：

话题：What is the essay/story about?

主题：What does the author want to say by talking about the topic?

话题结构与所叙述或议论的事件或议题的结构有关。作者通常会根据主题需要选择并凸显事件或议题结构的某些成分以构成话题结构。主题的传递通常有层级性。语篇的每个段落或成分会在不同层级表达主题不同维度的意义。主题结构构建的依据是作者对事件或议题的认识。

信息与观点（opinion）构成语篇的主要内容。不过信息是个非常难定义的概念。它通常与"资料"（data）和"观点"混淆。信息与资料的不同主要体现在加工处理方面。资料是用来描述那些没有经过处理加工的材料。信息是经过加工处理的材料。信息加工主要体现在两个方面：一是语言表述。作者会根据自己的意图选择相关词汇呈现信息。二是选择。作者在语篇里只选择与意图相符的信息。

信息与观点最大的不同是信息虽然经过加工处理，但它传递的是客观存在或有事实基础的材料，也就是说判断信息的标准是真实性。没有事实依据的信息是假信息。观点是作者的阐释（interpretation），其主要依据是主观判断，因此判断观点的标准不是真实性而是合理性。

信息结构指的是作者选择符合自己意图的信息并将其按照想要得到的认知效果进行排列的顺序。分析语篇信息时主要考虑的是三个问题：一是作者选择了哪些信息？二是作者如何排列这些信息？三是作者的排列顺序对读者的认知有什么影响？

语篇之所以能独立成章取决于各成分之间是否能形成**连贯**（coherence）关系。连贯指的是语篇成分之间的**关联性**（relevance）。与衔接（cohesion）不同，连贯一般没有形式标记。我们可以把连贯理解成语篇成分在概念层面的关联。不过关联究竟该如何理解，学界并没有共识。目前大多数学者接受的基本假设是：关联可以是逻辑关系或语篇成分之间在意义上形成的某种连续性（continuity）。我们把主题和话题视为理解语篇连贯的主要依据，因此与大多数语篇分析著作不同，我们对连贯的讨论并没有单列成章。我们认为语篇的话题和主题体现的是语篇两个不同层次的连贯关系。梳理语篇的话题结构和主题结构就可以厘清语篇的连贯。

衔接是相对具体的概念，指的是语篇成分的形式关联。Halliday和Hasan等学者发展的衔接分析框架是学界最具影响力的。根据他们的理论，衔接是通过**衔接手段**（cohesive ties）实现的。我们可以对比以下两个例子：

She couldn't find her book. John was here yesterday.（连贯）

She couldn't find her book. But John was here yesterday.（衔接）

在 Halliday 和 Hasan 的分析框架里，衔接分为**语法衔接**（grammatical cohesion）和**词汇衔接**（lexical cohesion）两大类。语法衔接主要由句子之间形成的**指代**（reference）、**替代**（substitution）、**省略**（ellipsis）和**连接**（conjunction）等四种语法关系体现。词汇衔接则是指借助词汇之间的**复现**（reiteration）和**搭配**（collocation）关系实现跨句意义关联。

词汇衔接，尤其其中的搭配关系是学界最有争议的。对于语篇词汇之间的关系，语篇分析里还有许多假说。Michael Hoey（2005）的**词汇关系**（lexical relations）理论从"词汇触发"（lexical priming）的认知角度对搭配关系进行了解释。他提出了**词汇组合**（patterns of lexis）①的概念。按照 Hoey 的假设，词语的使用不仅会触发读者的词汇联想，也会触发该词所属语义集（semantic set）的其他词汇。语义集属于词汇的概念域（conceptual domain），更常见的术语是语义场（semantic field）。任何词汇都有自己的语义场。如 father，这个单词的相关语义场是 family，提到 father 会激活 family 这个语义场，让人产生 mother、son 等相关的词汇联想。

作者在叙述或议论话题时，会像摄影那样选择特定的角度以凸显某些成分。这个角度就是语篇的**视角**（perspective）。作者通过视角提示读者语篇理解的切入角度，以此操控**意义潜势**（meaning

---

① 更常见的翻译是"词汇模式"。我们认为，由于 model 经常被翻译成"模式"，因而用"模式"很容易发生混淆。更主要的是 pattern 实际讨论的是词语之间的组合现象和关系。

potential）的实现。作者会根据自己的意图、所针对的读者、体裁等因素，选择视角的显性或隐性提示。

语篇的视角常与语篇的**焦点**（focus）一起讨论。焦点的作用是吸引读者的**注意力**（attention），让读者的意识聚焦。视角的作用其实就是聚焦读者的注意力。美国心理学家 William James 提出的**选择性注意**（selective attention）这个概念对理解视角和聚焦有很大的帮助。按照他的解释，读者注意力的聚焦意味着选择性地放弃焦点以外的内容，视野仅局限于所选定视角可及的范围。

不过，虽然语篇焦点是作者设定的，但焦点是否成立还取决于读者的识别和认可。读者如果没有相关知识或经验，就不一定能识别语篇的焦点。读者有时会根据自己的知识经验或需要，拒绝接受作者设定的焦点：

Reporter: Why do you rob banks?
William Sutton: Because that's where the money is. (Krifka 2000: 316)

记者的焦点是抢劫银行的动机，而 Sutton 不愿正面回答，因而拒绝接受记者的焦点。

语篇的视角一般会有**提示**（signalling）。提示是作者为了引导读者能按照他们设定的路径去理解语篇而设置的语言或非语言的线索。语篇的提示可以分成两类：一类是显性提示；另一类是隐性提示。显性提示通过倾向性明显的词汇或其他手段明示语篇的认知路径。显性提示虽然有较高的效率，但也会因操控痕迹明显而让身份或立场不同的读者产生抵触情绪。隐性提示主要是通过中性词汇或信息等进行暗示。读者是否能识别隐性提示取决于他们是否属于语篇所针对的对象，或他们是否具备相关的知识和经验。当然具体的语境也会影响读者对隐性提示的识别。隐性提示因掩盖了操控痕迹而不太容易引起读者的反感。

框架设定（framing）是另外一个分析作者如何操控读者认知的概念。这个概念的要点是：作者在叙述或议论某个话题时，会将该话题置于某一概念系统（system of concepts）之内，将它在被启用的概念系统中定位，赋予它在该概念系统内的意义（make sense）。这里说的概念系统并不一定是指系统知识体系，它也可以是经验或文化、传统习俗等。

框架（frame）在赋予话题系统内意义的同时，也限制了它的认知范围。框架的运作是个复杂的双向过程。作者为了激活所选择的框架，通常会通过**凸显**（salience）语篇某些成分来将读者的注意力引入特定的视角。读者的身份认同、知识结构和立场等许多因素会促使他们抵制作者的框架，将议题锁定在自己所认可的或所熟悉的认知框架之内，从而按照自己的，而不是作者所选用的框架去认知话题。

有两个概念与框架有密切关联。一是**图式**（schema）。图式由预存的各种知识性模块构成，与框架关系密切，也有学者认为框架和图式基本属于一个范畴。当图式被激活后，受众会按照图式的指向调动相关的资源，构建相应的认知语境，确立语篇成分之间的关联性。认知一旦由图式主导，思维会进入习惯轨道，思维的独立性和自主性会受到影响。社会文化习俗等对图式有重要的影响。在跨文化语境里，图式会形成冲突。

另外一个概念是**场域**（field）。场域指的是语篇所依托知识框架的归属领域（domain）。场域有不同层级和类别的划分标准，如科学、文学等知识体系的划分；科学又可以进一步细分为物理学、化学、生物学等；场域也可以按经济、政治、外交、教育等不同的社会活动类型划分。场域规定框架的知识范围。

尽管作者在构建语篇的过程中会极尽所能对语篇进行控制，但由于具有社会属性的语言让作者的表达无法摆脱语言的多义性和各种群体性特征，语篇内会存在许多**意义潜势**（meaning potential），即词语或信息各种意义组合的可能。有不少可能性与作者的意图并不一定一致。它们的存在使语篇内出现向心（centripedal）与离心（centrifugal）意义潜势之间的张力。语言的群体性特征也会使语篇出现**多声部**（multivocality）的状况。语篇的意义潜势和多声部状况是语篇理解多样性的主要根源。

语体（style）是个古老的概念，不同的分析框架有不同的分析参数。有的将语言使用与情境要求联系起来，如正式、非正式等；有的从语言形式的角度去描述语体，如会话、书面等；有的从效果角度去分析，如幽默、雅致等，有的根据表达方式，如简洁、滞重等。任何语篇都有其区别性（distinctiveness）特征。语篇分析的语体概念有所不同。语体在语篇分析里主要表示语篇的区别性特征。语篇分析主要从语篇的语言组合（patterning of language）和语篇策略等角度分析语体，将语体视作语篇表意的一个组成部分。

三、交际

语篇分析的基本假设是语篇认知是**作者**（author）和**读者**（reader）通过语篇发生的多主体交际活动。作者和读者之间形成的**主体间关系**（intersubjectivity）对语篇认知产生重要的影响。

一直以来，人们都以为作者既然是文本的创作者，那他/她自然是文本观点的始作俑者，对文本意义的确定有绝对裁定权（author-as-authority），理解文本因而也就是理解作者意图中的意义。语篇分析则对这样的观点提出了质疑。在语篇分析的框架里，语篇传递的观点究竟是作者本人的还是他们所归属团体的是不确定的。在许多情况下，即便作者是单数形式出现，但他/她实际上却是复数单位，代表某个群体发声。另外，作者在不同的话语活动类型或体裁中的地位和作用也不完全相同。在文学等活动类型里，作者对文本似乎有更多的个体主张权利，但在科学类的话语里，作者往往传递的是群体的观点。Erving Goffman（1981）有关作者角色的假设在语篇分析里很有影响。在他看来，作者可以分别或同时扮演三种角色：① **发声者**（animator）。发声者类似一个传声筒；② **作者**（author），也就是书写者；③ **责任者**（principal）。责任者是语篇思想内容的拥有者。

语篇分析不再把读者视为被动接收作者企图传递意义的一方。读者是主动参与者。他们根据自己的目的、认知结构和语境，对语篇进行解读，参与语篇意义的构建。McCarthy 和 Carter 用"协商"（negotiation）一词精准地描写了读者在语篇认知中的地位和作用。

有关作者和读者的分析，主要集中在**身份**（identity）、**立场**（stance）等方面。**身份**指的是作者和读者在构建或解读语篇时的自我认同。自我认同既可以指作者和读者对自己在社会中所担任社会角色（role）的认同，也可以指他们对社团归属（membership）的认同。由于身份体现的是作者和读者的社会属性，因此身份有强烈的意识形态色彩。身份认同是影响语篇构建和认知最重要的因素。

立场（stance）指的是主观倾向，包括态度、情感、价值判断等内容。作者会根据不同的目的、不同的读者、不同的活动类型和具体语境选择显性或隐性表达自己的立场。所谓显性，指的是作者直白、不加掩饰地明示自己的立场。隐性则指作者出于某种考虑，故意掩饰自己的主观感受，隐晦地暗示自己的立场。任何语篇类型，即便是科学报告都有作者立场的表达。不同体裁有不同的习俗和规约制约立场的表达方式。读者在语篇认知时也会采用各种立场。读者的立场会严重左右他们对语篇的解读。

读者定位（positioning）是分析作者与读者之间所形成的主体间关系的一个分析框架。Stuart Hall（1999）的理论是很有影响力的。定位指的是作者和读者通过语篇进行的关系定位。定位是一个充满张力的双向制约过程：一方面，作者在构建语篇的过程中会运用话语策略激活他们所要求读者采用的态度、相关知识和体验，诱导或迫使读者根据他们所认定的立场和视角去理解语篇，以此控制认知过程。另一方面，读者则会根据自己的身份认同、态度、知识结构和目的等因素，参照具体的语境，决定解读视角，自主建立与语篇的关系，以找到合适的解读角度。语篇认知的效率与读者定位有很大的关系。

四、语境

语境（context）是语篇分析最核心的概念之一。它指的是制约语篇构建和认知的系列影响因素。这些因素之所以能影响语篇的构建和认知，主要是因为这些因素向读者提供了处理语篇的信息线索。语境参数就是由这些因素组成。值得注意的是，不同的人群对语境参数的认定和参数的信息读取并不相同。读者会根据自己的认知结构、需求等从语境里有选择地确定语境参数并提取相关信息。另外，语境参数的可及性（accessibility）和关联性也会因为不同人群而变化。语境参数的可及性和关联性也会随着语篇认知的展开不断变化。

语境是个多层级的概念，它既包括语篇形式、体裁、互文性等与语篇本体有关的因素，以及时间、场景等与语篇使用环境有关的因素，也包括身份认同、主体间性、话语社团[①] 等与作者和读者有关的因素，还包括历史、文化、传统等影响语篇构建和认知的各种社会因素。我们把语境分成微观和宏观两个维度。微观语境的信息主要从语篇内提取。宏观语境的信息主要由语篇激活的各种语篇外资源组成。

语篇外的资源相对比较庞杂，涉及社会、文化、知识、传统等许多因素。语篇分析特别强调文化的作用，把它视为语篇构建和认知的根本依据。文化决定了几乎所有与语篇有关的内容。由于不同的群体有各自独立的文化，因此文化是导致语篇多样性的主要原因，也是造成语篇认知分歧的主要因素。

宏观语境的另外一个参数是语篇的**互文性**（intertextuality），即语篇之间的相互参照（referring）关系。虽然语篇独立成章，但无论从内容或表述上，它们都与其他共时的和历时的语篇有千丝万缕的联系。互文性体现的是语篇所承载的各种记忆，表明任何语篇离不开对已有话语资源的利用。互文性分显性和隐性两种。显性互文指的是有标记地将其他文本嵌入或移植到主文本。隐性互文通常指其他文本被无标记地融入主文本。

互文性不仅能帮助我们了解单个语篇与其他语篇的关系，还能使我们了解语篇与其他语篇在历时和共时层面的联系，了解所分

① 话语社团（discourse community）是话语分析里的一个术语，指的是在话语活动中形成的、有共同身份认同、遵守共同话语习俗和话语规约的交际群体。

析的语篇在知识体系中的具体位置。Porter（1986）有一个非常形象的说法，研究语篇的互文性就是在语篇中寻找其他语篇的踪迹（traces）。认识语篇间的关系是理解语篇的基本前提。

本章推荐书目

［1］黄国文. 语篇分析概要［M］. 长沙：湖南教育出版社，1988.

［2］曲卫国. 话语文体学导论：文本分析方法［M］. 上海：复旦大学出版社，2009.

［3］Baker, P. and S. Ellece. 2011. *Key Terms in Discourse Analysis*. London: Continuum.

［4］Carter, R. and A. Goddard. 2016. *How to Analyse Texts: A Toolkit for Students of English*. London: Routledge.

［5］McCarthy, M. 1991. *Discourse Analysis for Language Teachers*. Cambridge: Cambridge University Press.

［6］Paltridge, B. 2012. *Discourse Analysis: An Introduction*. London: Bloomsbury.

第二章　阅读与阅读教学

导引问题：

- 什么是语篇分析的阅读观？
- 语篇分析对阅读教学有什么重要帮助？

本章提要：

就阅读而言，教师和学生都是独立的主体。阅读教学的主体虽是教师，但教师的作用是为学生提供帮助，方便学生在阅读中自主形成自己的理解。教师不能代替学生理解语篇。理解课文只是教学的一个次要目的。阅读教学的主要目的是培养和发展学生的理解能力。阅读是认知的，而阅读教学则是元认知的。由于语篇理解受到主体、语境等各种因素的影响，阅读因而是一个不断变化的**动态过程**。阅读教学不能以某个终极理解结束。阅读教学应该通过展示理解在阅读中被反复修正、甚至推翻的动态变化过程，让学生体会**阅读的复杂性**和**理解的多种可能性**。

一、概说

McCarthy 和 Carter 有关 discourse 这个概念的解释会颠覆语言教学认知的观点意味着，如果要把语篇分析理论和方法引入教学，我们就必须根据语篇分析的理论框架重新审视阅读和阅读教学，从社会认知的角度去重新认识阅读、阅读教学、阅读教学的目的、教学中的师生关系、教学过程等问题。

阅读是读者的自主认知活动，阅读教学是教师帮助学生理解语篇的指导活动。就阅读而言，教师和学生都是独立的主体，他们各自形成的理解都有其合理性。阅读教学的主体是教师，但教师只是教学的主体。教师的指导是为学生的阅读提供帮助，如为学生提供各种指导以调动学生的认知资源，使他们能运用这些资源识别语篇的线索，从而方便学生自主形成自己的理解。教师的作用不是带领学生一起完成阅读，更不是替代学生理解语篇。

传统阅读教学的目的主要是理解课文，即"What does the text say?"然而，语篇认知应该只是教学的一个次要目的。阅读教学的主要目的应该是培养和发展学生的理解能力。理解能力应该至少涉及两个层面：认知与元认知。提醒学生语篇里有哪些语篇提示固然重要，但帮助他们如何识别语篇提示应该更重要。向学生提供理解课文的语境自然有益处，可教会学生如何认识语境提示、如何从语境参数里提取相关信息以自主构成理解所需要的语境应该对学生的帮助更大。告诉学生课文的主题或中心思想虽然能使学生理解课文，但这样授予式的理解并不能发展学生独立自主的阅读能力，极可能事与愿违，养成学生的被动期待，使他们阅读时不想依靠自己的判断而只仰仗权威的指点。也许我们可以这么说，阅读的目的是认知的，而阅读教学的目的则是元认知的。

语篇理解受到主体、语境等各种因素的影响，因此阅读是一个不断变化的动态过程。所谓动态变化，指的是语篇理解会根据不断产生的新的提示和新的语境因素不断修正相关的推断。这就意味着我们要在教学过程中让学生充分意识到理解不是简单的一次性解码

（decoding）而是复杂的持续（ongoing）推导（inferencing）过程，因而我们的教学过程应该是这个动态过程的真实展示。教学过程不能以某一个终极理解或"中心思想"的获得而结束。它应该是一次次理解在一次次阅读中被修正、甚至推翻的动态变化过程。在这个过程中，新的理解不断生成，语篇细节或线索被重新纳入视野，认知资源不断得到补充和扩大，学生的心态越来越开放。简言之，我们在教学过程中要让学生体会到的是课文的复杂性和理解的多种可能性。唯有如此，我们才可能避免 Susan Sontag 所批判的文本理解的单一化（impoverishment of a text）①。

二、阅读和阅读理解

1. 定义
有关阅读和阅读理解有许多定义，我们这里仅介绍两个与语篇分析有关的定义：

(Reading is) an interactive process in which the reader's prior knowledge of the world interacts with the message conveyed directly or indirectly by the text (Smith 1995: 23)

在 Smith 的阅读定义里有三个关键词语很好地体现了语篇认知的特点。第一个关键词是"互动过程"（an interactive process）。这个关键词强调的是语篇认知的主体性。既然是互动，读者的自主参与

---

① Sontag, S. 1996. Against interpretation. In. S. Sontag. (Ed.). *Against Interpretation: And Other Essays*. New York: Picador, 7.

是阅读的基本前提。第二个关键词是"读者已有知识"（reader's prior knowledge of the world）。这个关键词指出了读者理解所要具备的要素，即读者的已有知识是读者理解语篇的关键，也就是说阅读理解的实现不仅需要语篇线索，更需要相关知识对这些线索进行识别和解读。最后一个关键词是"文本直接或间接提供的信息"（the message conveyed directly or indirectly by the text）。这个关键词描述的是文本传递信息的特点，即有些信息可以直接获取，但有些则需要推导方可得到。

有关阅读理解的定义，我们选的是 Snow 的：

We define reading comprehension as the process of simultaneously extracting and constructing meaning through interaction and involvement with written language. (2002: 11)

Snow 的定义里有四个关键词语很好地体现了阅读理解的特征。"提取"（extracting）这个词表明任何理解都源于语篇，有语篇的依据。"建构"（constructing）这个词则告诉我们阅读不是简单地从语篇采撷信息，而是读者基于自己的认知框架对所提取的信息进行意义构建。要强调的是作者用 simultaneously（同时地）这个时间副词强调提取和构建并不是两个独立分离的过程。它们是一个过程的两个不同维度。第三个关键词"互动"（interaction）与前面提到的 Smith 对阅读的定义有明显的呼应。"参与"（involvement）这个关键词更是突出阅读理解过程中读者的自主性。Snow 对这个词的选择让我们想起了 Benjamin Franklin 的名言："Tell me and I forget; Teach me and I may remember; Involve me and I learn."。没有自主参与，与语篇的互动和意义建构自然也就无从谈起。

互动和参与都始于"提取"，也就是对语篇提示或线索的识别。

Duffy 对语篇线索提取的重要性有过很清楚的描写：

I have tried to demonstrate that comprehension is a continuous process of using text clues—mainly word meanings but also syntactic clues—to access relevant categories of prior knowledge and, on the basis of our own experience with those categories of knowledge, making predictions about what meaning is to come. (2009: 17)

不识别和提取语篇线索，读者已有的相关知识就无法激活，理解也就无从展开。值得注意的是，Duffy 这里用的是"预测"（prediction）。既然是预测，也就有预测的证明。阅读理解实质上就是一个预测、证明、修正的动态推导过程。

2. 阅读过程

阅读理解过程始于识别；预测是理解的第二步；根据语篇线索进行推导是第三步；推导结论的验证是第四步。

（1）识别（identifying）

识别语篇线索是理解的开始，对预测有着至关重要的影响。以 Life in a day[①] 这篇课文为例，课文一开始就提出了三个问题：

What do you love? What do you fear? What's in your pocket?

作者显然不是要求读者去分别回答这三个问题。他在这里应该是给出了理解这篇课文的提示或线索。love, fear 和 pocket 三个词，究竟哪个是提示呢？我们可以从三个词的关系进行推导。love 和 pocket, fear 和 pocket 这两个搭配与 love 和 fear 的搭配不一样。love 和 pocket 不属于两个同类的词语。love 和 fear 则属于同类词语，都比较抽象。

---

① 邹为诚 . 普通高中教科书　英语　必修第一册［M］. 上海：上海教育出版社，2020：6-7. 详细讨论请参阅"第四章　视角"。

这似乎在提示课文是从具体的 pocket 视角去理解 love 和 fear。

又如课文 The 1940s house[①]。这篇课文的题目直接就给出了调动相关认知资源的提示。理解这篇课文，学生需要有与 20 世纪 40 年代有关的历史文化知识。作者没有选择 family 而选择了 house 这个词可能也是一种提示。如果查阅《朗文当代英语在线词典》(*Longman Dictionary of Contemporary English Online*，后简称 *Longman Dictionary Online*)，我们可能会得到启发。词典是这么定义 house 和 family 的：

house: a building that someone lives in, especially one that has more than one level and is intended to be used by one family[②]

family: a group of people who are related to each other, especially a mother, a father, and their children[③]

再如课文 Blame your brain[④]。blame 和 brain 分别提示了讨论的立场和视角。brain 提示了课文所依据的认知框架，告诉学生理解这篇课文需要相关的科学知识。

（2）预测（predicting）

Duffy 把预测视为阅读理解最基本的步骤：

Predicting is fundamental to comprehension. Good readers anticipate

---

① 邹为诚. 普通高中教科书　英语　必修第一册［M］. 上海：上海教育出版社，2020：60-61. 详细讨论请参阅"第三章　语境"。

② https://www.ldoceonline.com/dictionary/house.

③ https://www.ldoceonline.com/dictionary/family.

④ 邹为诚. 普通高中教科书　英语　必修第二册［M］. 上海：上海教育出版社，2020：6-7. 详细讨论请参阅"第六章　语篇结构Ⅱ：话题结构和主题结构"。

meaning. They do this by predicting what they think is going to happen in the selection and by revising their predictions as they read. (2009: 101)

　　读者在阅读时通常都会根据语篇提供的线索对语篇的话题或主题做出某种预测。预测除了提出待证明的推导假设以外，一个重要的作用是相关的认知资源的调动。

　　我们在看到 A healthy mind in a healthy body[①] 这篇文章的标题时可能会做两个基本的预测。第一个预测有关这篇文章的话题，即文章讨论的是大脑与身体健康的关系。第二个预测有关文章的主题，即文章可能主张健康身体是健康大脑的前提。

　　（3）推导（inferring）

　　预测是否成立，这需要读者根据从文章正文提取的线索做推导。推导会根据读者已有的知识、语篇提示和语境参数，对预测进行核实或修正。我们在这里简单演示一下 A healthy mind in a healthy body 这篇文章的推导过程。

Good morning and welcome to *The Healthy Option*. Last week, we discussed the link between a balanced diet and good health; this week we're looking at the link between a healthy body and a healthy mind. More than 2,000 years ago in ancient Rome, the poet Juvenal said, "A healthy body produces a healthy mind."

For years, people had linked the two, but it was only in the 1960s that solid scientific evidence started appearing. In the decades that followed, study after study confirmed what the ancient poet had already known: keeping fit really does help the brain work better.

---

① 邹为诚. 普通高中教科书　英语　选择性必修第一册［M］. 上海：上海教育出版社，2021：12.

In the 2000s, a team of medical researchers found out that students who did exercise before or during classes performed better in their school work. They conducted an experiment where one group of students ran for 30 minutes on a treadmill, while another group didn't do anything in particular. The students were then given a problem-solving task. The students who had exercised did 10% better at solving the problem than those students who hadn't stepped on the treadmill. In another experiment, a different group of students did physical exercise for 40 minutes each day instead of 40 minutes a week, and their overall grades improved by 14%. As a result of this research, many schools across the US changed their timetables and even their classrooms to allow more time for physical activity. Students who had previously not been physically active during the school day now had a chance to exercise.

前面的两个预测成立吗？有关话题的预测应该没有问题。文章第一段告诉我们这篇文章的话题确实讨论的是健康与大脑的关系。这段还披露了题目出自于古罗马诗人 Juvenal 的话。Juvenal 的原话是 "A healthy body produces a healthy mind."。

有关主题的预测能成立吗？文章的第二段指出现代医学为 Juvenal 的话提供了科学证据，证明 "Keeping fit really does help the brain work better."。文章的第三段提供了实验证据：参加体育锻炼的学生比不参加锻炼的学生成绩好。根据这两段提供的线索进行推导，有关这篇文章主题的预测似乎成立。我们也许可以根据所提取的信息初步构建这样的主题：

A healthy mind needs a healthy body.

（4）评价（evaluating）

评价的要点就是对推导过程进行反思，以确定我们构建的主题不仅能从语篇里找到充分的证据，而且现有的语篇线索都支持这个推导。

反思过程要求我们更细致地识别语篇线索。还是以 A healthy mind in a healthy body 为例。我们会注意到，第二段在介绍科学依据时并没有用 healthy 这个核心词。作者在这一段里用的是 fit。第三段介绍的两个实验都只是与 exercise 有关，似乎强调的都是 fit，并没有提供任何有关学生健康方面的信息。

fit 和 healthy 是同义词吗？如果查 *Longman Dictionary Online*，我们会得到这样的结果：

healthy: physically strong and not likely to become ill or weak[①]
fit: someone who is fit is strong and healthy, especially because they exercise regularly[②]

参照词典的解释，两个词语虽然语义基本重叠，但侧重不同。healthy 侧重指不生病或不虚弱（not likely to become ill or weak），而 fit 则强调经常锻炼（especially because they exercise regularly）。词典的解释说明这两个词并不完全同义。英语里像 fit and healthy 的说法也可以证实两者的细微差异。这个差异重要吗？这自然是值得我们对推导进行反思的问题。

基于这样的反思，我们也许可以对文章话题所做的预测进行修正。文章虽然是讲健康与大脑（health and mind），但重点讨论的可能是锻炼与大脑运作的关系。据此，我们对前面推导出的主题也应该做相应的修正。文章的中心思想似乎更像是：锻炼对大脑运作有好处（Keeping fit really does help the brain work better）。这个主题与第三段的实验的关联性更强。

---

① https://www.ldoceonline.com/dictionary/healthy.
② https://www.ldoceonline.com/dictionary/fit.

这里还涉及到对阅读初期启用的认知框架的调整。作者对 health 的定义是基于锻炼与健康关系的认知框架。这个认知框架有依据吗？作者有关 health 的概念与世卫组织是一致的：

Health is a state of complete physical, mental and social well-being and not merely the absence of disease or infirmity.[①]

当然，我们还可以做进一步的反思，把理解推向更深层次，如 a healthy mind 与 the brain works better 同义吗？我们甚至还可以提出这样的疑问：既然作者的重点是 fit，那他为什么不用 fit body and fit mind 呢？

3. 阅读能力

阅读的这四个基本步骤（指识别—预测—推导—评价）表明阅读能力有认知（cognition）和元认知（metacognition）两个维度。没有元认知或反思这个部分，阅读可能会流于浅层或错过重要的语篇提示。现在倡导的批判性阅读实际上指的是就是阅读过程中的元认知，即阅读中对自己理解和思维过程要进行反思，对影响自己理解的各种因素要有一定的意识。根据这两个维度，阅读能力应该体现在对这两个问题的回答上。第一个是认知问题：

语篇传递的是什么信息？（What is the message of the text?）

第二个是元认知问题：

（1）我怎么断定这就是语篇要传递的信息？（How do I know that it is the message of the text?）

（2）我是否错过了什么线索或是否因为我个人的原因导致我

---

① https://www.who.int/about/accountability/governance/constitution.

对语篇做出这样的理解？（Is there anything I miss or in myself that prompts me to interpret the text that way？）

我们认为，就阅读能力而言，元认知能力是最重要的，因为没有经过反思的理解极可能会错失语篇中许多微妙的提示，或者是读者的理解是受自己或他人立场影响的结果。对于反思的重要性，Harvey 和 Goudvis 在 *Strategies That Work* (2017) 一书里说得非常明确：

> Active readers interact with the text as they read. They pay attention to their inner voice as they read, listen, and view. They develop an awareness of their thinking, learn to think strategically, and actively use the knowledge they glean. In this way, reading shapes and even changes thinking.

4. 阅读目的

有关阅读目的，学界有很多讨论，我们这里主要介绍的是 Rosenblatt（1994）的理论。她认为阅读目的可以分为获取信息（read for information）和感受体验（read for experience）两个类型。她称前者为"输出型阅读"（efferent reading），后者为"审美型阅读"（aesthetic reading）。输出型阅读的目的是为了获取信息，关注的只是结果。审美型阅读关注的则是过程，主要是为了感受在阅读过程中获得的知性和情感愉悦。

大多数阅读都属于输出型阅读。在这类阅读中，我们通常止步于信息获取。除非有其他原因，我们一般不会对语篇做进一步深层次的挖掘。简言之，输出型阅读关心的是"What does the text talk about?"很少会问"Why does the text talk about it this way?"

在输出型阅读中，我们往往会快速浏览甚至跳过一些与我们所想获取的信息关联性不大的部分。Poets.org 上有一篇介绍如何阅读诗歌的文章：How to read a poem[①]。文章很长，一开始有好几段有关文学阅读和理解特点的介绍。如果我们主要想从这篇文章里了解诗歌阅读的步骤（what），我们可能不会按部就班地顺读，会略过文章开始的那些段落，直接跳到文章列举的步骤：①Reading a poem aloud；②The line；③Starting the conversation；④Talking back to a poem；⑤Text and context；⑥Embrace ambiguity。对介绍这些步骤段落阅读的粗细取决于我们对步骤的了解程度。如第二个步骤可能太笼统，我们会阅读得仔细一些：

> ... Lines are often determined by meaning, sound and rhythm, breath, or typography. ...The relationship between meaning, sound, and movement intended by the poet is sometimes hard to recognize, but there is an interplay between the grammar of a line, the breath of a line, and the way lines are broken out in the poem—this is called lineation.

不过，阅读目的也可能在阅读过程中发生变化，输出型阅读也常常会变换成审美型阅读。如果我们仅仅想了解网络点餐服务的利弊，在阅读 A new way of eating: online food delivery services[②] 时可能会止步于获取相关的信息，如 online food delivery services 的好处是：providing jobs, benefiting consumers, having a variety of restaurants to choose from 等。它的问题是：food safety, couriers' violation of the traffic rules, packaging waste 等。

---

① https://poets.org/text/how-read-poem-0.
② 邹为诚. 普通高中教科书　英语　必修第一册［M］. 上海：上海教育出版社，2020：54–55.

Few people knew about online food delivery apps ten years ago, but today, many would find it hard to live without them. In China alone, over 400 million people use such apps. For better or for worse, online food delivery services have changed the way we eat, and they are also having a huge impact on our society.

These services have no doubt brought us many benefits. They provide jobs for millions of people and help restaurants find more customers. Since the apps are very convenient, they also benefit consumers: we can now have meals delivered at any time of day, despite bad weather or busy schedules. This is especially important for people who work long hours, since they might not have time to cook. Not only do these apps save time, they also provide us with a wide variety of restaurants to choose from. They have proved to be useful for retired people as well: seniors who live far away from restaurants and supermarkets can now get hold of meals and groceries more easily.

However, we must not forget the drawbacks of online food delivery services. For one thing, they make it even easier to order unhealthy food, high in sugar, fat and salt. Food safety is another problem: it can be hard to establish where the food actually comes from, and whether the owner is legally permitted to run a restaurant. As couriers need to deliver the orders as quickly as possible, some pay little regard to traffic rules. In recent years, there have been a number of terrible traffic accidents because of this. Moreover, the industry is creating unbelievable amounts of packaging waste: over a million tonnes of online food delivery boxes are thrown away every year. Experts assume that this number will continue to grow in the future, and this will have a negative impact on the environment.

There are many advantages of these services, but we need to make sure that we make the right choices in the long run. We should do our best to limit waste, especially when it comes to packaging. We also need to think about what we eat and the impact on our health. Next time you are thinking about ordering in, you should ask yourself whether you really need to. In most cases, it's better to walk over to the supermarket, buy the ingredients you need, and then cook them yourself.

但假如我们在获取信息过程中发现不能完全接受文章的观点而开始对文章提出质疑时,阅读类型就会发生转变。假设我们不同意这篇文章对网络点餐服务的利弊分析,我们会与文章进行商榷。如虽然网络点餐服务为许多人提供了工作,但它也使许多人因为饭店经营困难或饭店倒闭而失业。再如,出现食品安全问题是因为有关部门监管不到位,因而食品安全与网络点餐服务并没有直接的因果关系等。对文章的观点提出质疑表明我们开始聚焦文章的立论和论证过程。在这个转型过程中,除了信息,我们还获取了知性的愉悦。

注重阅读过程是审美型阅读的主要特征。在这类阅读中,我们通常会更关注语篇的具体细节,很少跳读,对语篇的叙述或议论会有较多的反思。审美型阅读能促使我们对语篇进行深层次思考。Rosenblatt 用"审美型阅读"这个术语的一个重要原因是这类阅读通常涉及文学阅读。文学类体裁的语篇往往要求读者透过话题深层次去思考和解读作品的意义 [1]。Robert Frost 的 The rose family 这首诗非常简单,仅从表层信息看,这首诗似乎没有提供任何新的信息。如果不对该诗做进一步深入的思考,我们很难有知性的愉悦。

The rose family

The rose is a rose,
And was always a rose.
But the theory now goes

---

[1] 请参阅"第八章　体裁:叙事类"。

That the apple's a rose,

And the pear is, and so's

The plum, I suppose.

The dear only knows

What will next prove a rose.

You, of course, are a rose —

But were always a rose.

　　我们会根据语篇提示提出许多疑问，如：为什么作者会提出 "The rose is a rose" 这样同义反复的主张？为什么第二行的时态不是第一行的现在时而是过去时？为什么会突然出现 the theory？ theory 前面为什么是定冠词 the？为什么这个 theory 会把苹果、梨、李子等与玫瑰等同起来？ The dear 指的是什么？为什么只有 the dear 知道？为什么要用 prove 这个词？为什么作者在最后会坚持说 "You, of course, are a rose"？为什么要用破折号引出 "—But were always a rose"？[①]

　　我们在前文指出过，审美型阅读并不局限于文学阅读。任何不满足于信息提取而关注语篇解读过程的阅读都属于审美型阅读。简而言之，输出型阅读与审美型阅读的主要区别是，前者止步于信息提取，而后者企图对语篇为什么以这样的方式呈现信息等做深层次的思考。如果我们在阅读 Journalists on the job[②] 时，仅提取课文给出的系列答案，我们的阅读就属于输出型。如果我们对课文选择从记者这个职业的角度讨论择业进行思考并提出疑问时，我们的阅读就转型了。我们根据这篇课文第一段的提示可以预测该课文的话题与

---

① 请参阅"第七章　语篇的词汇关系"。

② 邹为诚. 普通高中教科书　英语　必修第三册［M］. 上海：上海教育出版社，2021：6-7. 详细讨论请参阅"第四章　视角"。

如何择业有关：

Senior high school students in Shanghai recently had the opportunity to participate in the annual Career Day, where they got to follow a mentor for a day. In this way, students can see what their mentors do at work. This kind of direct experience of real workplaces can benefit students a lot. It may help them choose a future career. It may also open their eyes to new opportunities or jobs that they've never considered before.

可课文接下来的话题都是记者职业的要求和特点，我们获得的只是与记者职业有关的信息。记者职业特点与一般职业有什么关联吗？

三、阅读教学

1. 阅读能力的培养

Biancarosa 和 Snow 在 *Reading Next — A Vision for Action and Research in Middle and High School Literacy: A report to Carnegie Corporation of New York*（2006）一书中指出了一般阅读和阅读教学的最大区别：前者是获取信息或读懂语篇，而后者关注的是如何通过阅读具体语篇掌握阅读技能。阅读教学的重点不是 what，而是 how。Biancarosa 和 Snow 在列举了一系列阅读能力之后一言以蔽之地指出，阅读能力的核心内容就是 how：

... how to read purposefully, select materials that are of interest, learn from those materials, figure out the meanings of unfamiliar words, integrate new information with information previously known, resolve conflicting content in different texts, differentiate fact from opinion, and recognize the perspective of the writer — in short, they must be taught how to comprehend. (2006: 1)

这里的 how 其实就是语篇的元认知能力，也就是反思能力。所谓反思，其实就是有问题意识。就能力培养而言，教师如何激发学生对自己的理解过程提出问题，是阅读教学最重要的任务。教师也许可以从以下三个角度去启发学生反思：

（1）我的结论是否有充分的语篇证据？语篇里是否有其他不利于我得出这一结论的证据？

（2）我对语篇证据的理解是否有偏差？对这些证据是否有其他不同的解读？

（3）我所选择的角度和认知框架是否受到自己立场的影响？理解这篇语篇是否还有其他角度或认知框架？

我们也可以从语言、话题和主题三个层次去考虑阅读能力培养。语言理解能力是识别语篇提示最基本的能力。一般说来，语言理解能力包括两个基本内容：① 对词语一般意义和用法的理解，如前面我们提到的 healthy 和 fit。我们应该了解这两个词语在一般语境里的区别。只有了解了区别，我们才可能认识到作者选择的意图。② 词语在具体语境里表达的词义以及它们在语篇里所起的提示作用。还是以 A healthy mind in a healthy body 为例，我们在推导过程中至少应该考虑以下几个问题：

（1）既然 healthy 和 fit 有不同的侧重，作者为什么要用 healthy 而不是 fit 呢？英语里确实有"A fit body means a fit mind"一说 [1]。

---

① https://www.edutopia.org/exercise-fitness-brain-benefits-learning.

（2）作者在介绍现代科学发现时用的是 brain："Keeping fit really does help the brain work better"。既然如此，作者这里为什么要用 mind 而不是 brain 呢？"How does the mind work"与"How does the brain work"有什么不同？

（3）作者在同一篇文章里的词语切换究竟在给读者什么提示？

话题理解能力涉及运用相关认知资源理解话题的基本要点。如理解 A healthy mind in a healthy body 这篇课文要求学生运用相关的知识去考虑这么几个问题：

（1）body 和 mind 之间的关系；

（2）锻炼对 mind 或 brain 能有什么样的改善？

（3）unhealthy body 是否一定会导致 unhealthy mind？

对主题推导的反思主要针对的是作者所试图传递的信息，也就是语篇的主题，要考虑的不仅是对语篇的线索是否有充分的识别，相关信息的提取是否合理，还要对主题里的观点提出质疑。我们在前面谈到过，A healthy mind in a healthy body 这篇文章的标题里就给出了明确的主题提示，但如果我们注意到作者对 fit 的强调，我们就会意识到作者写这篇文章的目的并不是仅仅告诉古罗马诗人 Juvenal 的假设已经被现代科学证明。从反思的角度看，学生至少要考虑这么几个问题：

（1）并不是一流的学者都有一流健康的身体，如 Stephen Hawking 等。既然如此，作者为什么要这么说呢？

（2）作者介绍的实验都来自美国学校，因而作者可能针对美国不少学校体育锻炼时间安排的不足，从锻炼与学习效率的角度强调锻炼的重要性。

2. 课文和课文分析

我们通常将用于教学的语篇称为"课文"。课文这个术语意味着语篇在阅读教学和一般阅读中的作用有很大的不同。Nuttall（1996: 54）用"可利用性"（exploitability）这个术语来强调课文的特殊属性。Nuttall 所说的可利用性，指的是课文除了阅读目的以外，还有更重要的教学目的。从培养和发展学生的阅读能力的教学目的看，课文不是仅仅用来被学生理解。课文的主要用途是为训练学生的阅读能力和展示理解何以可能提供场所。也就是说，如果我们讨论完中心思想后就结束课文教学，我们只是把课文作为一般阅读材料。对于课文，我们应该在分析课文中更关注 how。

教师通常会在课堂里与学生分享自己对课文的理解。不过，从阅读教学的目的和课文的作用看，教师分享的不应该仅仅是自己得出的结论，更应该向学生展示自己的理解过程和结论的依据。Duffy 称教师的展示为思维示范（modeling the thinking）（2009: 52）是非常有道理的。只分享结论难免会出现把自己的理解强加给学生的结果。

有关教师对课文理解的分享，我们认为有必要消除阅读教学中另外一个更常见的误区，那就是教师对课文有一锤定音的阐释权威。之所以称之为误区，这是因为语篇阐释是基于读者的认知结构、阅读历史和生活体验与语篇互动后得出的结论。不同的认知结构、阅读历史和生活体验自然会产生不同的理解，学生在认知结构等诸多方面与教师存在很大的差异，他们的结论因而极可能和教师的不一样。但是不一样并不意味着不正确。理解是没有权威的。多样化的理解是阅读的正常现象。教师展示自己理解的主要目的如前文所说的，是展示推导过程，推导过程的展示会祛除阅读的神秘色彩，会让学生意识到理解与语篇提示识别、语境构建、认知资源等许多因素密切相关。Duffy 对教师分享理解的作用有非常到位的评论：

Students use your explanation as a guide, not as a script to follow. (2009: 52)

谈到教师解释的权威化，自然会联想到作者和评论家的解释权威。虽然作者在写作时有明确的意图并想方设法地设置提示以引导读者，但由于语言的歧义、语境的换置、读者的认知资源等各种复杂因素的影响，他们的努力并不能确保语篇不会引起不同的解读。Robert Frost 的诗歌 The Road Not Taken 就是一个很好的例子。这首诗的写作缘起于 Frost 和他朋友 Edward Thomas 的散步。Thomas 每到一个岔路口，总会举棋不定。每次做完选择后，他总是觉得应该走另外一条路。于是 Frost 写了这首诗讽刺了他。Frost 以为 Thomas 会把这首诗看成是一个玩笑，然而 Thomas 却不这样看 ①。

评论家常常会把语篇置于他们所熟悉的认知框架和知识图谱里，根据他们所信奉的理论去识别语篇线索，阐释语篇意义。他们会依照自己评论的目的系统强调该语篇某个维度的意义。评论家相对渊博的知识和娴熟的语言技巧，尤其是他们的社会地位，往往会赋予他们的解释较高的权威性。然而，参照语篇分析的基本假设，这种权威主要源于非认知的原因，如他们的社会地位和他们对某类认知资源的把握，并没有绝对的语篇依据。其实，因为所依据的理论不同，评论家对同一作品的评论也往往莫衷一是。如《普通高中教科书英语 必修第二册》有一篇课文节选于 Hemingway 的 The Old Man and the Sea。Hemingway 是公认的含蓄作家，因而评论家对这部作品主题的解读莫衷一是。有些评论家认为，这部作品讲的是 resistance to defeat；有些则认为该作品是有关 pride；还有评论家提出这部作品的主题与 man

---

① Orr, D. 2015. *The Road Not Taken*. New York: Penguin.

and nature 有关 ①。这些评论家的推导都有语篇线索的依据，在他们构建的语境里都有合理性。但如果把其中某个解读视为这部作品主题的终极性结论，这不仅无视语篇其他线索的存在以及对语篇线索各种解读的可能，对培养学生的自主阅读能力也没有任何益处。

3. 教师的角色

按照 Moreillon 的说法，教师的主要任务并不是简单回答 when、where、who、what、how 等在课文里能找到现成答案的问题。他们承担的任务要艰巨和复杂得多：

> Educators must strive to support students' thinking by modeling questioning that does not end with knowledge-level questions. They must model questioning that stretches readers beyond the facts found "on the line" (in the print or illustrations), to think between the lines, to think through and beyond the text. (2007: 59)

将学生的思路引向课文的深处和细微处方面，这是教师最重要的任务。教师的引导作用主要体现在两个维度。首先是语篇认知维度。由于各种原因，学生在阅读课文时往往没有相关知识的充分储备。教师因而有必要提前或适时干预，提供或者调动学生的相关知识资源。

不过，教师的干预是一把双刃剑。一方面，教师的知识结构相对完善，阅读经历也丰富，因此教师能较好地判断理解语篇时所需要的知识和语境信息。他们直接提供的信息通常关联性强，效率高。另一方面，教师的直接干预对培养学生对自己已有知识局限的意识以及补充相关知识储备的能力也有负面作用。自主发现自己知识不足的问题并进行自主修正，独立寻找相关资源，这是阅读能力的关

---

① https://www.litcharts.com/lit/the-old-man-and-the-sea/themes.

键要素。Snow 非常强调自主调动认知资源和自主修正的重要性：

Skilled readers are good comprehenders. They differ from unskilled readers in their use of general world knowledge to comprehend text literally as well as to draw valid inferences from texts, in their comprehension of words, and in their use of comprehension monitoring and repair strategies. (2002: 78)

其次，教师的作用在元认知能力培养方面有着不可或缺的作用。他们可以根据语篇理解的不同阶段和层面有针对性地提出系列元认知问题（how do you know）以提醒学生对自己的认知途径和过程进行反思。教师可以有针对性地适时介入，质疑学生推导依据的充分性。学生在阅读中往往会陷于最初构建的认知框架或自己对某一问题的态度等因素，有意无意地选择符合自己认知框架或态度的语篇线索，忽视与之不符的内容。在这种情况下，教师可以提供不同的认知框架，或者不同的语篇线索，甚至对同样的语篇线索做不同的解释，以帮助学生了解不同认知框架等对语篇解读的影响，以此促使他们反思自己所选择的视角和采用的认知框架。

当然，教师的作用远不止这些。必须强调的是，教师干预的依据不是基于自己的理解，而是针对学生在理解过程中产生的问题。不然，学生并不一定能理解教师干预的原因。Smith 曾强调指出：

It is not reading that many children find difficult, but the instruction. (2004: 3)

一句话，教师的作用不是提供答案，而是提供或帮助学生发现线索并根据这些线索进行推导。教师的作用是提出问题，让学生认识到语篇理解的复杂性。如果教师使学生觉得理解语篇很容易或迫使学生接受自己的理解，那教学就失败了。

4. 学生的角色

学生在阅读教学中也有双重身份。他们首先是一般读者。自主阅读课文是他们的基本任务。他们要充分利用已有的知识去识别课文的线索，并根据这些线索形成自己独立的阐释。Ricoeur 有一个比喻非常生动，读者（学生）是演奏家，不是听众。文本是谱子，只有通过他们的演奏，也就是阅读，文本才能产生意义：

> The text is like a musical score and the reader like the orchestra conductor who obeys the instructions of the notation. Consequently, to understand is not merely to repeat the speech event in a similar event, it is to generate a new event beginning from the text in which the initial event has been objectified. (1976: 75)

如果学生不进行自主阅读而以听取教师阅读的结论为目的，他们就成了聆听别人演奏音乐的听众，欣赏的只是别人对乐谱的理解。他们只是间接阅读者。唯有自己阅读，学生才能了解语篇的复杂性并体会阅读的知性愉悦。

其次，他们又是学习者。作为学习者，他们的任务不仅仅是理解课文，而是在教师的指导下通过反思自己的理解过程，提高自己的元认知意识，以发展独立阅读能力。简言之，学习者要提出的不仅仅是课文讲什么的问题。他们要就理解过程不断提出反思性问题，对自己、甚至教师的理解依据提出质疑。学完一篇课文后，如果仅仅知其然而不知其所以然，这说明学生只是完成了读者而不是学习者的任务。

我们这里借用 de Certeau（1984）的一个比喻。他曾把读者比作游客（Readers are travelers）。这比喻能很形象地形容课文、学生、教师三者的关系。课文是景点，导游的讲解虽然对欣赏景色会有很大的帮助，但它不能代替景色。游客不能只听讲解而不看景色，也不能只信讲解而不信自己的眼睛。

Readers are travellers; they move across lands belonging to someone else, like nomads poaching their way across fields they did not write, despoiling the wealth of Egypt to enjoy it themselves. (1984: 174)

本章推荐书目

[1] Biancarosa, G. and C. Snow. 2006. *Reading Next — A Vision for Action and Research in Middle and High School Literacy: A report to Carnegie Corporation of New York*. 2nd Edition. Washington DC: Alliance for Excellent Education.

[2] Duffy, G. G. 2009. *Explaining Reading: A Resource for Teaching Concepts, skills and Strategies*. 2nd Edition. New York: The Guilford Press.

[3] McCarthy, M. and R. Carter. 1994. *Language as Discourse: Perspectives for Language Teaching*. London: Longman.

[4] Smith, F. 2004. *Understanding Reading: A Psycholinguistic Analysis of Reading and Learning to Read*. 6th Edition. Mahwah, NJ: Lawrence Erlbaum.

第三章　语境

导引问题：

- 什么是语境？
- 语境对阅读理解有什么影响？

本章提要：

　　语境是理解语篇所需要的具体信息，通常由**作者**、**情境**、**语篇线索**等各种参数组成。只有那些被识别了的语篇提示才可能被读者列为语境构建的基本参数。语境构建最重要的步骤是从语境参数中提取相关信息。由于认知结构、阅读目的等不同，不同的读者对语篇提示会有不同的识别，对理解语篇所需语境参数的认定也会不一样。即便是相同的参数，不同读者提取的信息也不一定相同。不一样的信息提取必然导致不同的语境构建。不同的语境必然导致不同的理解。语境可以分为从语篇外获得资源的**宏观语境**和从语篇内获得信息的**微观语境**两个类别。

一、概说

　　"语境"（context）指的是理解语言行为所需的具体信息。Clark 和 Carlson 的定义是最经典的：

To sum up, context is information that is available to a particular person for interaction with a particular process on a particular occasion. (1981: 318)

语言理解之所以需要语境首先是因为许多语言表达式本身是多义的，因而也是含糊的，如：

A: The bill is large.

bill 有"账单"和"鸟嘴"的意思。没有语境提供相关信息就无法确定这句话里的 bill 究竟指什么。更重要的是，语言使用都出自于某种意图，也就是语用学所描述的"言外之力"（illocutionary force）。语言表达式本身不明示意图。即便确定了 bill 的意思，如果没有语言使用时其他具体信息，要理解 A 说这话的意图也是非常困难的。

语境通常由系列参数组成，这些参数与交际活动的构成要素有关。交际活动的第一要素是交际人，因此语境参数第一类别的信息是有关交际人或作者和读者，如他们的身份、立场、目的等各种相关信息。情境是交际活动的第二个要素，也是语境参数的第二个类别，具体包括言语行为具体发生的时空、场景、社会历史背景等信息。第三个语境参数类别与言语行为本体有关，如语言形式、话题、体裁等诸多信息。

不过，语境并不是一个自动形成的参数系列组合，它是读者从所选择参数里提取相关信息构建的结果。读者的选择不是任意的，它受到两个因素的影响。第一个因素是语篇的语境提示或线索（contextualization cues）。只有那些被识别了的提示才可能被读者列为语境构建的基本参数。语境提示可分为显性和隐性两种。显性提示通常有明确的词汇表述，相对容易识别，如 The 1940s house①。1940s 这个词语明确提示理解该语篇需要掌握 1940s 这个历史时期的信息。隐性提示虽然也是通过词汇示意，但其明示程度要低许多，如 house 这个词。这个词一方面显性提示需要具体了解 1940s 哪方面的信息，另一方面作者选择 house 而不是 family，这似乎又给出了隐性提示。

　　根据语篇提示选定参数只是语境构建的第一步。参数只是语境构建所需要的程序性（procedural）指令。语境构建最重要的步骤是读者从语境参数中提取相关信息。影响语境构建的第二个因素是读者的认知结构。由于认知结构、阅读目的等的不同，不同的读者对语篇线索会有不同的识别，对理解语篇所需语境参数的认定也会不一样。即便是相同的参数，不同读者提取的信息也不一定相同。不一样的信息提取必然导致不同的语境构建。如 1940s 涉及的时空范围很大，社会历史文化信息也非常多，究竟提取哪些信息构建理解这篇课文的历史语境，不同的读者会有不同的选择。这些选择对课文主题的阐释会有很大的影响。

　　按照 Sperber 和 Wilson（1995）提出的关联理论（relevance theory），语境构建是一个不断变化的动态过程。随着阅读的展开和深入，更多的语境线索会被识别，新的语境参数会被选用，因而最初构建的语境会被推翻或调整。语境的调整或重构意味着语篇理解就会发生变化。

　　我们这里有关语境提示或线索（contextualization cues）基本依据的是 Gumperz（1982）提出的概念：

————————

① 邹为诚.普通高中教科书　英语　必修第一册［M］.上海：上海教育出版社，2020：60-61.具体分析请参阅下面的讨论。

Roughly speaking, a contextualization cue is any feature of linguistic form that contributes to the signaling of contextual presuppositions. (1982: 131)

Gumperz 的定义里有两个基本要素：一是语言形式（linguistic form），即语境线索主要是通过语言表达的；二是语境线索提示的是语境预设（contextual presuppositions），也就是说语境线索提示的是语言理解的必要前提。

语境有多种分类，我们这里参照 van Dijk（2008: 19–20）的理论，把语篇语境分为宏观语境（macro-context）和微观语境（micro-context）两个类别。宏观语境参数的信息提取大多从语篇外资源获得，主要影响的是语篇的认知框架等，具体包括 ① 与作者有关的语境信息，如生活经历、创作活动和思想倾向等；② 与语篇有关的历史、社会、文化等信息；③ 与其他语篇的互文关系等。微观语境则指从语篇内提取信息而构成的语境。微观语境主要出现在语篇的语言层面，具体涉及词义关系、话题、主题等的理解。

二、语境与教学

语境意识是语篇意识的第一要素。语境意识的核心内容是对语境作用的认识，即任何语篇理解都是语境构建的产物。语篇的不同理解主要源于所构建语境的不同。就语境意识培养而言，关键是提高学生语境的敏感度，即要求他们拿到语篇时首先考虑语篇的语境构建。语境构建的基本内容是语境线索识别、参数选择和信息提取。

具体说来，可以让学生考虑这么几个问题：

（1）这篇课文给出了哪些语境线索？

（2）根据这些线索，我们应该选定哪些语境构建的参数？

（3）我们应该从这些参数里提取哪些关联信息？

（4）是否还有我们没有识别的语境线索？

（5）是否有构建不同语境的可能？

按照 Gumperz 的理论，语境线索是通过语言表达的，因此关注作者选择的语言表达形式是识别语境线索的关键，如在阅读 An experiment in education[①] 这篇课文时，我们首先要问的是：作者为什么要选择 experiment 这个词？这个选择是否在提示我们理解这篇课文所需要的语境信息呢？

信息提取需要一定的知识资源，尤其是宏观语境信息的提取。如何提高相关语境信息的可及性，这是很重要的问题。如果教师直接把自己构建语境时所提取的信息传递给学生，这虽然方便学生的语境构建，但也限制了学生参数选择和信息提取的自主性。在学生识别语境线索和确定相关参数后，我们可以提出这么几个问题供他们思考：

（1）这个参数所包含的信息涉及什么样的知识资源？

（2）判断知识资源的关联标准是什么？

（3）选择提取这些信息的依据是什么？

（4）如果提取其他信息，对理解会产生什么样的影响？

---

① 邹为诚．普通高中教科书　英语　必修第二册［M］．上海：上海教育出版社，2020：24-25．具体讨论请参阅"第四章　视角"。

三、宏观语境

任何语篇理解都是从宏观语境开始的。宏观语境的提示大多数是显性的。宏观语境包括许多参数，我们这里主要考虑的是两个参数类别：作者和背景。

1. 作者

对作者的了解程度会影响我们对语篇的期待、态度和理解。一般说来，有关作者的任何信息都可能为语篇理解提供线索。当然，作者只是个语境参数，究竟哪些与他们有关的信息可以提取为语境信息，这需要根据语篇的内容决定。

William Wordsworth 的诗 I wandered lonely as a cloud[①] 是一首经典的英语诗歌：

I wandered lonely as a cloud

I wandered lonely as a cloud
That floats on high o'er vales and hills,
When all at once I saw a crowd,
A host of golden daffodils;
Beside the lake, beneath the trees,
Fluttering and dancing in the breeze.

Continuous as the stars that shine
And twinkle on the Milky Way,
They stretched in never-ending line
Along the margin of a bay:
Ten thousand saw I at a glance,

---

① 邹为诚.普通高中教科书　英语　选择性必修第三册［M］.上海：上海教育出版社，2022：25.具体分析请参阅"第八章　体裁：叙事类"。

Tossing their heads in sprightly dance.

The waves beside them danced; but they
Out-did the sparkling waves in glee:
A poet could not but be gay,
In such a jocund company:
I gazed—and gazed—but little thought
What wealth the show to me had brought:

For oft, when on my couch I lie
In vacant or in pensive mood,
They flash upon that inward eye
Which is the bliss of solitude;
And then my heart with pleasure fills,
And dances with the daffodils.

William Wordsworth 是著名的浪漫主义诗人，一般认为浪漫主义创作思想和手法对理解这首诗会有很大的启发。但浪漫主义其实只是一个语境参数。参考 *Britannica* 的解释，这个术语里有许多不同的信息：

Among the characteristic attitudes of Romanticism were the following: a deepened appreciation of the beauties of nature; a general exaltation of emotion over reason and of the senses over intellect; a turning in upon the self and a heightened examination of human personality and its moods and mental potentialities; a preoccupation with the genius, the hero, and the exceptional figure in general and a focus on his or her passions and inner struggles; a new view of the artist as a supremely individual creator, whose creative spirit is more important than strict adherence to formal rules and traditional procedures; an emphasis upon imagination as a gateway to transcendent experience and spiritual truth; an obsessive interest in folk culture, national and ethnic cultural origins, and the medieval era; and a predilection for the exotic, the remote, the mysterious, the weird, the occult, the monstrous, the diseased, and even the satanic.[1]

Britannica 提供了以上 8 条相关信息，我们应该从 romanticism 这个参数里提取什么样的信息呢？

了解作者的生活经历对语篇理解有时也会有帮助，如这首诗是 1802 年 4 月 15 日 Wordsworth 和他的妹妹 Dorothy 在英国湖区去格拉斯米尔湖（Grasmere）经过格林可因湾（Glencoyne Bay）时写的。当时他看到一片水仙花时诗兴大发。这个背景知识对理解诗歌中提到的 vales and hills、the lake、the margin of a bay，还有 The waves beside them danced 等词语提供了很好的线索。

课文 An excerpt from *The Old Man and the Sea*[2] 是美国作家 Ernest Hemingway 的作品节选。Hemingway 的创作思想和他的其他作品的主题会为我们理解课文的这个片段提供思路，如学界讨论他的作品常提起的 the Hemingway code。*Britannica* 在解释 the Hemingway code 时专门提到了 *The Old Man and the Sea*:

To survive in such a world, and perhaps emerge victorious, one must conduct oneself with honour, courage, endurance, and dignity, a set of principles known as "the Hemingway code." To behave well in the lonely, losing battle with life is to show "grace under pressure" and constitutes in itself a kind of victory, a theme clearly established in *The Old Man and the*

---

① https://www.britannica.com/art/Romanticism.

② 邹为诚. 普通高中教科书　英语　必修第二册［M］. 上海：上海教育出版社，2020：60-61. 具体讨论请参阅"第六章　语篇结构Ⅱ：话题结构和主题结构"。

Sea.[1]

　　不过，课文只是小说的一个片段，因而这个 code 在多大意义上能帮助我们理解这个片段，这还取决于我们如何根据课文的线索从中提取与课文相关联的信息。

　　当然，不仅文学语篇的作者信息有助于理解，非文学语篇作者的信息同样能为理解语篇提供重要线索。如 Blame your brain[2] 的作者是 Nicola Morgan。她在自己的网站上是这样介绍自己的：

Nicola Morgan is one of our leading writers for teenagers: an award-winning novelist and expert in the teenage brain and mental health, who is invited all over the world to talk on a huge variety of fascinating topics. Nicola has won many awards, including Scottish Children's Book of the Year twice. Her novel, *Wasted*, was on lots of award lists and nominated for the Carnegie Medal. *Fleshmarket* is popular in schools and *Mondays are Red* continues to inspire and enthral. In 2018, she was awarded the School Library Association's prestigious award for Outstanding Contribution to Information Books. She has written about teenage brains, stress, anxiety, peer pressure and friendships, human behaviour, life online, body image and sleep.

Most importantly, Nicola cares about your wellbeing and has masses of science-based advice to help you be healthier, stronger, happier and more successful.[3]

---

① https://www.britannica.com/biography/Ernest-Hemingway.
② 邹为诚. 普通高中教科书　英语　必修第二册［M］. 上海：上海教育出版社，2020：6-7. 具体讨论请参阅"第六章　语篇结构Ⅱ：话题结构和主题结构"。
③ https://nicolamorgan.com/about-me/.

这段自我介绍最后一句话里的"cares about your wellbeing and has masses of science-based advice"显然是解读这篇课文的主题的重要语境信息。

Life in a day① 这篇课文主要介绍的是电影 *Life in a Day*。寻找课文提到的 Kevin MacDonald 导演的信息能让我们了解导演拍摄这部纪录片的指导思想。这对理解课文是非常有价值的。

MacDonald 之前拍摄过多部纪录片，如 *One Day in September*、*Touching the Void*、*State of Play* 等。这些纪录片能为我们了解他的创作思想和理解这篇课文提供重要的线索。Jeffrey Brown 在采访 MacDonald 导演时希望他能就课文第一段里的三个问题（What do you love? What do you fear? What's in your pocket?）做些解释。Brown 特别提到了"What's in your pocket?"这个问题。MacDonald 是这样回答的：

Well, that's a way of getting at themes to do with possessions, materialism, consumerism, inequality, because obviously what a farmer in Jaipour has in his pocket differs substantially to what an American teenager has in theirs. So it's a kind of interesting way into discussing that theme or the themes relating to possessions and what we own.②

MacDonald 对所收集到的视频处理过程的回顾对理解电影和课文的信息结构有非常大的帮助：

---

① 邹为诚. 普通高中教科书　英语　必修第一册［M］. 上海：上海教育出版社，2020：6-7. 具体讨论请参阅"第四章　视角"。

② https://www.pbs.org/newshour/arts/conversation-kevin-macdonald-director-of-life-in-a-day.

To begin with I had to sit back and just be nonjudgmental and just let material wash over me and sort of tell me what it wanted to say and listen to what it had to say. But then, of course, the time comes when you have to become the director and you have to say, OK, this is what I'm interested in, these are the themes that come out of this for me, these are my favorite clips for XYZ reason, and here is how I'm going to try and structure this. And really what we've done is we've structured it in kind of chronological order starting at midnight, ending at midnight ... But at the same time we're going through various thematics and so we approach some of that — the big issues of life and that's really what the movie is about.[①]

MacDonald 对纪录片主题的解释可以为我们对课文主题的推导提供依据：

I think that what people want to tell you is more or less that we are all fundamentally the same, and that sounds like kind of a cliche. ... There's a lot of emotion, a lot of laughter, a lot of things we all expect from seeing a movie. But what struck me was that everybody has ultimately got the same values, the same things that were important to them.

2. 背景

有关背景，我们这里主要讨论社会历史文化、作品创作、作品的互文关系等三个内容。

有关语篇历史文化背景的语境线索大多是显性的，语篇标题常常会有明确的提示。前面提到，The 1940s house[②] 这篇课文标题里的

---

① https://www.pbs.org/newshour/arts/conversation-kevin-macdonald-director-of-life-in-a-day.

② 邹为诚.普通高中教科书　英语　必修第一册［M］.上海：上海教育出版社，2020：60–61.具体分析请参阅下面的讨论。

1940s 直接明示我们理解这篇课文所需要了解的历史背景知识。这篇课文的第一段又明确说明 The 1940s House 是一项社会调查实验。这个说明为 Lyn Hymers 一家的活动提供了即时的背景知识：

> "There were many times when I thought, 'I can't do this. I am a 21st century woman. I don't work eighteen-hour days.' But then I'd stop and say, 'Hang on. In the 1940s, women didn't say they couldn't do it. They just got on with it.'" These are the words of 50-year-old Lyn Hymers, who took part in an experiment called *The 1940s House*. The purpose of the experiment was to see if a modern-day family would be capable of surviving in the 1940s.

这两种背景，尤其是社会调查实验的信息，是这篇课文不可或缺的宏观认知语境[①]。

在第一段开始的这几句话 "There were many times when I thought, 'I can't do this. I am a 21st century woman. I don't work eighteen-hour days.'" 里，a 21st century woman 是个重要语境线索。21st century women 有许多特点，究竟哪些特点是相关联的呢？这是我们在提取信息时要考虑的问题。理解 Lyn 的另外一句话 "Hang on. In the 1940s, women didn't say they couldn't do it. They just got on with it." 就需要我们了解生活在那个年代妇女的特点，以便理解两个时代女性的差异。同样，生活在那个年代的妇女也有许多特点，到底哪些信息是有参考价值的呢？

课文介绍了实验四个方面的内容。这四个方面构成了 1940s 年代物质生活的基本语境：

---

① 有关 1940s 这段历史信息，网上有许多资料。有关这项社会实验，可以参考 https://www.iwm.org.uk/learning/resources/the-1940s-house. 和 https://the1940sexperiment.com/.

54

（1）生活条件

Unfortunately, when they opened the door, all 21st century labour-saving devices immediately disappeared. There was no central heating or fridge in the house, but luckily they had a coal fire to keep them warm.

（2）安全

World War II started in 1939, and German planes were regularly dropping bombs over London. Although the war wasn't real for the Hymers, they spent a lot of time down in the hole.

（3）物资供应

In the 1940s, there was rationing of goods such as food and petrol. There wasn't much meat or milk, or many eggs, and the food was really boring. As a result, the family were often hungry, especially the children.

（4）家务

Things that Lyn did easily before, now became terribly difficult. She missed her washing machine most of all. "We had to boil the clothes and when the weather wasn't good, it was impossible to dry anything," said Lyn.

我们要考虑的问题是：

① 作者为什么选择这四个方面？ ② 这些方面与 surviving 有什么关系？ ③ 它们究竟考验的什么样的能力？ ④ 它们与前面提到的 1940s 妇女的特点又有什么关系？ ⑤ 它们与 Lyn 的态度又有

什么关系？

课文的最后一段提到了生活在 21 世纪有更好物质生活条件的 Lyn 却更想念那个物质匮乏的 1940s 年代：

> Today, Lyn is back in her modern, open-plan home, but surprisingly, she misses the 1940s house. The family grew closer, she feels, because they helpfully shared the hard work. In the evenings they played board games with the children, read books or just talked. Life in the 1940s wasn't easy, but an easier and more comfortable life doesn't necessarily mean a better life. "I would happily go back there," she says. "I loved that house where we all laughed and cried together as a family."

这是为什么？ Lyn 提到了一个理由："The family grew closer, she feels, because they helpfully shared the hard work"。理解这个理由需要我们了解 21 世纪生活形态和人际关系出现的变化，尤其是有关 being close 和 sharing 这两方面的变化。

这些新的语境线索可能会对我们思考课文主题产生影响。根据课文提供的信息，1940s 家庭成员 grew closer 是因为物质匮乏、生活不安宁迫不得已的选择。生活在 1940s 年代的人当时是怎么看待他们的生活呢？ 没有这些现代物质设备的他们是否会认同 Lyn 的感受呢？ 要回答这些问题，当然需要我们构建更大的宏观语境。不过，根据课文现有的语境线索，也许我们在思考中会产生这样几个问题：

（1）为什么 Lyn 一定要回到过去才可能重新找到家人间亲密的感觉呢？

（2）物质富裕了一定会使家人疏远？

（3）现代社会的人是否真的相互疏远了？

（4）现代社会是否真的不需要分享和分担（sharing）了？

（5）现代物质生活所带来的方便究竟是好还是坏？

值得注意的是，作者没有提供了解孩子想法的语境线索。他们是否会像 Lyn 一样希望回到物质匮乏的过去呢？他们对 closeness 和 sharing 又是怎么认识的呢？这自然又需要更多的语境信息。

The 1940s house 主要涉及的是社会历史背景语境。知识背景也是很常见的宏观语境参数。许多语篇的理解需要调动相关的知识资源。如 Going global[①] 这篇课文。标题里的 global 这个词虽然清楚地提示我们这篇课文所涉及的知识领域，可全球化是个涉及面很广的知识领域。理解这篇课文究竟具体需要提取全球化哪方面的知识信息，课文标题并没有明确告诉我们。这篇课文的宏观语境需要我们在阅读过程中不断地去细化调整。

课文的第一段似乎没有在讨论全球化问题，只给出了世界人口数量增加的信息：

The world's population reached five billion on the day I was born. That was in Indonesia back in 1987, and my parents were amazed that there were so many people on the planet. However, since then the population has continued to increase at an alarming rate. In October 2011, the seven billionth baby was born, and experts predict that there will be ten billion of us before the end of this century.

作者谈人口增量显然在提示这篇课文有关全球化的讨论与人口增长有关。人口是重要的语境参数。

作者在课文的第二段用了两个非常感性的例子帮助大家想象现

---

① 邹为诚. 普通高中教科书　英语　必修第二册［M］.上海：上海教育出版社，2020：42-43.

在人口数量之大的程度：

A number as big as seven billion is hard to imagine. If you said "hello" to a different person every second, it would take you 222 years to greet everyone on the planet. If seven billion people made a human chain with their hands, the chain would go to the moon and back nine times.

作者这么做显然是在强化人口这个语境参数。

课文的第三段谈到了人口增长速度越来越快的问题：

The growth of our human population is surprising. For more than two million years, humans moved around, finding plants to eat and hunting animals for meat. Then, just 10,000 years ago, we invented agriculture. At that time, there were only about five million humans, but this figure quickly doubled. The population reached a billion in 1805, and since then it has multiplied seven times. Experts believe that about 6% of all the humans that have ever lived are alive right now.

课文前三段有关人口增长的介绍基本明确了理解这篇课文需要的知识资源：全球化与人口的关系。如果查阅相关资料，我们会发现大多数有关人口与全球化的讨论都是从经济这个角度出发的。如有的研究提到了 "population dynamics have influenced globalization through effects on the distribution of labor and capital"[1]。不过，从课文在第四段指出的现象看，课文的角度不是经济问题：

The human population has never been bigger, but in some ways the

---

[1] S. J. La Croix, A. Mason and S. Abe. 2003. Population and Globalization. *Asia-Pacific Population & Policy*. East-West Centre, Number 64.

planet seems to be getting significantly smaller. In the past, travellers from Europe to Indonesia spent months at sea. Now you just have to sit on a plane for a few hours. When you arrived in another country a hundred years ago, you saw unfamiliar styles of clothing and buildings and discovered a completely different culture. In many places today, clothing and new buildings are very similar, and people enjoy the same sports, music, films and TV shows. We also buy the same products—smartphones, big burgers and T-shirts—from huge, global companies. Although we are on different continents, we are to a large extent starting to live the same lives.

这段开始的第一句话很容易让我们觉得作者会从因为人口增多而使地球变得越来越拥挤的角度去讨论全球化的后果。不过，作者却提到技术发展使地球变小，经济发展使文化差异消失了。

When you arrived in another country a hundred years ago, you saw unfamiliar styles of clothing and buildings and discovered a completely different culture. In many places today, clothing and new buildings are very similar, and people enjoy the same sports, music, films and TV shows.

作者在这段里列举的 clothing，new buildings，the same sports，music，films，TV shows，the same products—smartphones, big burgers and T-shirts—from huge, global companies 等指出了文化同化现象——经济领域发生的标准化或同化已经外溢到了文化领域。作者通过这个经济现象点出了课文审视全球化问题的视角：全球化使地球在文化意义上变小了，即作者构建的宏观语境是全球化与文化同化（globalization and cultural homogenization）。在这个语境里认识全球化问题需要全球化与文化同化方面的知识。

课文第五段专门提到了语言问题：

Even the languages that we use are becoming more global. There are around seven thousand languages in use today, but the number is decreasing fast. I grew up in a small village where everyone spoke Baras, one of Indonesia's local languages. Today, like most of the youth from my village, I live in the capital, Jakarta, and speak Indonesian there. The only regular Baras speakers at present are the older people who have stayed in the country, so the language is threatened with extinction. The same thing is happening around the world. Experts think that the number of different languages will halve to just 3,500 by the end of this century.

不仅是生活方式被同化，语言也出现被同化的趋势。作者为什么要专门提语言问题？要回答这个问题需要我们了解语言与文化的关系等知识内容。按照语言学的基本假设，语言是文化的载体。不仅文化价值、文化身份等的表达需要语言，文化习俗的存在也需要语言。皮之不存，毛将焉附？如果语言消亡了，文化自然就失去了存在的形式基础。作者通过许多语言消亡的事实提示的是全球化所造成的文化危机的深度。

作者在最后提出了单一文化和单一语言的弊病以及文化和语言多样性对人类是否有必要的问题：

Where will it stop? Will there be a time in the future when Earth's billions all speak just one language, and there are no cultural differences to divide us? Perhaps the planet would be more peaceful if this happened, but I must admit that the idea is quite disappointing, somehow. I prefer to think that, as our population grows, we can celebrate not the similarity but the wonderful differences of the human race.

作者在这里又给出了新的语境线索，引导我们的思考走向深入。要回答作者提出的问题，我们需要调取文化多样性方面的知识以构建这篇课文的宏观语境，即在文化多样性的知识背景下去认知全球化问题。

在文化多样性的语境里去重新阅读作者有关人口增长的描述，我们可能会理解作者深层的用意以及作者为什么说：

I prefer to think that, as our population grows, we can celebrate not the similarity but the wonderful differences of the human race.

如果全地球的人的语言、思想和举止都千篇一律，虽然大家可以和平相处，但这样完全同化的人类是否很可怕呢？

知识背景不仅对推导课文主题有重要价值，对理解课文里许多具体表述也必不可少。如理解 The good, the bad and the really ugly[1] 这篇课文不仅需要了解食品 pizza 和 burger 的区别，还需要了解 burger 在美国人食品中的地位，不然就不太好理解这篇课文最后的这句话：

I'd save some money and I wouldn't feel bad about eating burgers!

除了历史文化背景、知识背景以外，语篇的互文关系（intertextuality），即语篇之间的关系也是宏观语境的一个重要参数。不过，语篇的互文线索相对复杂。有些线索是显性的，如 Life in a day。大多数互文线索的识别受到我们的阅读经历和知识结构的影

[1] 邹为诚.普通高中教科书　英语　必修第一册［M］.上海：上海教育出版社，2020：42-43.具体讨论请参阅"第九章　体裁：非叙事类"。

响，如课文 A road less travelled①。只有读过 Robert Frost 那首 The Road Not Taken 的读者才可能识别这个线索。有时为了方便识别，文章会有相关的注解，如 Blame your brain②。课文提供了这样的互文注解：

This passage is heavily adapted from a section of *Blame My Brain—The Amazing Teenage Brain Revealed* by Nicola Morgan.

语篇的互文关系至少有两个类型：一种是与他人的作品的关系，如 A road less travelled；另一种是与作者其他作品的关系。考虑到有一些课文是原著的节选或改写，我们这里主要讨论第二种关系，即改写文本与原著的关系。了解原著为改写文本提供的语境非常重要。节选类的改写主要反映原著主题的一个维度，因此了解原著可以获得更宏观的语境。整篇改写通常与原著的主题有高度的一致，因此原著能给出更多的主题推导线索。

但凡改写，都会涉及对原著信息的取舍。阅读原著因而不仅为解读主题，而且为理解改写文本的细节也提供了语境。An excerpt from *A Walk in the Woods*③ 这篇课文是根据美国畅销书作家 Bill Bryson 写的 *A Walk in the Woods: Rediscovering America on the Appalachian Trail*（1998）这部作品改写的。课文是原著的节选式改写。如果阅读原著，我们可以发现原著能在多个方面为我们提供语境信息。

---

① 邹为诚.普通高中教科书　英语　必修第三册［M］.上海：上海教育出版社，2021：60-61.具体讨论请参阅"第六章　语篇结构Ⅱ：话题结构和主题结构"。

② 邹为诚.普通高中教科书　英语　必修第二册［M］.上海：上海教育出版社，2020：6-7.

③ 邹为诚.普通高中教科书　英语　选择性必修第一册［M］.上海：上海教育出版社，2021：72-73.具体讨论请参阅"第五章　语篇结构Ⅰ：信息结构"。

原著有关写作缘由的介绍对构建课文的宏观语境有重要的启示，如：

Following his return to America after twenty years in Britain, Bryson decided to reacquaint himself with his native country by walking the 2,100-mile Appalachian Trail, which stretches from Springer Mountain in Georgia to Mount Katahdin in Maine. The AT, as it's affectionately known to thousands of hikers, offers an astonishing landscape of silent forests and sparkling lakes—and to a writer with the comic genius of Bill Bryson, it also provides endless opportunities to test his own powers of ineptitude, and to witness the majestic silliness of his fellow human beings.[1]

虽然改写时删除的信息不一定会影响理解，但原著的有些信息能提供更充分的语境信息。这些信息为理解提供了方便。如课文的第一段是这样开始的：

It was perfect sleeping weather, cool enough to need a bag, but warm enough to sleep in your underwear, and I was looking forward to having a long night's rest, which is what I was doing when, at some point during the night, I heard a sound nearby that made my eyes fly open. Normally, I slept through everything—through thunderstorms, and through Katz's snoring, so something loud enough to wake me was unusual. There was a sound of bushes being disturbed—a click of breaking branches, a weighty pushing through low leaves and branches—and then a kind of large, frightening noise.

作者为什么要提 perfect sleeping weather？为什么要给出

---

[1] https://www.bookbrowse.com/reviews/index.cfm/book_number/132/A-Walk-In-The-Woods.

"Normally, I slept through everything—through thunderstorms, and through Katz's snoring" 这样的解释？"Normally, I slept through everything" 和 "a click of breaking branches, a weighty pushing through low leaves and branches" 显然有矛盾，因为如果他睡得很深，他自然不会听到 a click of breaking branches 等。为什么会出现这样的反常现象？课文并没有提供方便我们理解的具体语境。

　　作者在原著里提到的一些情况给了我们重要的语境线索。作者说，他在出发前曾读过一些书，还找了不少人了解路径情况。几乎所有人给他的信息都对他产生了负面影响，在他的潜意识里留下了阴影：

> Nearly everyone I talked to had some gruesome story involving a guileless acquaintance who had gone off hiking the trail with high hopes and new boots and come stumbling back two days later with a bobcat attached to his head or dripping blood from an armless sleeve and whispering in a hoarse voice, "Bear!" before sinking into a troubled unconsciousness.[1]

　　这个语境线索自然能解释前面出现的矛盾状况。其实让他这么惊醒的不完全是外部的声音，更多是他潜意识里的恐惧。

　　又如，如果对比课文和原著的这段对话，不难发现原著里的下划线部分其实对理解课文中两人对话的连贯非常重要。这些信息的省略增加了难度：

　　课文：

> I looked and looked, but I couldn't see anything but those two wide-set eyes staring from the near distance like eyes in a cartoon.

---

① Bill Bryson. 1998. *A Walk in the Woods: Rediscovering America on the Appalachian Trail*. New York: Broadway Books, 1.

"What are you doing, Bryson? Just leave it alone and it will go away."

"How can you be so calm?"

"What do you want me to do? You're crazy enough for both of us. I'm going back to sleep," Katz announced.

"What are you talking about? You can't go to sleep."

原著：

... I picked up a small stone and tossed it at it. I think it may have hit it because the animal made a sudden noisy start (which scared the bejesus out of me and brought a whimper to my lips) and then emitted a noise— not quite a growl, but near enough. It occurred to me that perhaps I oughtn't provoke it.

"What are you doing, Bryson? Just leave it alone and it will go away."

"How can you be so calm?"

"What do you want me to do? You're hysterical enough for both of us."

"I think I have a right to be a trifle alarmed, pardon me. I'm in the woods, in the middle of nowhere, in the dark, staring at a bear, with a guy who has nothing to defend himself with but a pair of nail clippers. Let me ask you this. If it is a bear and it comes for you, what are you going to do—give it a pedicure?"

"I'll cross that bridge when I come to it," Katz said implacably.

"What do you mean you'll cross that bridge? We're on the bridge, you moron. There's a bear out here, for Christ sake. He's looking at us. He smells noodles and Snickers and—oh, shit."

"What?"

"Oh. Shit."

"What?"

"There's two of them. I can see another pair of eyes." Just then, the flashlight battery started to go. The light flickered and then vanished. I scampered into my tent, stabbing myself lightly but hysterically in the thigh as I went, and began a quietly frantic search for spare batteries. If I were a bear, this would be the moment I would choose to lunge.

"Well, I'm going to sleep," Katz announced.

"What are you talking about? You can't go to sleep." (pp. 78–79)

原著更详细的信息为课文结尾的这一段话也提供了更具体的语境：

The bears—animals, whatever they were—drank for perhaps 20 minutes more, then quietly went away.

既然作者这么确定是 bear，那他为什么还会提到 "animals, whatever they were" 呢？原著里有这样一段话：

He nodded. "So you think it really was a bear?"

"Who knows?" I suddenly thought of the food bag—that's what bears normally go for—and spun my head to see, but it was safely suspended a dozen or so feet from the ground from a branch about twenty yards away. Probably a determined bear could have gotten it down. Actually, my grandmother could have gotten it down. "Maybe not," I said, disappointed.

四、微观语境

微观语境的构建是根据语篇内的语境信息构建的。微观语境对理解词义、信息、话题和主题有至关重要的作用。简言之，在语篇的微观层面，识别并理解词语的提示对正确理解语篇有着至关重要的作用。我们这里主要讨论两类微观语境提示：① 词义理解；② 信息理解。

1. 词语提示与词义理解

John Firth 有句名言，很好地阐释了相伴词语对理解词义的提示作用："You shall know a word by the company it keeps"。一般说来，词语提示涉及三种现象：

（1）同形词或同音词（homonyms）

如大家经常引用的例子：

We went to the bank yesterday.

这句里的 bank 究竟指的是银行还是河岸，这要取决于其他句子里出现的词语所给出的提示：

We could not cash our traveler's check.

cash our traveler's check 是与银行有关的活动，所以前句的 bank 指的便是银行。又如在 Going global① 里有这么一句：

At that time, there were only about five million humans, but this figure quickly doubled.

---

① 邹为诚.普通高中教科书　英语　必修第二册［M］.上海：上海教育出版社，2020：42-43.

figure 可以指数字，也可以指人物、身材等。这句前面的 five million humans 显然为理解后面的 figure 提供了语境。

（2）多义词

如 The 1940s house① 这篇课文里的词组 get on with：

In the 1940s, women didn't say they couldn't do it. They just got on with it.

get on with 至少有两个意思：a.continue；b.tolerate or become accustomed to。前面的 "women didn't say they couldn't do it" 为理解 get on with 在语篇里的具体意思提供了语境。

又如 Going global 里下面这句话里的 celebrate 这个词：

I prefer to think that, as our population grows, we can celebrate not the similarity but the wonderful differences of the human race.

按照 *Longman Dictionary Online* 的解释，celebrate 是个多义词，它至少有三个义项：

a. to show that an event or occasion is important by doing something special or enjoyable
b. to praise someone or something
c. to perform a religious ceremony②

这句里的 celebrate 到底是哪个义项？ similarity 和 differences

① 邹为诚.普通高中教科书　英语　必修第二册[M].上海：上海教育出版社，2020：6–7.
② https://www.ldoceonline.com/dictionary/celebrate.

给出的提示似乎表明在这个语境里，这些义项都不能很好地解释 celebrate。b 似乎最接近，但当我们说 celebrate differences 或 diversity 时，我们似乎不只是 praise。这句话出现在课文的最后一段。前面的讨论和最后一段首句 "Where will it stop?" 里的 stop 这个词，都似乎在提示，celebrate 在这里的意义并不完全在 *Longman Dictionary Online* 的三个义项范围内。

哈佛大学教育学院（Harvard Graduate School of Education）曾经举行过一个叫 Celebrating Differences 的活动[1]，该标题的副标题有个语境提示："An early-year lesson plan that helps students appreciate what makes us unique"。这个语境提示告诉我们，celebrating differences 不仅仅涉及 praise，还涉及 appreciation。网上还有篇文章的标题叫 9 Ways to Celebrate Diversity in the Workplace[2]。该文章介绍的具体方法给出了更具体的线索，如 "Pay attention to cultural nuances; Address communication barriers; Develop a cultural calendar"。这些示意 celebrate 还涉及行动线索，这对理解课文里的用法应该是有所启发的。

（3）特定含义

理解词语的特定含义常常需要了解语篇的主题或话题。如 Where history comes alive[3] 这篇课文中的 alive 一词按照 *Longman Dictionary Online* 的解释，alive 有三个基本含义：

a. still living and not dead;

---

[1] https://www.gse.harvard.edu/ideas/usable-knowledge/16/09/celebrating-differences.

[2] https://www.hrcloud.com/blog/9-ways-to-celebrate-diversity-in-the-workplace.

[3] 邹为诚. 普通高中教科书　英语　必修第一册［M］. 上海：上海教育出版社，2020：24-25.

b. continuing to exist;

c. full of energy ...[①]

它在 When history comes alive 这句话里究竟指的是哪个义项呢？课文的主题为 alive 的义项选择提供了具体的语境[②]。

Going global 里有这样一句句子：

The human population has never been bigger, but in some ways the planet seems to be getting significantly smaller.

地球自然不会变小，作者用 smaller 究竟想表达什么意思？这句话后面的句子为理解 smaller 提供了一个语境：

In the past, travelers from Europe to Indonesia spent months at sea. Now you just have to sit on a plane for a few hours.

但这个语境显然不能帮助我们理解作者为什么把下面这句也放在讨论 smaller 这个段落里：

When you arrived in another country a hundred years ago, you saw unfamiliar styles of clothing and buildings and discovered a completely different culture. In many places today, clothing and new buildings are very similar, and people enjoy the same sports, music, films and TV shows ...

课文有关 globalization and homogeneity 的主题就能为我们理解

---

① https://www.ldoceonline.com/dictionary/alive.

② 具体讨论请参阅"第五章 语篇结构 I：信息结构"。

smaller 这里的特殊含义提供了思路。

再如课文 The good, the bad and the really ugly[①] 中的 good、bad 和 ugly 三个词。虽然这些都是再常见不过的形容词，但如果脱离了课文 "I know what this food does to my body, but what does it do to the world around me？" 这个话题提示，这些词的意思同样很难确定。尤其是 ugly 这个词。这篇课文里，这个词几乎成了 bad 的最高级：have the biggest carbon footprint。

2. 词语提示与信息提取

词语提示不仅能帮助我们辨别词义，它们也能引导我们提取相关信息。如果不能正确识别和理解词语在语篇里的特定意义及其提示作用，所提取信息的关联性就可能出现问题。有一个叫 What's new? 的写作题目。具体的要求是这样的：

> Every year, many young people enter senior high school just like you. You may have something to say about your new school life, so send us a letter about it. We want to know what's different, what's similar and what's new.

different, similar 和 new 是三个很平常的形容词，但 different 和 new 同时出现，这就意味着在这个语境里，different 不等于 new。题目是 What's new？这就提示文章提供的信息应该主要与 new 有关。另外，题目要求里有 school life 这个词语。这个词语是重要的信息提取线索，因为它限定了信息的关联性。

不过有时词语提示并不会如此明显。我们需要在阅读时细细地去辨认词语的提示。如 "Practice makes perfect" 是很平常的谚语，但

---

① 邹为诚. 普通高中教科书　英语　必修第一册［M］. 上海：上海教育出版社，2020：42-43.

如果作为写作题目，我们就必须认真考虑 perfect 和 practice 同时出现是否意味着 perfect 在这里有微妙的语境提示作用。

根据 *Longman Dictionary Online* 的解释，practice 至少有两个语义项：a. regularly; b. improve：

when you do a particular thing, often regularly, in order to improve your skill at it[①]

practice 这个词本身并没有提示某项技能的掌握程度。不过，当它与 perfect 这个词一同出现时，practice 所要到达的高度就有了提示。这是 *Longman Online Dictionary* 对 perfect 的定义：

as good as possible, or the best of its kind[②]

据此，当 practice 与 perfect 一起用时，perfect 是有语境提示作用的。在这个语境里，practice 的目的不是为了基本掌握某项技能，而是要把已经基本掌握的技能练习到精湛的程度。*Longman Dictionary Online* 对这个习语也有解释：

if you do an activity regularly, you will become very good at it[③]

do an activity regularly 自然意味着有做这事的技能。假如我们写作时不注意 perfect 这个词在这里的提示作用，我们写的作文可能

---

① https://www.ldoceonline.com/dictionary/practice.

② https://www.ldoceonline.com/dictionary/perfect.

③ https://www.ldoceonline.com/dictionary/practice-makes-perfect.

会出现问题：

> An English proverb says, "Practice makes perfect." It means that it is practice that enables us to build up speed and efficiency. When we accomplish things without wasting efforts, it is the result of long practice.
>
> Our life abounds with examples of "Practice makes perfect." Take the study of English for example. Only through consistent practice can we memorize the words and master the grammar. And it is only through practice that we can become fluent in speaking and writing. Another good example is sports. Practice is the only way to become stronger and run faster. Besides, in team games, practice is what improves our sense of cooperation and helps the team win. Lacking practice, the team is doomed to fail. All evidence lends support to the fact that practice is the key to success in all fields.
>
> To sum up, the proverb has a profound and realistic significance: there can be no achievement which is not based on a solid foundation of practice.

作为提示语，perfect 只是提示 practice 的具体技能所能到达的高度。不同的技能有不同的高度标准，因此除了表示程度以外，它并没有任何其他具体含义。这篇文章的作者忽视了 perfect 这个词的语境提示作用，因而对题目的解释是不合适的：

> It means that it is practice that enables us to build up speed and efficiency. When we accomplish things without wasting efforts ...

speed, efficiency 或 without wasting efforts 是相对于某些技能而言的，并不是所有技能都必须达到的高度。且不说作者给出的例子是否与 speed 和 efficiency 有关，作者的例子基本忽视了 perfect 这个提示语的存在。第一个例子有关语言学习：

Take the study of English for example. Only through consistent practice can we memorize the words and master the grammar.

"memorize the words and master the grammar" 仅仅是掌握语言的基本练习要求，这些基本练习并不能达到语言学习的 perfect 高度。另外一个例子 "Practice is the only way to become stronger and run faster" 只表明 practice 能使人变得更强，跑得更快，但同样，更快和更强与 perfect 所提示的高度没有关联。

由于作者没有注意 perfect 的语境提示作用，因此文章的总结也完全忽视了 achievement 和 perfection 之间的区别：

To sum up, the proverb has a profound and realistic significance: there can be no achievement which is not based on a solid foundation of practice.

忽视词语的提示作用常常会导致文章提取的信息与题目要求发生背离。识别语境提示语并根据提示确定语境参数以提取相关信息是信息关联性的根本保证。

Why we should read classical literature[①] 这个议题似乎很简单，但如果忽视 why，read 和 classical 这三个词在这里的语境提示作用，在提取信息时就可能会发生偏差。在讨论 read classical literature 时提 why，这就意味着重点应该不在 classical literature 本身，而在 read，也就是说，why 在这里提示我们这里构建的语境是阅读，而不

---

① https://highschool.latimes.com/beacon-park-school/opinion-why-we-should-read-classical-literature/.

是经典本身。classical 这个词语提示的是，我们在讨论 why 时关注的不是一般文学阅读，而是经典文学阅读的益处，即经典文学提供的帮助是非经典文学无法提供的。下面这篇文章似乎忽略了 why，read 和 classical 这三个词的语境提示：

The term "classical" is used for the literature of any language in a period notable for the excellent quality of its writers' works. It is also a term used to note that something is pure, genuine and worth remembering. While other literary efforts come and go, some literature, because of its high quality, gets preserved over time.

In the fall of 2016, my parents agreed to send me to a specialized academy in China for one year that focuses on reading, studying, and memorizing classical literature from all around the world, such as the Analects of Confucius, Sanskrit poetry, and European and American writers like Shakespeare, Spenser, Byron, Dickinson, and Frost. We also read nonfiction excerpts of significant writings by Churchill, Albert Schweitzer, and Martin Luther King, among others.

After settling in and beginning to make new friends, I delved into the works of great thinkers and writers. The literature we read during this year has influenced me a lot. For example, "Of Study" by Francis Bacon, has changed the way I think about studying. Bacon's observation that "studies serve for delight, for ornament, and for ability" made me think of studying in a new way, not as a burden or obligation, but as an activity that is meant to give joy and enhance our thinking, speaking, and writing abilities and add charm to our personality.

Most of the teachers at this school had graduated from top colleges and had great backgrounds. Many used to be professors but chose to teach at a school that focused on classical literature instead. I think it is because they knew how important classic literature is in our daily lives that they made this life choice.

Classic literature is important because it opens up a perspective to different worlds and historical perspectives. Readers understand places like America or Russia better when they have read its literature. Books like *Gone With the Wind*, *Of Mice and Men*, *A Tale of Two Cities*, *War and Peace*, etc., weave a tale of history and friendship into the bleak times they depict. I also gain more knowledge when I read classical literature because many stories are based on history. Studying history suddenly becomes exciting when I look at the past through the vibrant characters in these stories.

To be honest, I prefer historical fiction the best because seeing all the characters battle against terrible circumstances is very motivating. Knowing that there are people in worse situations helps me be more positive in my everyday life. These novels have great passages that have inspired me. For example, "The strongest of all warriors are these two — Time and Patience," and "Tomorrow is another day," have helped me overcome many difficulties in my life.

Reading classic novels has also improved my overall vocabulary and writing skills because writers from an older time period have unique styles of writing. I especially enjoy Shakespeare's plays like *Hamlet* and *A Midsummer's Night's Dream*. Shakespeare even created a few of the words used in everyday language. These great works taught me old English and grammar.

Reading classic literature teaches us life lessons through human history. These books are like a mirror through which we can see the lives of others. We can make ourselves better by comparing their good deeds and their bad points. Books like *Oliver Twist*, *Moby Dick*, *1984*, *To Kill a Mockingbird*, *Animal Farm*, etc., give us the opportunity to learn a lot from the characters animating these novels. We can essentially shape our personality and inner self through classic literature.

作者在第一段里对 classical 的界定没有考虑 why 和 read 的提示，仅仅从作品本身的品质而不是作品可能产生的效果去定义 classical：

The term "classical" is used for the literature of any language in a period notable for the excellent quality of its writers' works. It is also a term used to note that something is pure, genuine and worth remembering. While other literary efforts come and go, some literature, because of its high quality, gets preserved over time.

作者在定义里选择的 pure, genuine 和 worth remembering 等词语只能帮助读者构建何以为经典的语境，却很难帮助他们构建 read classical literature 有什么益处的语境。这两个语境的参数不同，所需要提取的信息自然也大不一样。

虽然作者在具体讨论中所提取的信息基本围绕阅读所产生的积极影响，但他在讨论影响时又忽视了 classical 这个词语：

For example, "Of Studies" by Francis Bacon, has changed the way I think about studying. Bacon's observation that "studies serve for delight, for ornament, and for ability" made me think of studying in a new way, not as a burden or obligation, but as an activity that is meant to give joy and enhance our thinking, speaking, and writing abilities and add charm to our personality.

这里提到的 "Of studies" 确实是经典作品。但这个例子只能证明 Bacon 的这句话有醍醐灌顶的作用，但与他界定经典时用的 pure, genuine 和 worth remembering 等词语好像没有太大的关联。作者接下来又指出：

Classic literature is important because it opens up a perspective to different worlds and historical perspectives.

这里提取的信息与前面的经典定义也没有任何关系。另外,我们要问的是,难道打开我们视野的一定是经典文学?非经典文学就一定不能打开我们的视野?紧接着的这句话暴露了作者实际上无视了 classical 的提示,并没有区分经典和非经典文学:

Readers understand places like America or Russia better when they have read its literature.

作者列举 historical fiction 时,显然也忽略了 classical 的提示:

To be honest, I prefer historical fiction the best because seeing all the characters battle against terrible circumstances is very motivating. Knowing that there are people in worse situations helps me be more positive in my everyday life.

文章最后的两个例子同样与 read classical literature 无关:

Reading classic novels has also improved my overall vocabulary and writing skills because writers from an older time period have unique styles of writing.

Reading classic literature teaches us life lessons through human history.

阅读任何小说,甚至书籍都能拓展我们的词汇量,对我们的写作也会有帮助。如果说经典作品对我们的写作有帮助是因为它们有较早历史时期独一无二的语体风格的话,那时代不同了,带有历史印记的语体是否能符合不同时代的要求呢？经典作品之所以成为经典难道仅仅是因为它们的历史性？撇开历史性，经典作品对我们的语言学习和写作究竟有什么特别的帮助呢？第二个例子也有同样的问题。我们阅读任何历史书籍都可能会获得 life lessons，为什么一定要读 classical literature 呢？ classical literature 究竟能给我们哪些不同于非经典文学的启示呢？

由于作者回答这个题目时没有很好地考虑 why，read 和 classical 这些词语的语境提示，结果导致所提取的信息与题目出现了严重的偏差。

本章推荐书目

[1] Brown, G. and G. Yule. 1983. *Discourse Analysis*. Cambridge: Cambridge University Press.

[2] Clark, H. H. and T. B. Carlson. 1981. Context for Comprehension. In. J. Long and A. Baddeley. (Eds.). *Attention and Performance IX*. Hillsdale, NJ: Lawrence Erlbaum.

[3] Duranti, A. and C. Goodwin. (Eds.). 1992. *Rethinking Context: Language as an Interactive Phenomenon*. Cambridge: Cambridge University Press.

[4] Hymes, D. 1964. Introduction: Toward Ethnographies of Communication. *American Anthropologist*. 66(6): 1–34.

[5] Van Dijk, T. 2008. *Discourse and Context: A sociocognitive approach*. Cambridge: Cambridge University Press.

第四章　视角

导引问题：

- 什么是语篇的视角？
- 语篇视角对理解语篇有什么作用？

本章提要：

　　视角指的是语篇叙述或议论所选择的**角度**。任何视角的确定都离不开语篇的提示。作者通常会凸显某个语篇成分以引导读者从他们的角度去理解语篇。根据视角提示的凸显度，视角提示可以分成**显性**和**隐性**两大类。提示是否能被读者识别以及读者是否会按照该视角的引导去理解语篇与读者的知识结构、身份认同等有很大的关系。语篇分析的视角有思想、叙事、时空、身份、认知等五个维度。语篇视角是理解语篇的关键因素，它能帮助我们了解作者所采用的认知框架、相关语境线索和作者的立场，方便我们调动理解语篇所需要的相关认知资源。

一、概说

　　"视角"（perspective）类似相机取景，指的是语篇叙述或议论所选择的角度。任何语篇都会按照不同的目的和所针对的读者选择特定的视角去叙述或议论某个事件或观点。

语篇视角的识别取决于语篇"凸显"(salience)成分的识别。为了取得最佳的交际效果,作者通常会凸显某个语篇成分以引导读者从他们的角度去理解语篇。不过凸显是个相对概念,凸显程度首先是由它与其他成分所形成的关系所确定的。其次,凸显是否能被读者识别并按照该视角的引导去理解语篇与读者的知识结构、身份认同等有很大的关系。

语篇分析的视角和文学批评的视角(point of view)并不完全是一个概念。文学批评里的视角主要指叙事视角。叙事视角主要有以下三个类别:

(1)无所不知的作者(omniscient author)视角。大多数文学作品都属于这一类,如小说 *The Last Leaf*、*The Old Man and the Sea* 等;

(2)第三人称叙事(third person)视角,即作者通过作品中的人物叙述故事,如 Scot Fitzgerald 的名著 *The Great Gatsby* 等;

(3)第一人称叙事(first person)视角,即作者选择作品人物中的一位以第一人称进行叙述,如小说 *Frankenstein*[①]。

按照语篇分析的假设,视角是任何语篇的必要成分。语篇视角通常涉及五个维度:

(1)思想视角。思想视角提示作者在语篇中表达的思想倾向,也就是作者的立场。思想视角的提示分显性和隐性。显性提示多采用倾向性明确的词语,如:

What you did is <u>not acceptable</u>.

---

① 邹为诚. 普通高中教科书 英语 选择性必修第三册[M]. 上海:上海教育出版社,2022:60–61.

隐性提示则通过相对中性的词语操控或信息选择等手段实现，如：

An experiment in education[①]

（2）叙事视角。文学批评的视角基本属于这个维度。叙事维度的提示语通常是人称。

On my way to school, I saw him.

Lyn is back in her modern, open-plan home, but surprisingly, she misses the 1940s house.

（3）时空视角。时空视角提示作者在叙事或描写时选择的时空参数，最常见的提示手段是时间和地点状语，如 now，then，2023，或时态等。

Nowadays many people contact their friends via WeChat.
In the 1940s, these chores were like a full-time job.

常见的地点状语有 here、there、down、up 等，以及由各种介词如 behind、beside、under、in 等引导的表达地点的状语。

We are celebrating our victory here.

动词 go、come、bring、take 等也常用来做空间提示。

---

① 请参阅后面（p. 106）的讨论。

I got there early and <u>went</u> straight to the office.

He <u>brought</u> me a gift.

（4）身份视角。身份视角指的是作者在语篇里所显示的身份认同。身份视角的提示也分为显性和隐性。显性提示通常通过词语明示。

<u>As a teacher</u>, I believe we should encourage students to read more.

隐性身份提示则会通过叙事角度、信息选择等手段提示。

We use hundreds, maybe even thousands of different words every day. Many of them have been part of our vocabulary since early childhood, but the words that fascinate us are the other ones, the ones that didn't even exist a few years ago. As the world changes, the vocabulary that people use moves on too. In fact, experts estimate that at least 4,000 new English words are coined every year. <u>Have you ever stopped to wonder where they come from and why they have the meanings that they do?</u>[①]

（5）认知视角。认知视角一般提示作者叙述和议论时所选择的认知框架，引导读者依照该框架去理解语篇。认知视角大多有明确的词语标识，有些则相对隐晦。

<u>Legally speaking</u>, he should not be held accountable for what happened yesterday.

Blame your <u>brain</u>.

---

① 邹为诚. 普通高中教科书　英语　选择性必修第三册［M］. 上海：上海教育出版社，2022：72.

视角和语境是两个不同的概念。视角是语篇叙述或议论问题或事件的角度，而语境是理解语篇所需要的信息资源。视角与语境的关系是，语境的激活往往与视角提示有关。视角与立场也不同[①]。视角给出的是识别作者立场的线索，而立场表达的是作者具体的思想倾向。

二、视角与教学

语篇视角的识别是理解语篇的关键因素，因为一方面识别视角提示能帮助我们了解作者所采用的认知框架、相关语境线索、作者的立场等，另一方面确定视角能有利于我们对学生预存的知识和经验做出预估，从而提前进行适当的干预。

视角教学要注意两个问题：一是任何视角的确定都离不开提示。视角的识别必定有语篇的依据。二是提示的识别与学生的相关知识储备和阅读经验有关。不同的学生可能会识别不同的视角，这要求我们在教学中要保持高度开放的心态。只要学生能找到识别的依据，我们就应该承认这种识别的可能性。

如果我们判断学生识别视角提示有困难，那就有必要进行提前干预，介绍相关的背景知识。介绍背景知识的目的不是直接告知视角提示，而是为学生自主识别视角提供有关联的依据。

我们在语篇视角讨论时可以考虑以下几个具体问题：

（1）语篇的标题有可供判断视角的提示吗？

（2）语篇的开始部分是否有帮助我们识别视角的信息？

---

① 请参阅"第十章　立场"。

（3）语篇的正文是否呼应我们识别的视角？

（4）作者为什么要选择这样的角度？

（5）语篇的视角如何影响语篇的议论或陈述？

（6）作者的视角选择是否会影响我们对所讨论议题或事件的看法？

考虑到我们的相关知识、生活经历和阅读经验往往会对视角识别有牵制，从而导致我们会有意无意选择性地注意语篇凸显的内容，我们有必要通过提问促使学生对自己的识别有一定的反思：

（1）我们对语篇视角的识别为什么会聚焦这些凸显成分？

（2）我们的相关知识和立场对凸显的注意是否有影响？

（3）我们的识别是否受到了别人的启发而不是源自语篇本身？

讨论视角的时候还要考虑语篇体裁对视角选择的影响。许多叙事类语篇的标题通常只涉及题材（subject matter），明示的只是话题，对语篇的视角几乎很少提示，如 A day in the life of a digital human，文学名著 The Old Man and the Sea 等。有些文学类作品的标题有象征意义的提示，如 The Last Leaf, The Road Not Taken 等，但作者究竟是从哪个视角去构建象征意义，标题并没有给出提示。

三、视角提示的基本方式

视角提示与凸显有关。作为视角判定依据的凸显却也是智者见智的事情。就提示方式而言，我们识别视角时通常会考虑这么四个基本问题：

（1）作者为什么要选择这样的修饰语？

（2）作者为什么要选择这样的名词或动词？

（3）作者为什么要这样排列语篇的主语？

（4）作者为什么选择这样的信息或信息排列？

我们接下来分别从词语、主语和信息层面讨论语篇视角的提示方式。

1. 词语提示

词语是提示语篇视角最常见的方式。修饰语是凸显性最强的，如：

The confusing way Mexicans tell time①

之所以判定 confusing 这个词语提示视角是因为它明确提示墨西哥人的时间观念与主流观点的不同。我们会期待语篇的讨论会聚焦墨西哥人时间观念与主流时间观点的不同之处。

要注意的是，confusing 也可以视作宏观语境线索，提示讨论语篇需要调动主流时间观的知识资源。由于 confusing 这个词语涉及判断，因此这个词语在提示视角的同时，似乎也提示了立场。说"似乎"是因为虽然视角有提示立场的作用，但立场需要通读全文后才能确定。这篇文章末尾的表述表明 confusing 不能代表作者的立场：

Difficulty in explaining what I have come to call "Ahorita Time" is a reflection of different cultural understandings of time.

我们可以比较下面两个标题：

---

① 束定芳.普通高中教科书　英语　必修第一册［M］.上海：上海外语教育出版社，2020：20.

What is a vocation and how can you find yours?①
Finding one's true vocation②

第一个标题给出的 what 和 how 提示的仅仅是文章的话题。这篇文章究竟从哪个视角讨论 what 和 how，我们需要从文章的正文里去找线索：

Identifying your vocation is one of the most important things you can do in life. After all, once you <u>find and pursue your true calling</u>, you can do the work you feel you were meant to do. <u>Following your passion</u> is not only personally fulfilling but can also put you in a great position to help others.

这段里的划线部分提示了文章讨论职业的视角。这在这篇文章讨论 what is a vocation 时也得到了证明：

"Vocation" comes from the Latin word "vocare," which means "to call." Rather than simply what you do for a living, it has to do with your purpose in life—what you feel "called" to do. However, you can earn a living while pursuing your vocation.

作者在课文 Finding one's true vocation 的标题里加了 true 这个词。true 之所以成为视角提示是因为它暗示作者的切入点不是 find，也不是一般的 vocation 概念，而是 vocation 不同于一般理解的角度。课文的第一段证实了这一点：

---

① https://blog.mvnu.edu/what-is-a-vocation-and-how-can-you-find-yours.
② 邹为诚. 普通高中教科书　英语　选择性必修第二册［M］. 上海：上海教育出版社，2021：6.

What to do next?

It was a big question. I had gone out into the world to fend for myself. I had gained a livelihood in various vocations, but no one was impressed with my successes. I had once been a grocery clerk, for one day, but had consumed so much sugar that I was fired. I had studied law an entire week, and then given it up because it was so tiresome. I had been a bookseller's clerk for a while, but it was too stressful. The customers bothered me so much that I could not read with any comfort. I had been a private secretary, a silver miner, and amounted to less than nothing in each, and now—

作者，也就是 Mark Twain，有过各种能糊口度日的职业，但他并不满足于从事一个仅能糊口的职业。他也有过其他不错的工作，但这些工作却不符合他的性格和兴趣，如他不愿意接受打扰太多而影响他读书时间的工作等。Mark Twain 讨论职业的视角显然和一般世俗观点大不一样。

直接用名词或动词等提示语篇视角的情况也很普遍，如课文 The influencers[①]。词典告诉我们这个词用的场景是：

a person who is able to generate interest in something (such as a consumer product) by posting about it on social media[②]

作者选择 influencer 这个词意味着他讨论的推销与一般的推销不同。课文第一段的例子有导向作用，这段里 "Welcome to the world

---

① 邹为诚. 普通高中教科书　英语　选择性必修第一册［M］. 上海：上海教育出版社，2021：42-43. 请参阅"第九章　体裁：非叙事类"。

② https://www.merriam-webster.com/dictionary/influencer. 我们这里选用 *Merriam-Webster* 是因为 *Longman Dictionary Online* 没有收录这个词。

of stealth marketing" 这句话直接与标题呼应，清楚地点明了课文的视角：

> Imagine this: you are in a café when you hear a young man talking about a new computer game. He's explaining its amazing features to a girl, who then asks where she can buy it. Nothing unusual, you might say, until after 15 minutes, they move to another café and have an identical conversation. On your way home, a "tourist" in the street asks you to take a photo with their camera. You do and, afterwards, they tell you how they bought the camera recently and how it's on special offer. <u>Welcome to the world of stealth marketing.</u> You may say you haven't met a stealth marketer yet, but that's the point. Contrary to what you might expect, this practice is quite common.

有些视角提示相对复杂，如 Blame your brain[1]。作者这里选择 brain 这个词似乎表明课文是从生理学的角度讨论问题的。*Longman Dictionary Online* 词典对 brain 的定义是：

> the organ inside your head that controls how you think, feel, and move[2]

课文在第一段提出了问题之后，马上就给出了生理学的一些结论：

> Scientists know that a brain chemical called dopamine causes this feeling of enjoyment. What has dopamine got to do with you? Well, some scientists believe that dopamine levels are sometimes lower in teenagers

---

① 邹为诚 . 普通高中教科书　英语　必修第二册［M］. 上海：上海教育出版
　　社，2020：6-7. 请参阅"第六章　语篇结构Ⅱ：话题结构和主题结构"。
② https://www.ldoceonline.com/dictionary/brain.

than they are in children. This means that some teenagers might need to take more risks to get the same "wow" factor.

不过，标题里 blame 这个词的作用不能忽视。blame 提示课文的角度不完全是生理学的。如何判断这篇课文的视角，我们还需要在课文里寻找其他提示，如四个小标题：①The "wow factor"；② "I just feel like it；③Pressure from friends；④What you can do。小标题有两个是不支持生理学视角的，尤其是最后一个。这给多少有点宿命论的生理学解释打上了问号。

许多标题并没有视角的提示，如课文 The story of a T-shirt[①]。作者选择 story 这个词只是告诉读者他关注的是与 T-shirt 有关的故事。作者究竟关注的是 T-shirt 哪个意义上的故事呢？我们需要到课文里去寻找线索。课文的第一段给出了具体的视角提示——These clothes make people's dreams come true：

Lagos, Nigeria—Yaba market is busy, hot and dusty. People are looking around the second-hand shops, picking through piles of old clothes, and they're all searching for deals. The market is flooded with cheap clothes from America and Europe, and they usually sell out fairly quickly. "These clothes make people's dreams come true," says Abeke, a shop owner. "Everyone wears them. When they put them on, you can't tell the difference between the rich and the poor." At the front of Abeke's store is a cotton T-shirt with the words "Get Real". It's picked up by a young guy who looks at it carefully. He tries it on and smiles—it fits him and it looks good. It's a simple T-shirt, but it has a long story.

---

① 邹为诚. 普通高中教科书　英语　必修第三册［M］. 上海：上海教育出版社，2021：24-25. 请参阅"第七章　语篇的词汇关系"。

2. 主语提示

主语提示也是视角提示的常见手段。根据 Kuno（1976）的移情（empathy）理论，句子的主语通常是句子的凸显点，说话人的陈述角度通常是主语。他理出了两个重要线索：

（1）主语线索

John hit Mary.

（2）所有格线索

Mary's husband hit Mary.

虽然 Kuno 讨论的是句子层面的问题，但我们认为移情理论的适用性不局限于句子。语篇内句子主语的分布和出现频率也可能是语篇视角提示的方式[①]。语篇的主语提示主要有两种情况：① 标题里的主语结构。如果标题由句子承担，句子的主语极可能是语篇的视角。② 语篇内句子主语的分布。主语的分布和出现频率提示语篇切入的角度。如：

Older people have a better quality of life than younger people.[②]

作者用 older people 作标题句子的主语显然是在提示文章的讨论是从 older people 的视角展开的。

---

① 请参阅：曲卫国.话语文体学导论：文本分析的方法［M］.上海：复旦大学出版社，2009.

② 邹为诚.普通高中教科书　英语　选择性必修第四册［M］.上海：上海教育出版社，2022：42.

又如下面这篇文章的标题：

Journalists on the job[①]

journalists 这个主语提示有关 job 的讨论是从 journalist 的角度展开的。在前面提到的 Finding one's true vocation 里，所有格 one's 的出现表明 true 的意义应该是从个人的视角去判断的。

The confusing way Mexicans tell time[②] 这篇课文的主语分布和出现频率也典型地呼应了标题里 confusing 这个词给出的提示：

When I first set foot on Mexican soil, I spoke Spanish well. So when I asked a local ice-cream seller for an ice-cream, and he said "ahorita," which directly translates to "right now," I took him at his word, believing that its arrival was immediate.

I sat near his shop and waited. Half an hour passed and still no ice-cream arrived, so I asked again about it. "Ahorita," he told me again. His face was a mix of confusion and maybe even embarrassment.

I was torn. Waiting longer wasn't pleasant, but I felt it was impolite to walk away, especially if the ice-cream was now being delivered just for me. But finally, after waiting too long, I made a rush for the nearest bus to take me home. As I left, I signalled at my wrist and shrugged to the ice-cream seller. Obviously I couldn't wait any longer and it really wasn't my fault. His face was, once again, one of total confusion.

This experience faded from my memory until years later when I came

---

① 邹为诚. 普通高中教科书　英语　必修第三册［M］. 上海：上海教育出版社，2021：6.

② 束定芳. 普通高中教科书　英语　必修第一册［M］. 上海：上海外语教育出版社，2020：20.

back to live in Mexico. I discovered that understanding "ahorita" took not a fluency in the language, but rather a fluency in the culture. When someone from Mexico says "ahorita," it should almost never be taken literally; its meaning changes greatly with context. As a linguist told me, "Ahorita could mean tomorrow, in an hour, within five years or never." It is even used as a polite way of saying "no, thanks" when refusing an offer.

Difficulty in explaining what I have come to call "Ahorita Time" is a reflection of different cultural understandings of time. Since I moved to Mexico, my attitude towards time has changed dramatically. I don't worry so much about being late; I am generally still on time for appointments, but when I'm not, I don't panic. Ironically, it would seem that "Ahorita Time" has actually allowed me to live far more in the "right now" than I ever did before.

主语"I"的分布情况和出现频率显然在告诉读者，课文的视角是"I"。课文对跨文化交际里自我中心的审视和批判就是从这个视角发动的。

同样的主语分布结构在 The story of a T-shirt[1] 也存在，以课文的第一段为例：

Lagos, Nigeria—Yaba market is busy, hot and dusty. People are looking around the second-hand shops, picking through piles of old clothes, and they're all searching for deals. The market is flooded with cheap clothes from America and Europe, and they usually sell out fairly quickly. "These clothes make people's dreams come true," says Abeke, a shop owner. "Everyone wears them. When they put them on, you can't tell the difference between the rich and the poor." At the front of Abeke's store is a

---

[1] 邹为诚. 普通高中教科书　英语　必修第三册［M］. 上海：上海教育出版社，2021：24-25.

cotton T-shirt with the words "Get Real". It's picked up by a young guy who looks at it carefully. He tries it on and smiles—it fits him and it looks good. It's a simple T-shirt, but it has a long story.

这段主要有三类主语：Yaba market, People 和 clothes。第一类是地点，Yaba market 以销售价格极其低廉的商品出名。第二类是人：people，they，Abeke (shop owner)，a young guy 等。这里的 people 有两个类别：店主和淘旧货的顾客。第三类是商品，clothes 和 a cotton T-shirt with the words "Get Real" 以及 T-shirt 的代词 it 等。商品主语最多。最后几句非常清楚地点出了课文的视角：

It's picked up by a young guy who looks at it carefully. He tries it on and smiles—it fits him and it looks good. It's a simple T-shirt, but it has a long story.

问题形式标题的主语视角提示功能通常不明确，如 Is chocolate the answer?[①] 在这种情况下，文章的视角提示有可能出现在文章的第一段：

The latest World Happiness Report says that prosperity is not the main reason for happiness. If you suffer real hardship, you are unlikely to be happy, but once your basic needs are met, money and material things become less of a necessity. Happiness depends more on recognizing the things you have and appreciating them, rather than getting more things.

---

① 邹为诚.普通高中教科书　英语　选择性必修第一册［M］.上海：上海教育出版社，2021：6—7.请参阅"第七章　语篇的词汇关系"。

这段的主语有三个类别：①prosperity, money and material things；②you, your basic needs；③happiness。这三类主语形成的三角关系可能在提示这篇文章的视角：物质满足与幸福之间的关系。值得注意的是，这里只有 you，也就是人是施事主语。除了主语以外，最后一句话里 recognize, appreciate, have 和 get 四个动词也进一步提供了讨论这个三角关系的线索。

3. 信息提示[①]

语篇的信息选择和信息结构是识别语篇视角的另外一种方法。语篇里出现的信息是作者根据其视角选择的，根据语篇所选择的信息和信息排列的逻辑我们就可能找到语篇的视角。

Journalists on the job[②] 是一个很好的例子。根据标题，这篇课文是从 journalist 角度去讨论职业选择问题。journalist 是个很宽泛的角度。我们需要从信息选择的角度使视角变得更具体。课文罗列的系列问题提供了作者选择信息的基本思路，这些思路为具体理解文章的视角提供了进一步的线索。这七个问题表面上在讨论 journalist 的职业特点：

（1）What makes a good journalist?

（2）Would all writers make good journalists?

（3）How do you spot a good news story?

（4）Do journalists always write true stories?

（5）Should news stories appeal to the readers' emotions?

（6）What is challenging about working as a journalist?

① 请参阅"第五章　语篇结构Ⅰ：信息结构"。
② 邹为诚.普通高中教科书　英语　必修第三册［M］.上海：上海教育出版社，2021：6-7.详细讨论请参阅"第四章　视角"。

（7）What makes the work of a journalist valuable?

不过从这七个问题抽象出的相关信息：①curiosity and love；②focusing；③keeping eyes and ears open；④sources；⑤benefiting others；⑥time pressure；⑦purpose 等，也许能使我们不仅找到它们之间的内在关联，也找到这些信息与择业的关系，从而确定课文讨论择业的视角。能让我们有好奇心和激情，能让我们聚精会神，能让我们保持开放心态和敏感，能让我们寻找各种信息源，能让我们感到所做的职业对他人有帮助，能让我们感受争分夺秒的压力，能让我们感到自己的价值等，这些难道不是我们在择业时应该考虑的因素吗？细细想来，所有这些因素都与个人体验、发展和价值等有关。作者的这七个问题显然在提示讨论择业的具体视角。

分析语篇的信息选择不仅能使我们对视角的认知具体化，也常常能让我们反思最初的视角识别。这里以 The Road Not Taken[①] 为例。诗歌标题里的 Not 似乎提示诗歌的视角针对的是没走的路。不少评论认为这首诗的话题是选择，尤其是所放弃的选择对人生的影响。不过，如果细细分析每一诗节的信息，我们也许会对诗歌的视角产生不同的解读。诗歌的第一段是这样的：

> Two roads diverged in a yellow wood,
> And sorry I could not travel both
> And be one traveler, long I stood
> And looked down one as far as I could
> To where it bent in the undergrowth;

---

① 邹为诚.普通高中教科书 英语 选择性必修第四册［M］.上海：上海教育出版社，2022：44.

第一诗节里的信息非常多，几乎每一行都有不同的信息。第一行说的是诗人来到了岔路口；第二行表达的是诗人的遗憾；第三行提供的信息是，由于一个人不能同时走两条路，他不得不做选择；第四行叙述诗人尽力观察眺望，寻找选择的依据；第五行描写诗人的努力程度，他看到了目力所能及之处。

作者选择的这五条信息似乎不仅冗余而且自相矛盾。到了岔路，必然得选择。一个人自然不可能走两条路。第五行有关小路的拐弯尽头的信息似乎否定了第四行诗人极目远眺的意义，因为小路拐弯尽头意味着无论诗人怎么努力，无论眺望时间多长都是无用功。作者第一段的信息选择是否有暗示诗歌的视角呢？

诗人在第二诗节里提供了至少三种信息：

Then took the other, as just as fair,
And having perhaps the better claim,
Because it was grassy and wanted wear;
Though as for that the passing there
Had worn them really about the same,

诗人先是用标题里出现过的动词 take 宣布了他的决定，并提供了该决定的依据：just as fair, having perhaps the better claim。诗人这里选择的 claim 这个词尤其值得玩味。*Longman Dictionary Online* 的解释是：

a statement that something is true, even though it has not been proved[①]

_____

① https://www.ldoceonline.com/dictionary/claim.

也就是说这个 better claim 实际上是诗人的主观认知。下面一句 because 引导的句子 "Because it was grassy and wanted wear" 进一步证实了这仅仅是推导。不过，有意思的是，诗人紧接着提供的信息又否定了他的推导："Though as for that the passing there/Had worn them really about the same"。不能说诗人没有进行过推敲，但为什么他的推敲会被简单的现实状况轻易推翻呢？诗人给出这样的信息又想做什么样的提示呢？

诗人在第三诗节的信息可以分为两类：

And both that morning equally lay
In leaves no step had trodden black.
Oh, I kept the first for another day!
Yet knowing how way leads on to way,
I doubted if I should ever come back.

前两句的信息为推测的否定提供了进一步的依据。两条路的状况其实是一样的。后三句写出了他上路后的心理活动。和第二段提供的信息一样，这也是一个自我否定过程。诗人虽然说 "I kept the first for another day"，但 "Oh" 这个感叹词表明他实际上此时心里清楚，一旦踏上了一条路，路路相连，恐怕就不会再回头了。这个自我否定信息又在提示什么呢？

第四节提供的是假设性的将来信息：

I shall be telling this with a sigh
Somewhere ages and ages hence:
Two roads diverged in a wood, and I—
I took the one less traveled by,

And that has made all the difference.

耐人寻味的是，诗人又提到了感叹。将来的感叹与前面的感叹是同一种情绪吗？与前面两段描写心理过程时都出现的自我否定信息不同的是，这个段落里似乎没有相互矛盾的信息，诗人的语气似乎显得非常肯定。这又是为什么？为什么诗人在讲述自己那时做出的决定时用了破折号"—"呢？由破折号引出的陈述句，语气会那么肯定吗？这个破折号是否对诗人所说的"I took the one less traveled by,/And that has made all the difference."提出了质疑呢？

有关 Robert Frost 这首诗的评论太多了，而且大多数评论都围绕一个视角：选择的后果。我们这里无意否认这个视角的合理性，但这首诗的每一段都有相互矛盾的信息排列，这难道不在传递什么含义吗？

也许应该我们重新审视题目，该思考一下，作者为什么不用 chosen 而用 taken？*Merriam-Webster* 定义 choose 的第一个义项是：

to select freely and after consideration①

按照词典的定义，选择行为有两个要素：① 自由；② 思考。可诗歌第一节告诉我们，一个人不能同时走两条路，但到了岔路口的他又不得不前行。他其实并没有选择的自由。他不能看到路拐弯后的状况，也就是无法推断选择的后果，因此他的思考是无效的。特别值得一提的是，诗人在前几个诗节里多次提到他面临的选择项是相同的。没有不同选择项的选择还是选择吗？诗人提供的这些信息

① https://www.merriam-webster.com/dictionary/choose.

难道不是在提示我们或许应该从另外一个视角去解读这首诗吗？

四、视角与连贯

语篇视角所激活的认知框架是统辖整个语篇连贯的重要机制。语篇连贯的依据不是简单的逻辑关系，而是语篇的话题和主题。作者根据话题或主题结构所设定的视角为理解语篇成分之间的连贯提供了关键思路。

Life in a day[①] 这篇课文的标题只笼统介绍了文章的话题，并没有给出该话题是从哪个视角切入的任何提示。我们需要从课文的正文，尤其是第一段去寻找视角的线索。值得注意的是课文开门见山提出了三个问题：

What do you love? What do you fear? What's in your pocket? These are the questions from the film *Life in a Day.*

识别这篇课文视角的重要线索是第三个问题里的名词 pocket。love 和 fear 是抽象名词，是我们人生最重要的情绪；pocket 则是具体名词，里面的东西是每天陪伴我们的普通生活用品。据此，我们也许可以假设，作者之所以选择 pocket 这个代表普通日常生活的具像作为视角去讨论 love 和 fear，是因为他赋予了 pocket 重要的象征意义：

---

① 邹为诚．普通高中教科书　英语　必修第一册［M］．上海：上海教育出版社，2020：6-7.

What do you love? What do you fear? What's in your pocket? These are the questions from the film *Life in a Day*. Director Kevin Macdonald asked people around the world to answer the questions and send in a video clip from a typical day. He was interested in creating a picture of the world, a digital time capsule for the future. On 24 July 2010, people from Africa, Europe, America, Antarctica and Asia recorded events on their mobile phones and digital cameras and uploaded them onto the Internet. In all there were 81,000 video clips. It took Macdonald and a team of researchers seven weeks to make them into a film.

The film starts at midnight. The moon is high in the sky, elephants are washing themselves in a river in Africa and a baby is sleeping. At the same time, in other parts of the world, people are getting up, brushing their teeth and making breakfast. In the next minutes of the one-and-a-half-hour-long film, we watch everyday routines from more than 140 different countries and see the connections between them. In one short scene an American girl is playing with her hula hoop. In another, a child is working at a shoeshine stand in Peru. One looks well off, the other is poor, but then the shoeshine boy shows us his favourite thing—his notebook computer. He's very proud of it because he earned the money to pay for it.

"We all care about the same things," says the director and in some ways he's right. Family and friends are the things most people love and many of them are keen on sports, like football. But then one man says he loves his cat and another loves his fridge because it doesn't talk back!

Monsters, dogs and death are the things most people fear. One young girl is worried about growing up and a man in Antarctica says, "I'm afraid of losing this place." But when asked, "What's in your pocket?", the answers are surprising. We don't see an ID card, a shopping list, or a bus ticket. Instead, one person has a paper towel, and another shows us a button. A poor man says he has nothing. He's not ashamed of his poverty—he's simply happy to be alive.

The film ends just before midnight, with a young woman in her car. It's raining outside and she's recording a short clip on her phone. "I just want people to know that I'm here," she says. In other words, she wants to show that her life matters. Even though their lives are very different, the people in *Life in a Day* have one thing in common: each of them is able to find meaning and happiness, no matter what his or her life is like.

课文的第一段是介绍背景，为我们构建宏观语境提供线索。课文从第二段开始讲述纪录片的内容，或者说第二段是 Life in a day 的开始。令人深思的是，Life in a day 开始的时间是午夜（midnight）。

一日之计在于晨，通常一天都是从早晨开始的。为什么这部影片选择从 midnight 去设置一天的开始呢？回答这个问题需要考虑课文的视角以及由视角激活的认知框架。也许我们可以换个角度思考：一日之计在于晨，英国诗人 Robert Browning 有一首诗是这么写的：

The year's at the spring

The year's at the spring,
The day's at the morn;
Morning's at seven;
The hillside's dew pearled;
The lark's on the wing;
The snail's on the thorn;
God's in His heaven—
All's right with the world!

如果选择从 morning 开始，则无论选择哪里的 morning 作为起点多少有"以某个区域为基点"的嫌疑。课文的视角是任何人的 pocket，选择 midnight 作为起点就可以避开以某个区域为观察点的嫌疑。

作者在这段里提供了一系列信息，如 elephants washing themselves in a river；a baby is sleeping；people are getting up，brushing their teeth and making breakfast 等。这些信息之间的关联是什么呢？答案自然可以有很多。有一点是可以肯定的，这些活动是人和动物每天要做的事情，是最基本、最自然的日常活动。作者这里特意提到的是 Africa 而不是其他发达的大洲，动物也是非洲的 elephants。这与作者的认知框架有关联吗？

作者在这一段里用 routine 直接点出了 pocket 日常生活的象征意义：

... we watch everyday <u>routines</u> from more than 140 different countries and see the connections between them.

作者接下来选择了两个非常具体的例子：

In one short scene an American girl is playing with her hula hoop. In another, a child is working at a shoeshine stand in Peru. One looks well off, the other is poor, but then the shoeshine boy shows us his favourite thing—his notebook computer. He's very proud of it because he earned the money to pay for it.

根据主语出现的次数，这段的视角显然聚焦在 Peruvian boy 身上。值得深思的是，作者在这么简短的段落里对 American girl 和 Peruvian boy 做了一系列的对比：

（1）American girl 在玩 vs. Peruvian boy 在工作

（2）American girl 富裕 vs. Peruvian boy 贫困

（3）hula loop vs. notebook computer

（4）hula loop 的来源？ vs. Peruvian boy earned the mony for the computer

作者为什么要做这些对比呢？从 pocket 这个视角看，这些对比产生的差异该如何解释呢？

作者在第三段借导演之口提示了他的答案：

"We all care about the same things," says the director and in some ways he's right.

由于各种原因，我们的日常活动形式不同，口袋里装的东西也不同，我们喜欢的东西不一样，但我们都有共同的关注。不过，作者为什么要用 in some ways 这个立场标识语呢[①]？作者为什么一方面说 care about the same things，但另一方面却又列举这些不同的喜好呢？

Family and friends are the things most people love and many of them are keen on sports, like football. But then one man says he loves his cat and another loves his fridge because it doesn't talk back!

与前两段不同，第四段侧重的是 fear。作者选择了三类信息：monster, dog and death。monster 是现实世界不存在的想象之物，death 则是无法逃避的自然规律。它们是恐惧的两个源头。可作者为什么在这里要选择 dog 呢？同样值得考虑的是当作者提到害怕长大的姑娘时，他并没有给出任何身份信息：

One young girl is worried about growing up

---

① 请参阅"第十章 立场"。

但讲述那位男子的恐惧时却专门提到了 Antarctica。这是为什么？这两者之间有联系吗？值得深思的是，为什么作者特别提到 ID card，shopping list，bus ticket 等这些不是大家口袋里所携带的东西？为什么作者提到的却是 paper towel 和 a button？作者为什么说口袋里空无一物的 poor man 不为自己的赤贫感到羞愧？如果我们将 paper towel 和 a button，甚至空无一物的口袋与 ID card，shopping list，bus ticket 做词汇关系的对比[①]，我们是否能发现它们的本质不同呢？

作者在这段说 a poor man 不感到羞愧的原因是 "he's simply happy to be alive"。我们又该如何从 pocket 的角度去理解他的幸福感呢？

课文的最后一段引用了雨中坐在车子里的年轻女子的这样一段话：

"I just want people to know that I'm here," she says. In other words, she wants to show that her life matters.

作者为什么不选择阳光明媚的白天而是午夜时分的雨天？"Her life matters" 与前面 "he's simply happy to be alive" 之间有什么关联吗？课文的最后一句话在点出了课文主题的同时，也解释了选择从 pocket 看 love and fear 的理由：

Even though their lives are very different, the people in *Life in a Day* have one thing in common: each of them is able to find meaning and happiness, no matter what his or her life is like.

pocket 这个视角显然提供了一条连贯线索，指出不管口袋里

---

① 请参阅"第七章　语篇的词汇关系"。

有什么，我们共同关注的是生命的本体和本意，而不是像 ID card、shopping list、bus ticket 等人生的附加意义。

An experiment in education[①] 的视角提示相对微妙。作者用 experiment 这个词不仅告诉读者课文的话题，而且还暗示了他讨论这个教育题材的视角。experiment 的意思是测试新假设或新方法，因此这个词也间接地提示了这篇课文有挑战传统教育观念的意图。作者从挑战的视角选择信息，构建了语篇成分之间的连贯。

The best programme on TV last night was the first episode of a new series about education, and it was set on a farm. But this farm is not for animals; it's for children. The farm has been converted into a school for one class of difficult students. And it's the job of one man to try and teach these students something in the two weeks they are there.

The class is a group of 16 boys and girls, aged 13 and 14, who have all been expelled from schools at least once. Their previous teachers said that they were "unteachable" and, judging by their behaviour in the programme last night, it isn't hard to see why. The teacher who has to deal with this class is 40-year-old Philip Beadle. Before working in education, Mr Beadle played in a rock band. He gave up music eight years ago to become a teacher. At his first school, he helped his students to get the best English marks the school had ever seen. As a result, he was made Schoolteacher of the Year.

In the programme last night, we saw the students have their first lesson with Mr Beadle. He started by playing a game, where he and the students pointed at each other and said something funny about the other person. This might not sound very educational, but it caught everyone's attention. After that, Mr Beadle took his class outside for an English lesson. At their

① 邹为诚.普通高中教科书 英语 必修第二册［M］.上海：上海教育出版社，2020：24-25.

previous schools, most of these students refused to read in front of their classmates, so Mr Beadle took them to a field to read to some cows. Each student read a brief quote from a Shakespeare play to them, and the students seemed to enjoy it. In the next scene, Mr Beadle took them to another field to teach them basic punctuation. He did this through another game where he asked the students to jump around, clap their hands and shout, "question mark!" and "semicolon!" Everyone seemed to enjoy this strange way of learning. By the end of the episode the students were indeed starting to accept their new teacher. Some of them even said he was "all right".

I really enjoyed this show because the teacher had such a positive effect on the students. If, like me, you are amazed by this experiment in education, you'll want to watch the whole series. Personally, I can't wait to see what happens next!

作者在第一段提供了课文的语境。课文介绍的是有关教育的电视系列节目。实验的地点是农场，针对的对象是困难学生（difficult students）。困难学生和农场场景的选择暗示课文的角度与一般的教育讨论大不相同。

作者在第二段给出了学生和教师的信息。他选择的信息与挑战的角度高度契合。这些学生的年龄大多是 13 或 14 岁，都曾经被学校开除过。年龄信息非常重要，因为这个年龄段的孩子逆反性强，还处于成形期（formative period）。开除的信息同样重要，因为这条信息表明传统教育方式对这些孩子不起作用。

教师信息也是从 experiment 的角度选择的。首先是年龄：40-year-old Philip Beadle。40 岁这个年龄段的人有了较丰富的生活经验，但兴趣和思想还没有被完全固化。教师从教前的 rock band 经历也很有针对性。rock music 是一种具有奔放特质的音乐风格，不受正统音乐的束缚。Mr Beadle 的非正规教师背景提示他对教育的理解和做法会与传统正规教育有很大的不同。

课文的第三段是重点。作者在介绍实验时有意识地选择了三个活动：

（1）playing a game, where he and the students pointed at each other and said something funny about the other person.

（2）Mr Beadle took them to a field to read to some cows.

（3）another game where he asked the students to jump around, clap their hands and shout, "question mark!" and "semicolon!"

作为 experiment，作者的选择揭示了传统教育存在的根本问题。虽然作者没有明说第一个活动与教育的关系，但 "but it caught everyone's attention" 这句话点明了传统教学存在的问题。教学首先要吸引学生的注意力，而传统教学最大的问题就是无法吸引这些学生的注意力。让这些学生对牛朗读的第二个活动似乎很怪诞。然而这不仅仅是好玩，更重要的是这么做能让他们无所顾忌，帮助他们克服学习困难时所产生的自卑心理。第三个活动是让学生在游戏中学习，也就是通常所说的寓教于乐。游戏不仅能让学生感到快乐，互相间产生互动，也能使他们身心投入。这三个活动的效果是明显的：

By the end of the episode the students were indeed starting to accept their new teacher. Some of them even said he was "all right".

因为是 experiment，所以作者选择这三个活动实际上依据的是教育学的基本原理。注意、自信和兴趣，这是学习所需要的三大要素。传统教育恰恰在这些方面出现问题，导致教学无法吸引困难学生的注意力，触发他们的兴趣，因而也无法使他们身心投入。作者对传统教育的挑战就从传统教育存在的主要问题着眼。作者的这个视角决定了课文的信息选择和排列，统辖了课文的连贯。

本章推荐书目

［1］曲卫国. 话语文体学导论：文本分析的方法［M］. 上海：复旦大学出版社，2009.

［2］Kuno, S. 1976. The Speaker's Empathy and Its Effect on Syntax: A reexamination of Yura and Kureru in Japanese. *The Journal of the Association of Teachers of Japanese*. 11(2/3): 249–271.

［3］Montgomery, A., A. Durant, N. Fabb, T. Furniss and S. Mills. 1992. *Ways of Reading: Advanced Reading Skills for Students of English Literature*. London: Routledge.

［4］Simpson, P. 1993. *Language, Ideology and Point of View*. London: Routledge.

第五章 语篇结构Ⅰ：信息结构

导引问题：

- 什么是语篇信息？
- 语篇的信息结构是如何影响理解的？

本章提要：

　　信息是语篇的主要内容构成。信息是按照一定意图加工处理后用于语篇的材料。语篇呈现的信息只是作者根据自己的意图从实际状况中选用的部分信息。语言表达方式会对信息的真实性和信息的作用产生重要影响。信息的信度与信息源有重要的关联。信息结构（information structure）指的是信息的排列顺序。信息结构的构建依据并不是事件在实际状况中的发生顺序，而是作者的表达意图和作者想取得的认知效果。信息结构主要有**时间、因果、认知顺序**等多个维度。了解语篇的信息选择和信息结构对认识作者的立场以及他们对语篇认知过程的操控有重大帮助。

一、概说

　　结构（structure）是一个关系集（relation set）。语篇结构指的是语篇成分之间的关系以及基于这些关系所构成的成分关系集。由于语篇有多个不同层级的成分组成，因而语篇结构也相应有不同层级的结构。本书主要讨论语篇三个不同层级的结构：信息结构、话题结构和主题结构。

信息是语篇的主要内容构成，因而是语篇内容的第一层级。信息的选择和排列通常在表层受到话题的制约，由此话题是语篇内容的第二层级。信息和话题都受到语篇主题的统辖，故而主题是语篇内容的第三层级。

语篇分析有关结构的讨论深受 Anthony Giddens 的建构理论（construction theory）的影响，通常把结构认知视作是一个读者与语篇动态互动的构建过程，将结构定义为建构，强调读者自身的认知结构、社会文化习俗以及其他各种语境因素对结构认知过程的动态制约。

本章主要讨论语篇的信息结构。信息是一个很难界定的概念。许多英语词典对 data（资料），fact（事实）和 information（信息）不做特别的区分，如 *Longman Dictionary Online*：

information: facts or details that tell you something about a situation[1]
data: information or facts[2]
fact: a piece of information that is known to be true[3]

不过，从语篇分析的角度看，这三个词还是有重要区别的。资料通常用来描述那些没有经过处理加工的材料。信息通常是按照一定意图加工处理过的材料。事实通常指事件在加工处理前的实际状

---

[1] https://www.ldoceonline.com/dictionary/information.
[2] https://www.ldoceonline.com/dictionary/data.
[3] https://www.ldoceonline.com/dictionary/fact.

况，信息则是指事件经加工处理后在语篇内的呈现。

信息与观点也是经常容易混淆的一对概念。*Longman Dictionary Online* 是这么解释 opinion 的：

... your ideas or beliefs about a particular subject[①]

既然信息是加工处理过的材料，那它似乎也是对实际状况的看法或阐释，究其实质，信息也应该可以算作观点。我们认为，信息和观点的主要区别是两者的证明方法不一样。信息传递的内容尽管被处理加工过，但该内容有一定的事实基础，因而判断信息的依据是真实性。没有事实依据的信息是假信息。观点则不同，观点表达的是个人对事实等的阐释（interpretation），是个人的主观判断，因此判断观点的依据不是真实性而是合理性。不合理观点是错误观点。

之所以需要将资料和事实与信息区分开来，一个重要原因是一旦资料和事实在语篇里出现成为信息后，它们就失去了客观独立性，只为语篇服务。

区别信息和观点是了解语篇信息结构的第一步。以 Ideal beauty[②] 的第一段为例：

Nigerian teenager Happiness Edem had just one aim in life: to put on weight. So she spent six months in a "fattening room" where her daily routine was to sleep, eat and grow fat. She went in weighing 60 kg, but came out weighing twice that. In some parts of Africa, being fat is desirable because it is a sign of attractiveness in women and power and wealth in

---

① https://www.ldoceonline.com/dictionary/opinion.
② 邹为诚. 普通高中教科书　英语　必修第三册［M］. 上海：上海教育出版社，2021：42-43.

men. However, in magazines and in the media we are bombarded with images of slim women with a fair complexion and handsome, broad-shouldered young men. It is fairly rare to see short-sighted, middle-aged models. Some people question these shallow beauty ideals. Is one idea of physical beauty really more attractive than another?

这一段有八句句子。前三句叙述的是 Happiness Edem 做的事情：

（1）Happiness Edem had just one aim in life ...

（2）she spent six months ...

（3）She went in weighing 60 kg ...

只要 Edem 做过这些事情，这些信息就是真实的。接下来的三句叙述的是非洲某些地方的状况：

（1）In some parts of Africa, being fat is desirable ...

（2）However, in magazines and in the media we are bombarded with images of slim women ...

（3）It is fairly rare to see short-sighted, middle-aged models.

如果非洲任何地方都没有这些实际状况，这三句里的信息就是假消息。同样如此，只要有人提出质疑，第七句 "Some people question these shallow beauty ideals." 就是真实信息。第八句 "Is one idea of physical beauty really more attractive than another?" 属于观点类，因为它表达的是主观判断，是阐释性的，所以无法用真实性去判断。

语篇的信息呈现受到三个因素的制约。第一个因素是作者的意图。语篇信息是作者根据自己构建语篇的意图选用的，因此只是实际状况的一部分。第二个因素是信息传递方式。语言是信息的主要载体，不同的语言表达方式会对信息的真实性和信息的作用产生重要影响。第三个因素是信息源。信息的信度与信息源有重要的关联。即便信息相同，如果信息源不同，信息的信度受到质疑的程度就不同。

　　信息源通常涉及两个问题：一是谁说的？即提供信息的人是否具有相关的资质或权威。二是源于什么样的知识框架？即信息是否与大家相信的知识体系相符合。如对于"Are apples healthy food?"这个问题有两个回复。第一个回复是营养学博士的，其解释框架是现代生物学的：

> Apples are healthy foods; they are a source of insoluble fiber that improves intestinal transit and combats constipation. Apples are also a source of vitamins, minerals, and bioactive compounds that help control hyperglycemia, insulin resistance, and other health benefits.[①]

另外一个回复提供的信息源于不同的知识体系：

> ... different apple colors represent different parts of the body. Red apples protect the heart and vessel. It also reduces the content of lipids as well. Green apples are probably the most beneficial. Although representing the liver, they are said to detoxify the inner body, promote teeth and bones growth, and help fight depression. Yellow apples help protect eyesight.[②]

究竟相信哪种解释，这完全取决于读者对知识体系的态度。

　　信息在语篇中的效率与信息排列顺序有关。信息结构指的就是信息的排列顺序。信息结构的构建依据并不是实际状况的顺序，而

---

① https://microsoftstart.msn.com/en-us/health/ask-professionals/apple?questionid=el9ax4v3&type=nutrition&ocid=entnewsntp&source=bingmainline_nutritionqna.［2023-04-24］.

② https://techforhunt.com/why-apple-eating-is-important-in-traditional-chinese-medicine/.［2023-11-26］.

是作者的表达意图和作者想取得的认知效果。信息结构有多个维度，我们这里主要讨论三个维度[①]：① 时间；② 因果；③ 认知顺序。

（1）时间维度

信息排列与事件发生的顺序可以形成时间上的正向顺序关系，van Dijk 提供了这么一个例子：

She went straight to her room and, before she sat down at her desk, she took off her hat and touched her face with a powder puff.

这里信息陈述与事件发生的时间顺序基本一致。不过，信息排列顺序与事件发生的时间顺序也常常不一致：

She sat down at her desk after she took off her hat.

按照时间维度排列信息似乎具有相对的客观性，方便掩饰作者的选择痕迹。

（2）因果维度

信息排列的顺序有时会从因果维度展开。作者会根据自己的需要，或先聚焦因，或先强调果：

John was ill. He didn't come.

这两句之间虽然没有衔接连词，但两句的因果关系非常明显。如果把两句的顺序换一下，因果聚焦的先后就不同：

[①] 我们这里主要依据的是 Van Dijk, T. 1977. *Text and Context: Explorations in the Semantics and Pragmatics of Discourse*. London: Longman.

John didn't come. He was ill.

作者常用连词或副词对句子之间的关系进行标注，以凸显因果关系的顺序：

John didn't come because he was ill.

因果维度的排列对认知的影响主要体现在语境构建上。先提到的部分会成为后出现部分的语境。

（3）认知维度

信息排列的认知维度是学界较有争议的一个假设。van Dijk 认为，按认知原理，信息排列应该有一定的规律可寻。符合认知规律的信息排列，读者相对容易接受：

The early Australian Aborigines made the land navigable through songs, dance and paintings.[①]

为什么是 songs 和 dance 排在前面，而 paintings 排在最后？古人就有这方面的假说：言之不足，歌之咏之，歌之不足，舞之蹈之。绘画似乎应该是比歌舞相对晚发生的事情。如果我们把顺序换一下，可能会产生不同的感觉：

The early Australian Aborigines made the land navigable through paintings songs and dance.

---

① 邹为诚. 普通高中教科书　英语　选择性必修第三册［M］. 上海：上海教育出版社，2022：18-19.

这里我们要专门介绍 van Dijk 提出的"常规排序序列"（normal ordering）假设。根据这个假设，物体的结构对认知过程有重要影响。如我们通常先注意物体的整体，然后才关注物体的组成部分；先看到的是较大的物体，然后才注意到较小物体；先观察物体外部，然后再考察物体内部。van Dijk（1977: 10）提出了七个常规排序序列：

a. General（A）—particular（B）

b. Whole（A）—part/component（B）

c. Set（A）—subset（B）—element（C）

d. Including（A）—included（B）

e. Large（A）—small（B）

f. Outside（A）—inside（B）

g. Possessor（A）—possessed（B）

必须强调的是，许多学者对这个假设的认知依据提出了异议。我们无意在这里讨论学界的分歧。不过，我们认为常规排序序列这个假设对分析信息结构对语篇理解的制约有很大的帮助。这个假设能让我们注意到信息排列顺序的异常（deviation），能提高我们对排列顺序的敏感度，从而在阅读中对语篇的信息结构提出这样的问题：

a. 作者把 B 信息放在 A 信息前面想要凸显什么？

b. 凸显这条信息对理解语篇会产生什么影响？

我们可以通过对比以下两篇报道的信息结构来看不同的信息选择和信息排列顺序会产生什么样的认知效果。

报道 A

4 Chinese teens among 5 people killed in Canada crash

Five people — four teenagers and a 42-year-old woman — were killed in a two-vehicle crash in Huntsville, Canada, on Saturday, according to the Ontario Provincial Police (OPP).

The teenagers from the Greater Toronto Area were between the ages of 15 to 17 and have been identified as Chinese students. The woman from Huntsville was identified as Jessica Lynn Ward, a mother of two.

Police received the call around 11:10 pm for the crash on Highway 60 near Hidden Valley Road, seven kilometres from Huntsville. Three of the four teenage victims and the woman died at the scene, and one of the teenagers died in the hospital, according to OPP.

The teenagers were heading west in a Mercedes SUV, while the woman was traveling east in a Ford SUV. The highway was closed for several hours while police investigated. Police haven't yet revealed the cause of the collision or the identities of the teenage victims. They are still investigating the incident and asking anyone with footage of the collision to contact the OPP in Huntsville.

The Chinese Embassy in Canada and the Chinese Consulate General in Toronto immediately activated the emergency response mechanism, according to a statement from the Chinese consulate on Monday.

The consulate verified the situation with the OPP at the earliest opportunity and has established contact with the relatives of the international students.

The Chinese Ambassador to Canada Cong Peiwu and Consul General Luo Weidong in Toronto have expressed their condolences to the families of the victims.

The consulate is closely monitoring the situation and making every effort to handle subsequent matters properly. It also reminded students in Canada to pay attention to traffic safety.[1]

---

[1] https://global.chinadaily.com.cn/a/202311/28/WS65656c93a31090682a5f0644.html.

报道 B

Four Chinese students killed in fatal crash in Huntsville, Ont.

Four Chinese students were among those who died in a fatal motor vehicle collision in Huntsville, Ont., over the weekend, officials have confirmed.

The two-vehicle collision took place around 11 p.m. on Saturday, Nov. 25, involving a westbound Mercedes SUV and an eastbound Ford SUV on Highway 60, according to Huntsville OPP.

Five people died in the crash. Police say four of the victims were teens from North York and Richmond Hill. The other victim was a 42-year-old woman from Huntsville. She was pronounced dead at the scene, police said.

"One of the individuals in the Mercedes SUV was transported to hospital and succumbed to his injuries there," police said.

On Monday, the Consulate-General of the People's Republic of China in Toronto released a statement confirming that Chinese officials verified the collision with the OPP and contacted the families of the foreign students involved.

According to a GoFundMe page, Jessica Lynn Ward was the woman involved in the collision.

"Jessica leaves behind her two precious children (aged 17 and 14) to deal with this unimaginable loss," reads the GoFundMe page.[1]

如果对比两篇报道的前面几段，我们会发现它们的信息选择和排列不太一样。报道 A 一开始就提到了 five people were killed，只说了 teenagers，没提国籍。不过在提及女性死者时，提到了具体的

---

[1] https://globalnews.ca/news/10117806/four-chinese-students-killed-fatal-huntsville-crash/.

年龄:

Five people — four teenagers and a 42-year-old woman — were killed in
a two-vehicle crash in Huntsville, Canada, on Saturday, according to the
Ontario Provincial Police (OPP).

报道 B 只提了四个学生,并没有提年龄,但提了国籍:

Four Chinese students were among those who died in a fatal motor vehicle
collision in Huntsville, Ont., over the weekend, officials have confirmed.

报道 B 不像报道 A 那样直接指出还有一位女性死亡。不过报
道 B 用了 among 这个介词,提示除了四位中国学生外,还有其他
人。报道 B 的信息排列似乎违反了"常规排序序列",因为通常报道
会先报道死亡人数的总数。

两篇报道提及信息源时的措辞也不一样。报道 A 更具体: the
Ontario Provincial Police;报道 B 则笼统: officials have confirmed。

报道 A 在第二段提到了学生的国籍和他们的年龄。在这段里还
增加了那位女性的具体姓名以及她的家庭情况:

The teenagers from the Greater Toronto Area were between the ages of
15 to 17 and have been identified as Chinese students. The woman from
Huntsville was identified as Jessica Lynn Ward, a mother of two.

由第一段的 general 到第二段的 particular 似乎与"常规排序序
列"相符。报道 B 在第二段还是没有提及在车祸中死去的女性,却
在给出车祸具体时间的同时特别提到了两辆车车型的信息细节:

The two-vehicle collision took place around 11 p.m. on Saturday, Nov. 25, involving a westbound Mercedes SUV and an eastbound Ford SUV on Highway 60, according to Huntsville OPP.

报道 A 的第三段叙述的是警察的接警时间，车祸发生的具体地点以及他们到场后所发现的情况：

Police received the call around 11:10 pm for the crash on Highway 60 near Hidden Valley Road, seven kilometres from Huntsville. Three of the four teenage victims and the woman died at the scene, and one of the teenagers died in the hospital, according to OPP.

报道 B 的第三段也引用了警察的话以及警察到场后发现的情况：

Five people died in the crash. Police say four of the victims were teens from North York and Richmond Hill. The other victim was a 42-year-old woman from Huntsville. She was pronounced dead at the scene, police said.

值得注意的是，报道 B 在这个时候才提供了总的死亡人数。那位女性死者和学生的年龄才被提及。与报道 A 不同的是，报道 B 没有提当场死亡的三位学生，只提 42 岁的女性当场死亡。值得注意的是，这段里的地点状语与前面的 westbound 和 eastbound 相呼应，提示了不同车型的归属。

报道 A 在第四段提到了车型号，描述了车祸发生的具体状况。除此之外，还再次提到了警方的调查：

The teenagers were heading west in a Mercedes SUV, while the woman was traveling east in a Ford SUV. The highway was closed for several hours while police investigated. Police haven't yet revealed the cause of the collision or the identities of the teenage victims. They are still investigating the incident and asking anyone with footage of the collision to contact the OPP in Huntsville.

报道 B 的第四段非常短，直接引用了警察的话。警察只提了其中一位学生送医不治的情况，并再一次提到了学生汽车的车型：

"One of the individuals in the Mercedes SUV was transported to hospital and succumbed to his injuries there," police said.

如果对比前四段，不难看出两篇报道有不同的信息选择和排列。两篇报道不同的信息结构使它们的视角不相同：报道 A 的切入点是一起涉及学生和中年妇女的车祸，中国学生很年轻，15—17 岁，而中年妇女则有家庭。而报道 B 则突出中国学生开的是豪车。报道 B 将女性死者信息延后所产生的一个效果是，不仅学生自己付出了代价，而且还使当地的中年妇女赔上了性命。报道 B 有些信息的选择，如有关具体出发地的交代也似乎有某种责任的暗示：中年女子是 Huntsville 的当地人，当地人自然熟悉路况，而学生则是从 North York 和 Richmond Hill 来的，他们对路况不一定熟悉。

值得注意的是，报道 A 有多次提及事件还在调查中的信息。报道 B 却没有这方面的信息。报道 A 选择以与中国领事馆有关的信息结束报道，信息的选择和排列符合对这种问题处理的期待：

a. activated the emergency response mechanism;

b. verified the situation and established contact;

c. expressed their condolences;

d. monitoring the situation and reminded students in Canada to pay attention to traffic safety

报道 B 提到了中国领事馆，但它却以 GoFundMe page 提供的信息结束报道。有关中国领事馆的信息只有两条：

a. verified the collision;

b. contacted the families

对比之下，报道 B 提供的信息让人感觉中国领事馆非常 businesslike。GoFundMe 是个众筹平台。选择这个平台披露中年女性死者的具体信息还是意味深长的。报道借该平台不仅提供了女性死者名字的信息，还特意提到了她两个孩子的年龄：

Jessica leaves behind her two precious children (aged 17 and 14) to deal with this unimaginable loss.

信息的呈现方式需要特别注意，如报道 A 提及了中国学生的年龄，通篇没有表示情感色彩的形容词。报道 B 并没有提及中国学生的年龄而是用了 teens 这个词。该报道通篇只有两个形容词 precious 和 unimaginable，但这两个形容词都用来描写 Jessica 的家庭。

二、信息结构与教学

信息结构是语篇的基本内容构成。唯有了解语篇的信息选择和信息结构，我们才可能认识作者的立场以及他们对语篇认知过程的操控。

在教学过程中，我们可以把信息分析分为三个基本步骤：

（1）甄别信息与观点；

（2）了解作者的信息选择。了解作者信息选择是为了了解是否有其他相关信息没有被作者选用，以对作者信息选用的目的和效果做出判断；

（3）确定作者选用信息的排列顺序。判断作者的信息排列是否有特别之处，以及这样排列会有什么样的凸显效果。

具体说来，在分析语篇的信息结构时，我们可以考虑以下几个问题：

（1）语篇为什么要提供这些信息？

（2）是否有重要信息被忽略？

（3）语篇的信息是否可以分成不同板块？

（4）板块间的相互关系是什么？

（5）语篇的信息源是否可靠或有多源性？

对于信息结构，我们应该提醒学生考虑这么几个问题：

（1）为什么语篇以这条信息开始？

（2）语篇的信息排列有什么依据？

（3）语篇的信息排列与语篇的话题或主题有什么关系？

（4）语篇的信息排列顺序与一般认知有不同吗？

（5）语篇的排列顺序对我们的认知有影响吗？

就信息与观点的关系而言，我们可以请学生思考这么几个问题：

（1）信息是为观点提供依据还是为引出观点？

（2）信息是否有与观点不同的暗示？

三、信息结构分析

分析语篇信息选择和信息结构的目的是解读语篇的主题和了解作者是如何操控信息以表达主题的。最重要的是考虑两个问题：第一，作者选择了哪些信息？第二，作者这样排列信息凸显了什么？

课文 Where history comes alive[①] 描写了东西方两个不同的城市。比较课文对西安和佛罗伦萨的介绍，我们会发现作者在介绍两个城市时所选择的信息有很不同的侧重：

Xi'an, China

Xi'an is no doubt one of the most popular tourist destinations in China. Every year, millions of travellers visit the Terracotta Army of Emperor Qin Shihuang about 42 kilometres from the city centre, which is one of the most amazing historic sites in the world.

As one of China's great former capitals, Xi'an grew to be the largest city in the world during the Tang Dynasty, a golden age of art and poetry. Chang'an, as it was known at the time, was the starting point of the Silk Road, which connected China to the world. It was here that Xuan Zang set out on his famous travels, which became the basis of *Journey to the West*. Historic sites from that time include the two Wild Goose Pagodas and the remains of the Daming Palace, which was the centre of the Tang court.

Today, Xi'an is a modern city, at the heart of China's Belt and Road Initiative, but its long history can be seen everywhere: it is one of the few cities in the world that still have city walls. The wall, almost 14 kilometres in length, was originally built for the purpose of defence, but nowadays, it's a great

---

① 邹为诚. 普通高中教科书 英语 必修第一册［M］. 上海：上海教育出版社，2020：24-25.

way to experience Xi'an: from here, you can get an amazing view of the city.

Florence, Italy

Florence, one of the famous historic cities in Italy, is the birthplace of many amazing ideas and discoveries!

Florence's history is alive with the memory of a time when art, culture and science were being "reborn". In the late 13th century, the Renaissance began here before spreading to the rest of Europe. At that time, Michelangelo, Leonardo da Vinci and Galileo were some of the people living, working and studying in Florence. During this period, they, along with other great minds, contributed valuable artworks and made important scientific discoveries.

Florence is filled with art, science and history museums and ancient buildings, as well as historic universities. You can visit many of these places to experience and admire the amazing work and discoveries that happened during the Renaissance period. An example is Michelangelo's famous statue *David*, which he completed between 1501 and 1504. Another must-see is the University of Florence. It was started in 1321 and many famous people studied there in the Renaissance period, including Leonardo da Vinci.

In Florence today you can experience the old and the new. Historic sites are neighbours with fancy restaurants and high-end shops. While you are trying the delicious local food, you can decide which interesting places to visit next.

让我们先看有关西安的信息。这部分的第一句就提示了信息选择的角度——tourist destination:

Xi'an is no doubt one of the most popular tourist destinations in China.

有意思的是，作者接下来选择的旅游信息并不在西安，而是离西安中心有 42 公里远的秦始皇陵兵马俑。

Every year, millions of travellers visit the Terracotta Army of Emperor Qin Shihuang about 42 kilometres from the city centre, which is one of the most amazing historic sites in the world.

作者在第二段提供了一系列与西安历史有关的信息：

（1）the largest city in the world during the Tang Dynasty；

（2）a golden age of art and poetry；

（3）the starting point of the Silk Road；

（4）Xuan Zang set out on his famous travels；

（5）the Wild Goose Pagodas and the remains of the Daming Palace

唐朝是中国历史上一个辉煌的时期，唐诗是中国文学的瑰宝，丝绸之路更是对外交流史上的壮举。玄奘不仅是汉传佛教佛经的翻译家，更是旅行家和文化传播者。他为了求法解迷惑从长安出发，经姑臧出敦煌，辗转新疆及中亚等地到达印度摩揭陀国王舍城。大雁塔是玄奘为保存由天竺经丝绸之路带回长安的经卷、佛像等而主持修建的，因而大雁塔是文化融合的象征。大明宫不仅仅代表中国古代建筑艺术的顶峰，奠定了中国的宫殿建筑制度，而且它对日本等亚洲国家的宫殿建筑也产生了重要影响。据考证，日本平城京、平安京宫城无论是宫殿布局还是与城郭的位置关系，在很大程度上都是模仿了唐大明宫。

对了解西安历史或西安旅游而言，这些信息确实很重要。不过，作者聚焦西安的唐代历史究竟是出于什么样的考虑？这个信息排列顺序依据的是什么？

课文的第三段则是西安的现代信息。作者具体提到的信息有：

（1）Xi'an is a modern city, at the heart of China's Belt and Road Initiative；

（2）it is one of the few cities in the world that still have city walls

这篇课文的标题是 Where history comes alive。作者在第一、第二段选择的古代信息和第三段的现代信息之间有呼应吗？我们究竟应该如何根据第三段的信息理解在西安历史变得鲜活起来呢？

第三段的一带一路的信息相对容易理解。一带一路是现代中国提出的倡议，是丝绸之路的延续，与玄奘的文化传播壮举有清楚的呼应，因而它是 "history comes alive" 的重要标志。可作者为什么要选择在第三段，也就是介绍现代西安时提到古城墙呢？

> The wall, almost 14 kilometres in length, was originally built for the purpose of defence, but nowadays, it's a great way to experience Xi'an: from here, you can get an amazing view of the city.

作者在介绍古城墙时为什么要专门讲古城墙是为了防卫而建造的呢？为什么作者建议读者从古城墙这个点去俯瞰西安呢？

对比西安，有关佛罗伦萨描述的第一句就提示信息选择的角度完全不同：

> Florence, one of the famous historic cities in Italy, is <u>the birthplace of many amazing ideas and discoveries</u>!

　　这句的核心词语是 the birthplace of many amazing ideas and discoveries。这使有关佛罗伦萨信息的选择更多与人类精神文明发展有关联。这部分的第二段提供了这么几条信息：

　　（1）memory of a time when art, culture and science were being "reborn"；

　　（2）In the late 13th century, the Renaissance began here before spreading to the rest of Europe；

　　（3）Michelangelo, Leonardo da Vinci and Galileo were living, working and studying in Florence

　　特别值得一提的是三位人物的选择。Michelangelo 被世人称为意大利文艺复兴的三杰之一。他的艺术风格影响了许多艺术家，他作品的艺术生命到现在还依然强劲。Da Vinci 是三杰中的另外一杰。虽然他的艺术作品与 Michelangelo 的一样出类拔萃，但他的成就并不局限在艺术领域，他的贡献是全方位的。Galileo 则与前两位不同，他被誉为"现代科学之父"。他在人类思想解放和文明发展的过程中作出了划时代的贡献。

　　该部分的第三段提到了：

　　（1）museums, ancient buildings 以及 historic universities

　　要强调的是 historic universities 现在还在运作。

　　（2）Michelangelo's famous statue *David*, which he completed between 1501 and 1504

　　这座雕塑是公认的体现文艺复兴人文主义思想的典范。Michelangelo 通过人体赞美了人的力量，表达了人打碎了中世纪的思想桎梏而获得新生的主题。

　　（3）the University of Florence 这所历史悠久的大学

这所学校不仅见证了意大利的文艺复兴，更见证了文艺复兴对后世科学和人文的影响。

作者最后一段有关佛罗伦萨今天状况的信息选择与西安也明显角度不同：

（1）Historic sites are neighbours with fancy restaurants and high-end shops;

（2）While you are trying the delicious local food, you can decide which interesting places to visit next.

梳理完作者所选择的信息之后，我们可能要回答以下几个问题：

（1）作者是在做两个城市的历史对比吗？

（2）作者的不同选择是出于什么样的视角呢？

（3）作者的视角与"history comes alive"有什么关系呢？

信息的排列顺序不仅能为推导语篇主题提供线索，同时也能对作者的立场有所提示。一般来说，阅读议论文时，我们通常会期待一般的总结性信息，然后再进入具体的讨论，也就是general—particular 的常规排序序列。

Ideal beauty[①] 这篇课文却没有遵循这个序列。它以非典型的 Nigerian teenager Happiness Edem 的具体信息开始。如果我们注意到了信息的排列顺序与常规排序序列不符，"作者到底想凸显什么呢？"这一问题便会产生：

Nigerian teenager Happiness Edem had just one aim in life: to put on weight. So she spent six months in a "fattening room" where her daily

---

① 邹为诚.普通高中教科书　英语　必修第三册［M］.上海：上海教育出版社，2021：42–43.

routine was to sleep, eat and grow fat. She went in weighing 60 kg, but came out weighing twice that. In some parts of Africa, being fat is desirable because it is a sign of attractiveness in women and power and wealth in men. However, in magazines and in the media we are bombarded with images of slim women with a fair complexion and handsome, broad-shouldered young men. It is fairly rare to see short-sighted, middle-aged models. Some people question these shallow beauty ideals. Is one idea of physical beauty really more attractive than another?

Ideas about physical beauty change over time and different periods of history reveal different views of beauty, particularly of women. Egyptian paintings often show slim dark-haired women as the normal practice, while one of the earliest representations of women in art in Europe is an overweight female. This is the Venus of Hohle Fels and it is more than 35,000 years old. In the early 1600s, artists like Peter Paul Rubens also painted plump, pale-skinned women who were thought to be the most stunning examples of female beauty at that time. In Elizabethan England, pale skin was still fashionable because it was a sign of wealth: the make-up used to achieve this look was expensive, so only rich people could afford it.

Within different cultures around the world, there is a huge difference in what is considered beautiful. Traditional customs, like tattooing, head-shaving, piercing or other kinds of bodily changes can express social position, identity or values. In Borneo, for instance, tattoos are like a diary because they are a written record of all the important events and places a man has experienced in his life. For New Zealand's Maoris they reflect the person's position in society. Western society used to have a very low opinion of tattoos. Today they are considered a popular form of body art among the new generation.

For Europeans, the tradition of using metal rings to stretch a girl's neck may be shocking, but the Myanmar people consider women with long and thin necks more elegant. In Indonesia, the custom of sharpening girls' teeth to points might seem very odd while it is perfectly acceptable in other places to straighten children's teeth with braces. Wearing rings in the nose or plastic surgery might be seen as ugly and unattractive by some cultures, but it is commonplace in many others.

It appears that through the ages and across different cultures, people have always changed their bodies and faces for a wide variety of reasons: sometimes to help them look more beautiful, and sometimes to enable them to show social position or display group identity. Whether it is wearing make-up or decorating the body with tattoos, rings and piercings, different cultures view these things with different eyes. Does this mean that we are all beautiful in our own way?

从这篇课文的宏观结构看，它一共有五个段落。每个段落都有各自的信息维度。第一段涉及 beauty 理念的共时冲突；第二段涉及 beauty 理念的历时变化；第三段涉及 beauty 习俗的象征意义；第四段涉及 beauty 习俗引起的 culture shock；最后一段总结陈词并提出新的问题。

从各段落的信息排列看，每个段落似乎都有两个信息板块组成，一个板块有关非欧洲的信息，另一板块则与欧洲有关。两个信息板块的基本排列顺序也大致相同，第一板块是非欧洲的，第二板块是欧洲信息。唯一没有按照这个排列的是最后一段。不过这一段只有观点，并没有信息。值得思考的是，每段虽然信息排列相同，但它们之间的关系和作用似乎不完全一样。

第一段第一板块主要介绍 Nigerian teenager Happiness Edem 的相关信息。第二板块由 however 引出。虽然作者没有明说，但从内容上看，这里介绍的是欧洲人的 beauty 观。这块的信息相当笼统，只提到了 magazine 和 media。这两块信息形成鲜明的两个反差：fat vs. slim。由于两个板块的具体程度不一样，这个板块的排列顺序似乎是 specific vs. general。之所以说"似乎"，是因为 Edem 的审美观实际上与欧洲人是两个不同体系，但作者的这个排列顺序却造成两者是同一体系的错觉。这段最后的问题更是强化了这种错觉：

Is one idea of physical beauty really more attractive than another?

第二段讲的是 beauty 观的历时变化。第一板块介绍的是 Egyptian paintings 里描绘的 slim dark-haired women，第二板块则是有关欧洲人的 beauty 观念。与第一段相比，有关欧洲的信息要更详细、更具体。这个板块提到了多个历史信息，如 the Venus of Hohle Fels, Peter Paul Rubens, Elizabethan England 等。

值得注意的是，不仅两块的信息具体程度有差异，内容也有差异。第一块只有 Egyptian paintings。由于没有其他信息呼应这段第一句提到的 "change over time" 和 "different periods of history reveal different views of beauty"，这个板块的信息不能体现 Egyptians 审美观的历时发展和变化。欧洲信息板块有两个时段的信息，35,000 years 和 early 1600s。这两个不同时段自然能显示出欧洲 beauty 观的历时变化。从时态上看，第一板块是一般现在时，而第二板块则是过去时。这样的信息选择是否在提示我们课文的认知框架呢？

第三段主要介绍各 beauty 习俗在不同文化中的意义。这一段的第一个板块明显长于第二个板块，内容十分具体，提到了 Borneo 和 Maoris 的 tattoo 象征意义。这些审美习俗被作者归入 traditional customs。值得注意的是，这个板块里的信息呈现用的是一般现在时。第二板块只有两句话，第一句是西方社会过去对 tattoo 的否定性评价，第二句则介绍了西方新一代人对 tattoo 的接纳。两句话用了过去和现在两个不同的时态，这不仅与第二段呼应，反映出西方审美态度的变化，而且还给人现代西方社会已经跳出 tradition 的感觉。两个板块的内容也形成对比。与第一板块信息不同的是，有关西方社会的介绍没有提任何象征含义或社会意义。审美仅是人体艺术。

第四段的第一板块与前面不同，是由欧洲人对其他文化具体实践的 "shocking" 反应开始。这段对非欧洲人习俗的介绍非常具体，内容也非常奇特：

the tradition of using metal rings to stretch a girl's neck may be shocking, ... Indonesia, the custom of sharpening girls' teeth to points ...

虽然这段里提到的 "straighten children's teeth with braces, wearing rings in the nose or plastic surgery" 没有地域标识，但根据这篇课文的表述规律，这些没有地域标识的实践极可能是欧洲的。

第五段是基于信息的总结性观点综述。要问的问题是，这里的观点主要对应的是哪些信息呢？这段的第一个观点是：

It appears that through the ages and across different cultures, people have always changed their bodies and faces for a wide variety of reasons: sometimes to help them look more beautiful, and sometimes to enable them to show social position or display group identity.

这个观点的核心词语是 have always changed。不过，从课文提供的信息看，这个观点应该不对应非西方的审美实践。

这段里的第二个结论似乎也与前面的信息有不相符之处：

Whether it is wearing make-up or decorating the body with tattoos, rings and piercings, different cultures view these things with different eyes.

如第三段所提供的西方社会信息，欧洲人是有变化的：

Western society used to have a very low opinion of tattoos. Today they are considered a popular form of body art among the new generation.

据此，我们应该考虑作者提供的信息是否回答了他在第一段提出的"Is one idea of physical beauty really more attractive than another?"这个问题。同时也要考虑作者为什么要在最后一段提出"Does this mean that we are all beautiful in our own way?"这个完全不同的问题。最后一段的这个问题显然是对第一段问题的修正。将physical beauty 进行比较意味着我们采用的是某一个文化的标准。课文给出的不同文化的不同信息显然表明这样的比较不合适。另外一个值得思考的问题是，课文其实只提供了作者或西方人审视其他文化的信息，并没有给出任何非西方人判断西方文化的信息。作者的这种选择又意味着什么呢？

　　信息呈现的方式也是分析语篇信息的一个重要内容。An excerpt from *A Walk in the Woods*[1] 是叙事类体裁。作者的信息呈现方式对我们了解作者笔下人物的心理有非常大的影响。以课文的第一段为例，作者在这段提供了许多信息，但呈现的方式却不完全一样：

It was perfect sleeping weather, cool enough to need a bag but warm

---

[1] 邹为诚.普通高中教科书　英语　选择性必修第一册［M］.上海：上海教育出版社，2021：72–73. 这篇课文改编自 Bill Bryson 写的 *A Walk in the Woods*。我们这里根据原著，对课文稍作了改动。请参阅"第三章　语境"。

enough to sleep in your underwear, and I was looking forward to having a long night's rest, which is what I was doing when, at some point during the night, I heard a sound nearby that made my eyes fly open. Normally, I slept through everything—through thunderstorms, and through Katz's snoring, so something loud enough to wake me was unusual. There was a sound of bushes being disturbed—a click of breaking branches, a weighty pushing through low leaves and branches—and then a kind of large, frightening noise.

简单地整理后，我们发现这段至少有三类信息呈现方式和三个信息系列。三类信息呈现方式分别是：

（1）以"客观"事实方式呈现：cool weather, a sound nearby that made my eyes fly open, which is what I was doing, Normally, I slept through everything, sound of bushes being disturbed, a click of breaking branches

（2）以心态描写方式呈现：perfect sleeping weather, I was looking forward to having a long night's rest

（3）以推测方式呈现：something loud enough to wake me was unusual, a weighty pushing through low leaves and branches, then a kind of large, frightening noise

三个信息系列：

I.

（1）perfect sleeping, cool weather（天气）

（2）I was looking forward to having a long night's rest（心态）

（3）which is what I was doing（行动）

（4）There was a sound nearby that made my eyes fly open.（突发事件）

II.

（1）Normally, I slept through everything（原因）

（2）something loud enough to wake me was unusual（推测）

III.

（1）sound of bushes being disturbed, a click of breaking branches（动静）

（2）a weighty pushing through low leaves and branches（推测）

（3）then a kind of large, frightening noise（推测）

第一个信息系列是：天气—心态—行动—突发事件。在一个凉爽的晚上，人很疲劳而且很想睡，按理应该会入眠很快。然而，作者在描写行动时却用了过去进行时态，拉长了入眠的进程，这一方面与前面描写的情况有矛盾，另一方面却也似乎对这一过程会有事件发生进行了提示。

第二个系列是原因系列：原因—推测。原因在前，作者似乎强调结果不应该发生。值得注意的是，对结果的描述只是作者的推测。

第三个系列是：动静—推测—推测。有关动静的信息显然与前面 something loud enough 的推测不完全相符。disturb 和 click 这两个词似乎并没有给人有出现庞然大物（weighty）的感觉。后面的两个信息好像都是来自作者的推测：weighty 和 frightening。

作者应该期待这些信息会使读者产生疑问。一个平素睡得很沉、不容易惊醒，且又很累的人，通常很少会被外部树枝断裂声惊醒。可从他这么快就做出的推测看，一定是事出有因。他一定在这之前受到了什么惊吓或心理暗示。课文是节选，原著中有一段证明了他曾受到过心理暗示：

Nearly everyone I talked to had some gruesome story involving a guileless acquaintance who had gone off hiking the trail with high hopes and new boots and come stumbling back two days later with a bobcat attached to his head or dripping blood from an armless sleeve and whispering in a hoarse voice, "Bear!" before sinking into a troubled unconsciousness.①

作者信息选择所激活的认知框架为理解主人公接下来产生熊的联想提供了语境：

Bear!
I sat up and reached quickly for my knife, then realized I had left it in my pack, just outside the tent. ...

本章推荐书目

[1] 曲卫国. 话语文体学导论：文本分析的方法 [M]. 上海：复旦大学出版社，2009.

[2] Van Dijk, T. 1977. *Text and Context: Explorations in the Semantics and Pragmatics of Discourse*. London: Longman.

[3] Eco, U. 1990. *The Limits of Interpretation*. Bloomington and Indianapolis: Indiana University Press.

[4] Halliday, M. A. K. 1967. Notes on Transitivity and Theme in English. *Journal of Linguistics*. 3: 37–81.

---

① Bill Bryson. 1998. *A Walk in the Woods: Rediscovering America on the Appalachian Trail*. New York: Broadway Books.

第六章　语篇结构Ⅱ：话题结构和主题结构

导引问题：

- 什么是语篇的话题和主题？
- 语篇的话题结构和主题结构之间有什么关系？

本章提要：

　　话题是语篇叙述或议论的内容，通常由具体的议题或事件组成。话题成分之间的关系主要由图式或知识体系决定。图式的文化属性意味着不同文化的话题有不同的界定和构成。语篇话题的构成成分是作者按照其意图选择的结果。语篇主话题和次话题之间的关系构成语篇的**话题结构**。**主题**是作者通过语篇想表达的观点，通常比较抽象。**主题结构**指的是语篇的主位主题和语篇各部分的次位主题之间的关系集。话题有相对的确定性，而主题的解读和主题结构的认定是一个开放的动态过程。多样性主题理解是语篇认知的常态。

一、概说

　　话题（topic）指语篇叙述或议论的内容，即语篇讲些什么（aboutness），通常由比较具体的议题或事件组成，如：The story of a

T-shirt[①]，这篇课文的话题是 T-shirt。又如 A question of taste[②]，taste 则是这篇课文的话题。

话题成分之间的关系主要由图式（schema）或知识体系决定。图式的文化属性意味着不同文化对话题可能有不同的界定和构成。以 A question of taste 为例，如果这个话题的讨论是以科学知识为基本框架，话题的界定和相关成分会相当技术：

The word taste, or gustation, to give its full name, refers to what is detected by the taste cells, located on the front and back of the tongue and on the sides, back and roof of the mouth. These receptor cells, or taste buds, bind with molecules from the food or drink being consumed and send signals to the brain. The way our brains perceive these stimuli is what we refer to as taste, with there being five recognised basic tastes: salty, bitter, sweet, sour and umami.[③]

这个框架里的讨论会有很多术语，如 taste bud, gustation, receptor cell 等，对话题成分之间关系的解释通常都会依据某个科学分支展开。

如果从一般图式的角度讨论 taste，taste 的定义往往专业性没有那么强，如 *Longman Dictionary Online* 的定义：

the feeling that is produced by a particular food or drink when you put it in

---

① 邹为诚.普通高中教科书　英语　必修第三册［M］.上海：上海教育出版社，2021：24-25.请参阅"第七章　语篇的词汇关系"。

② 邹为诚.普通高中教科书　英语　选择性必修第一册［M］.上海：上海教育出版社，2021：60-61.请参阅"第九章　体裁：非叙事类"。

③ https://www.fifthsense.org.uk/what-is-taste/.

your mouth①

　　这类定义选用的词语相对通俗易懂，专业术语非常少，因而理解这类话题关系仅需要一般的常识。

　　语篇大多由主话题（global topic）和主话题内的各个次话题（local topic）组成。主话题和次话题之间的关系构成语篇的话题结构。主话题是语篇讨论的主要内容，次话题则是主话题的各个维度，也就是主话题的下位话题。话题结构可以用下面的图表表示：

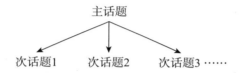

　　主话题统辖次话题，但次话题之间的关系主要与它们所涉及的主话题的多个维度有关。有一点需要特别强调，话题通常有多个维度。虽然认知框架或图式对话题的构成有影响，但主话题选择多少次话题，这主要由作者根据所要表达的主题决定。也就是说，语篇的主题决定语篇的话题结构。这意味着，虽然次话题的上位关联单位是主话题，但语篇的主题常常会凌驾于话题之上，直接决定次话题的关联性。据此，我们可以得出另一个结构图表：

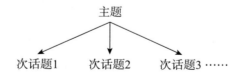

　　考虑到话题成分间的关系认定受到认知框架或图式以及语篇主题的双重制约，我们将话题结构和主题结构合在一起讨论。

　　主题（theme）指的是作者通过语篇想表达的观点，也就是通常

---

① https://www.ldoceonline.com/dictionary/taste.

所说的中心思想(main idea)。主题是基于话题抽象出的观点,因而有"以小见大"或"一叶知秋"的价值。

主题与话题主要有四大区别:① 话题比较具体,由具体事件或议题构成,因而话题是语篇的表层内容;主题则比较抽象,表达的是超越具体事件或议题的深层意义。② 话题与其成分的关系受到知识体系或图式的制约,而主题与其成分的关系受到作者的思想的左右。③ 话题的呈现可以是句子或单词,但主题的表达一定是陈述句(statement)。④ 有关话题和主题的提问也不一样:

话题:这篇语篇讲什么?

主题:作者通过这篇语篇想表达什么意思?

Emily Dickinson 曾经写过这样一首短诗:

A word is dead
When it is said.
Some say.
I say it just
Begins to live
That day.

我们可以用一个单词或词组总结这首诗的话题,如这首诗讨论的是语言的生命。之所以说这个总结仅仅是话题,是因为它并没有告诉我们作者的观点是什么。阐述作者的观点,也就是这首诗的主题,我们需要用一句陈述句,如"It is use that gives life to a word"。

主题结构指的是语篇的主题和语篇内各部分主题之间的关系集。为了方便区别,我们称语篇主题为"主位主题",语篇内各部分的主题为"次位主题"。和次话题一样,次位主题表达的是主位主题的一个维度,我们也可以用这样一个图表来表示它们的关系:

次位主题选择的依据主要是作者想表达的意图。与话题不一样，次位主题与主位主题的关系要复杂得多。它们可以涉及多个知识框架或图式。

如果将主题和话题合在一起考虑，我们可以得出以下的图表。主位主题统辖一切，主话题仅统辖次话题。我们用虚线表示主位主题统辖的范围：

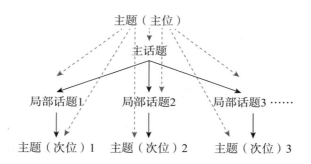

由于话题构成的基本依据是认知框架或图式，对话题结构的认定相对容易达成共识，话题因而具有相对的确定性。主题是作者的意图，是必须通过推导获得的深层含义。尽管作者会提供各种语境线索引导读者的推导，但这个推导过程受到许多因素的影响。主题的解读和主题结构的认定于是具有相对性和不确定性。也就是说，语篇的主题阐释是一个开放的动态过程，其多样性理解是语篇认知的常态。

语篇的体裁是影响语篇主题表达形式的主要因素。体裁的影响主要表现在两个方面：第一，作者通常会在非叙事类的语篇中，如议论文、说明文等，直接陈述语篇的主题。作者往往不会在叙事类语篇，尤其是文学类里明示语篇的主题。第二，不同体裁的主题解读方式不一样。在叙事类作品，尤其是文学作品里，主题的解读常常是通过联想挖掘作品的象征意义，也就是说叙事与主题并不构成逻辑关系。非叙事类语篇主题的阐释主要是通过推导，因而语篇内容和主题有较强的逻辑关系。

二、话题、主题与教学

语篇的理解通常可以分为两个阶段：第一个阶段是理解和分析话题；第二个阶段是破解主题。这两个过程往往是互相渗透的。

话题的确定相对容易，因为作者通常会在标题或在正文的开篇处给出明确的提示。但话题的确定仅仅是第一步。更重要的是话题构成成分，也就是话题结构的认识。话题通常与图式或知识框架有关。不同文化习俗对话题的基本构成有很大的影响。缺乏相应的图式或忽视不同文化的不同图式构成会造成话题结构分析的困难。图式之所以重要是因为在话题分析过程中，我们首先要考虑该语篇的话题结构与话题的一般构成是否一致，语篇的话题结构是否凸显或舍弃一般话题的某些成分。我们可以考虑以下这些问题：

（1）这篇语篇的话题是什么？

（2）一般来说，这个话题有哪些次话题组成？

（3）这篇语篇的话题结构有什么不同？

（4）语篇的次话题选择究竟凸显主题的什么内容？

（5）语篇的次话题是如何与主位话题或主题相关联的？

主题的解读要复杂得多。在主题解读的过程中，我们要考虑两个方面：① 主题解读的语篇依据。虽然主题的认识因各种主体因素的影响有高度的相对性和不确定性，但这并不意味着读者可以无视语篇线索，无制约地任意发挥。② 认知框架。根据语篇线索激活的认知框架能提供主题解读所需要的相关知识，有利于将解读引向深入。认知框架的关联性是影响主题解读的关键因素。也许我们可以提出这样一些问题供学生思考：

（1）该语篇的主题是什么？

（2）判断主题依据的是哪些语篇线索？

（3）解读主题依据的是哪种认知框架？

（4）语篇的线索是否能激活其他的认知框架？

（5）语篇的主题是否有其他解读的可能？

三、话题结构和主题结构分析

任何语篇理解都是从话题认知开始。我们这里先用 Henry A. Dobson 的短诗 A kiss 作为例子。

A kiss

Rose kissed me today,

Will she kiss me tomorrow?

Let it be as it may,

Rose kissed me today.

But the pleasure gives way

To a savor of sorrow:—

Rose kissed me today,—

Will she kiss me tomorrow?

这首诗的话题结构很简单，标题就是主话题：A kiss。当然如果把 "Rose kissed me today" 当成主话题也可以。这首诗的次话题也不难识别。每两行成一个次话题：

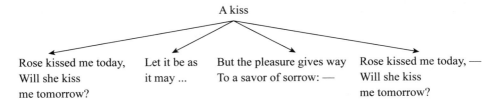

A kiss

Rose kissed me today,
Will she kiss
me tomorrow?

Let it be as
it may ...

But the pleasure gives way
To a savor of sorrow: —

Rose kissed me today, —
Will she kiss
me tomorrow?

如果我们选择从内心活动这个认知框架去思考这些问题，也许我们可以做这样的假设：这些次话题描写的是主人公被 Rose 亲吻之后的内心活动。主人公出现的四种心理活动传递了两个信息：

（1）主人公爱上了 Rose，不然他不会出现这样的心理活动；

（2）主人公并不能确定 Rose 是否爱他。kiss 虽然可能是 Rose 表达爱恋的方式，但也可能是她的一时冲动之举。

次话题 1 "Will she kiss me tomorrow?" 表达的是什么意思呢？是疑虑还是期待？这自然不好判断，不过有一点是肯定的。诗人通过这个问题暗示作者期待 Rose 此举不是一时冲动。次话题 2 说的是自我安慰："Let it be as it may/Rose kissed me today"，但诗人通过 "Let it be as it may" 这个表达式传递了主人公对未来会发生什么事并没有任何把握的无可奈何的心情。次话题 3 显示作者起初的喜悦经过这些内心活动被忧愁侵蚀了："But the pleasure gives way/To a savor of sorrow: —"。诗歌的最后两行乍一看是次话题 1 的重复，但前一行和行尾的破折号提示了这两行表露的是不同的情绪："Rose kissed me today,—/Will she kiss me tomorrow?" 如果次话题 1 里有任何热情的期待，两个破折号则将其完全打消了。

也许我们可以就此建立这样的话题结构，话题连贯的依据是事件引发各种心理活动：

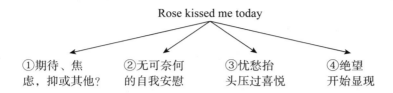

显然，这首诗次话题选择的依据是不自信或悲观情绪。如果主导的是自信，次话题可能就不是这些内容。梳理完诗歌的话题结构之后，我们要问的第二个问题是：这首诗通过 A kiss 这个话题想传递什么信息呢？即这首诗的主题是什么？

如前所述，主题是语篇的深层次意义。这首诗描写了被亲吻后的复杂心情。就文学解读而言，kiss 或 "Rose kissed me today" 的象征意义就是作品的主题。如果我们联想 kiss 的象征意义是爱情，次话题 1 的主题可以理解为爱情会产生渴望；次话题 2 的主题是爱情会导致焦虑；次话题 3 的主题是爱情会造成悲伤，次话题 4 的主题便是绝望等。也许我们可以根据次主题的这些关联，推导出这首诗的主题：

对爱情的渴望会导致乐极生悲。

不过，如果换个认知框架，我们会发现不仅仅是爱情，任何渴望都可能触发这样的心理过程。如果这个推导成立，那 kiss 这里不仅仅代表爱情，它可能具有更广的外延。

不过，我们这里并没有考虑这样一个问题：主话题叙述的是事实，而次话题所描写的都源于主人公内心的活动。这些心理活动有依据吗？诗歌没有提供任何线索。也许，焦虑等情绪并没有现实依据。如果从这个角度去考虑，也许我们可以推测诗歌主题不是说对爱情的渴望等会导致乐极生悲，而是焦虑或悲观都源于人内心的期待。当然，这首诗的主题解读还有许多其他的可能。

和诗歌一样，作者写小说不是为了叙述一个话题而是要表达一个观点。和诗歌一样，小说的主题也与话题的象征意义有关。同样和诗歌一样的是，小说的话题相对容易确定，主题却有各种解读的可能。

课文 An excerpt from *The Old Man and the Sea*[①] 是 Hemingway 同名长篇小说的节选。课文叙述了老人与鲨鱼对峙的一个场景片段。由于课文是节选，因此课文的话题与小说的话题并不一定一致。课文引言里的提问给出了这段节选的主话题："Can the old man survive a shark attack?"

The old man took one look at the great fish as he watched the shark close in. I cannot keep him from hitting me, he thought, but maybe I can get him.

The shark closed fast on the boat and when he hit the fish the old man saw his mouth open and his strange eyes and his sharp teeth as he drove forward in the meat just above the tail. The old man could hear the noise of skin and flesh ripping on the big fish when he threw the fishing spear into the shark's head at a place where the line between his eyes crossed with the line that ran straight back from his nose. There were no such lines. There was only the heavy sharp blue head and the big eyes and the powerful teeth. But that was the location of the brain and the old man hit it. He hit it with his wet, bloody hands driving a good spear with all his strength. He hit it without hope but with determination and complete hatred.

The shark turned over and the old man saw his eye was not alive and

---

① 邹为诚.普通高中教科书　英语　必修第二册［M］.上海：上海教育出版社，2020：60-61.

then he turned over once again, wrapping himself in the rope. The old man knew that he was dead but the shark would not accept it. Then, on his back, with his tail still moving and his mouth opening and closing, the shark swam over the water as fast as a speedboat. The water was white where his tail beat it and three quarters of his body was clear above the water when the rope broke. The shark lay quietly for a little while on the surface and the old man watched him. Then he went down very slowly. "He took about forty pounds," the old man said aloud. He took my spear too and all the rope, he thought, and now my fish bleeds again and there will be others. He did not like to look at the fish any longer since the shark had bitten it. When the shark had hit the fish, it was as though he himself were hit. But I killed the shark that hit my fish, he thought. And that was the biggest shark that he had ever seen. And he had seen big ones in his lifetime. It was too good to last, he thought. I wish it had been a dream now and that I had never caught the fish.

"But man is not made for defeat," he said. "A man can be destroyed but not defeated." I am sorry that I killed the fish though, he thought. Now the bad time is coming and I do not even have the spear. The shark is terrible and able and strong and intelligent. But I was more intelligent than he was. Perhaps not, he thought. Perhaps I was only better armed.

课文一共有四段。我们可以尝试给每个段落确定一个次话题：①the approach of the shark；②the attack and counterattack；③the shark's death；④the old man's reflection。由此我们得出以下话题结构图：

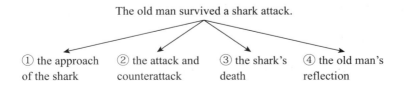

The old man survived a shark attack.

① the approach of the shark　② the attack and counterattack　③ the shark's death　④ the old man's reflection

　　这个话题结构描写的只是整个事件（event）的基本过程，但从课文的信息内容来看，还有两个重要的内容需要考虑：一是枪鱼（marlin），即课文里的 the fish 与老人的关系，鲨鱼攻击这条鱼对老人意味着什么；二是老人的心理活动。

　　这篇课文几乎每一段都有叙事视角的变换。第一段的第一句是第三人称叙事视角（The old man took one look ...）。第二句立刻转成第一人称（老人）的叙事视角（I cannot ...）

　　第二段虽然只有第三人称叙事视角（The shark closed fast on the boat ...），但这段里只有第一句是描写鲨鱼的活动。从第二句开始，虽然叙事视角还是第三人称，但所见所闻似乎都是从老人视角获得的，如："The old man could hear the noise of skin and flesh ripping on the big fish ..."。虽然没有明确标注，但 "There were no such lines. There was only the heavy sharp blue head and the big eyes and the powerful teeth. But that was the location of the brain ..." 等明显是老人的所见和所思。又如："He hit it without hope but with determination and complete hatred." 描写的也只能是老人的内心活动。

　　第三段也是以第三人称叙事视角开始。不过，几乎也都是老人的所见所闻。如："The shark turned over and the old man saw his eye was not alive ... The old man knew that he was dead but the shark would not accept it. ..." 除此之外，还有老人的言语和思想活动，如："'He took about forty pounds,' the old man said aloud. He took my spear too and all the rope, he thought, ..."。

　　第四段写的是老人的心理活动，以直接引语 "But man is not made for defeat" 和 "A man can be destroyed but not defeated" 开始。值得思考的是，紧接着的这句 "I am sorry that I killed the fish though, he thought." 似乎并不支持前面两句话。他为什么要对自己 "killed the fish" 这件事感到遗憾呢？人们通常对 defeat 的解释是人不会认输，即人的意志不会被摧毁。然而 "But I was more intelligent than he was. Perhaps not, he thought. Perhaps I was only better armed." 这些话似乎强调的不是不屈的意志。在这段里，老人还提到 "Now the bad time is coming and I do not even have the spear."。没有鱼叉也就是没了武器，这使得 "better armed" 这个假设都变得不确定。

"But man is not made for defeat" 和 "A man can be destroyed but not defeated" 被许多人理解为小说 *The Old Man and the Sea* 的主题。从整部小说去理解，这个解读自然成立，但课文只是小说的一个节选。根据 Hemingway 描写的这些心理活动，这两句话能抽象成课文的主题吗？怎么理解老人下面的这些心理活动与这两句话的关系呢？

He hit it without hope but with determination and complete hatred.

When the shark had hit the fish, it was as though he himself were hit. But I killed the shark that hit my fish, he thought.

I wish it had been a dream now and that I had never caught the fish.

I am sorry that I killed the fish though, he thought.

But I was more intelligent than he was. Perhaps not, he thought. Perhaps I was only better armed.

在考虑课文主题和主题结构时，也许我们要做三个象征意义的联想：

（1）the fish 象征什么？

（2）shark attack 象征什么？

（3）老人的反击象征什么？

就主题而言，也许我们可以把 "Can the old man survive a shark attack?" 这个问题改成："What did the old man survive?"

虽然非文学类的叙事在主题解读上没有那么复杂，但由于许多叙事的主题是隐性呈现的，因此主题的解读还是具有不确定性。

Island story[1] 这篇课文的标题是个名词词组，它只给了一个笼统的话题提示。究竟这个 island story 的具体内容是什么，我们需要正文提供更多的线索：

"When I was a little boy, I loved to go fishing in the sea with my spear," says John Sailike, sadly. "When I leave the island, I'll lose the sea and the happiness of this place. I'll miss the sound of the waves at night ... I won't hear it any more."

John is a fisherman from the Carteret Islands in the South Pacific, a beautiful and peaceful semicirclea of white sand, palm trees and crystal clear waters. Each day, he goes out in a small boat to catch fish for his family, while his wife looks after the children and grows vegetables in their garden. The family lives in a wood hut with sand floors and they don't use much electricity, so when the sun goes down, it is usually time for bed. This peaceful, underdeveloped place has a tiny population and only one contact with the outside world—a ship which brings supplies from Bougainville, a large island 86 km away. But all this is about to change, because John, along with 3,000 other people, is leaving his island home. The question is, why?

Take a closer look at the islands and the reason becomes clear. The Carterets are the victim of global warming. High tides often flood across

---

① 邹为诚. 普通高中教科书　英语　选择性必修第一册 [M]. 上海：上海教育出版社，2021：24-25.

the villages and wash away people's homes. Salt water from the sea is overflowing into vegetable gardens and destroying fruit trees. It's polluting the fresh water supply too. Islanders are struggling to survive on coconut milk and fish, and children are suffering from malnutrition. The dying trees are home to mosquitoes that spread diseases, like malariaa. John and his fellow islanders are facing great challenges, and they know that life on the island is coming to an end.

Experts predict that the Carterets will be under water in the not-so-distant future. Before then, the islanders will relocate to places like Bougainville and rebuild their lives. This move will provide people with food and shelter, but what will happen to their culture? The islanders have songs for different everyday activities, and traditions and celebrations linked to the sea. They also have their own language, called "Halia". If they coexist with other cultures, this may die out.

"We're losing our home, our identity, our whole life," says one islander. "We hope the world is listening." It is. In recent years, articles in international newspapers, online videos and an Oscar-nominated documentary film called Sun Come Up have talked about the Carteret Islands. People have supported the islanders and as a result, they have turned their anger and frustration into action. People are also looking for ways to preserve the islanders' way of life and record their language and traditions for future generations.

Back on the island, John Sailike is getting into his boat for the last time. He's saying goodbye to his home and to his ancestors. He does not know what the future will bring; he does not know if his culture will survive. He is the human face of climate change.

　　课文一共有六段，每一段都有不同的次话题。第一段的话题讲述 Sailike 要离开他生活的岛屿的悲伤之情；第二段的话题有关他和家人在岛上的生活；第三段的话题是全球变暖是他们被迫离岛的原因；第四段的话题是重新安置对他们文化的打击；第五段的话题描述了各地为保存 Carteret Islands 文化所做的努力；第六段的话题与第一段呼应，再次讲述 Sailike 离岛的心情。与第一段话题不同的是，这段更多提到的是迷茫。

参照前面的做法，我们也为这篇课文做个话题图表。我们在前面讨论话题时曾指出，话题与主题不同，可以由一个词组或句子担任。课文的标题较笼统，只是划定一个话题域。我们在做这个话题表时可以选择课文原来的标题，也可以根据课文的内容选择更具体的主话题，如"Sailike is leaving his island"。究竟"Island story"和更具体的"Sailike is leaving his island"哪个更合适？也许次话题与主话题的关联程度分析会给我们一定的启示。假设我们选择 Sailike is leaving his island，视角应该在主语 Sailike：

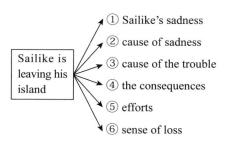

依据关联度判断，似乎次话题①、②、⑥与 Sailike 有直接的关联，但次话题③、④和⑤的关联度要低很多，因为这些次话题的重点是 Island 的生活和文化。这可能是为什么课文的标题是 Island story，凸显的不是 Sailike 而是 Island 的原因。

作者通过讲述 Carteret 岛屿的故事想传递什么信息呢？或者作者是根据什么样的认知框架去解读岛屿故事的意义呢？要解读这篇课文的深层主题，我们必须首先从话题提供的线索着手。次话题③、④、⑤、⑥提供了主要线索：global warming 对人类生活产生了灾难性影响。作者在课文的最后一句话更是明确提示了 Sailike 遭遇的典型性：

He is the human face of climate change.

从主题的角度看，六个次话题揭示了全球变暖灾难性影响的六个维度（次主题）：

（1）人们被迫离开家园；

（2）人们被迫放弃原有的生活方式；

（3）生存环境日益恶化；

（4）文化无法延续；

（5）保留文化的努力；

（6）人们对出路感到迷茫。

根据这样的分析，我们也可以说这篇课文的话题是全球变暖对岛民生活的影响。这篇课文的主位主题是什么呢？六个次位主题应该是给了我们一定的启示。

大多数非叙事类体裁语篇的主题是显性呈现的。语篇标题或篇首段落常常在抛出话题的同时提出语篇的主题。虽然有些语篇的标题只提及话题，但作者会通过正文的一系列讨论，将读者带入主题。分析非叙事类语篇时要特别留意话题和主题的区别，区分讨论的内容和作者想通过这些内容表达的观点。

Blame your brain[①] 这篇课文的标题貌似话题和主题同时提出：青少年的行为受生理因素的控制。但读罢全文后就会发现，作者在这篇课文里表达的观点并不仅仅是"青少年的许多问题与大脑里多

---

① 邹为诚.普通高中教科书　英语　必修第二册［M］.上海：上海教育出版社，2020：6-7.

巴胺水平的高低有关"这样消极的观点。青少年的行为受生理因素的控制或大脑多巴胺水平高低的影响只是个话题。

It's a fact: many teenagers take more risks than children and adults. The question is, why? Check out the latest studies and think about what you can do about it.

The "wow" factor

Have you ever been on a roller-coaster ride? How did you feel when you got off? Excited? Amazed? This is the "wow" factor, the feeling of pleasure we get when we take and survive a risk. Scientists know that a brain chemical called dopamine causes this feeling of enjoyment. What has dopamine got to do with you? Well, some scientists believe that dopamine levels are sometimes lower in teenagers than they are in children. This means that some teenagers might need to take more risks to get the same "wow" factor.

"I just felt like it"

Have you ever done something dangerous or frightening without thinking about what happens next? When an adult asks a teenager, "What were you thinking of when you did that?" a common reply is, "I just felt like it." But the question misses the point, because the point is that the teenager might not have been thinking at all! The teenager didn't plan to take a risk: it just "happened". A few years ago, scientists made a surprising discovery: the teenage brain goes through many physical changes, and some parts of it develop later than others. The last part to fully develop is the frontal cortexa. This is the area of the brain which allows us to do things such as controlling feelings and making good decisions.

Pressure from friends

Have you ever taken a risk to impress your friends? Even teenagers who are not usually big risk-takers may suddenly do something dangerous because they want to show off or fit in. If you look at statistics, boys often take more risks than girls, perhaps because they don't want to look bad in front of their friends—though girls dislike that too. Boys are more likely not to wear seat belts, more likely to get into an argument or a fight, and more likely to smoke and drink. But is taking risks really the best way to get people to respect, notice and like you?

What you can do

There's no easy solution, but try to make good choices and be independent. Don't get pushed into doing things by your friends. You can get your dopamine fix in lots of other exciting ways. Roller coasters, skateboarding and surfing will all give you the same "wow" factor. And if you're around 17, stop worrying, because your brain has reached the point where you can more easily make wise decisions. You've survived up until now, so you've achieved a lot—well done!

　　这篇课文的次话题相对较容易识别，除了第一段，其他段落都有副标题（subtitle）。作者在第一段用 why 引出课文讨论的议题："Why do many teenagers take more risks than children and adults?" 第二段的标题是 The "wow" factor，这段的话题是冒险行为与多巴胺的分泌水平（dopamine level）的关系。第三段 "I just felt like it" 讨论的是主观感受和大脑的关系。第四段 Pressure from friends 是有关同伴压力与冒险行为的关系。作者在最后一段 What you can do 里介绍该如何应对成长期间多巴胺等问题。

　　但课文的主话题和次话题之间的关系似乎不太好确定。有些次话题与主话题的关联似乎不是很密切，如第四、第五这两个次话题似乎与大脑对行为负责的关联不大。次话题之间的关系也不是很强，如第四个次话题与第二个之间似乎没有关系，最后一段回答的也不是第一段的问题。

要厘清这篇课文的话题结构或主话题到底是什么，可能需要对这篇课文的主题和认知框架进行推导。如果课文的主题就是 Blame the brain，我们就很难解释次话题 ④ 和 ⑤ 的关联性。如果课文的认知框架是生理学的，诸如"make good choices and be independent"的建议与生理解释就自相矛盾。

也许这篇课文的宏观语境能给我们启发。根据课文的注释，这篇课文是根据 Nicola Morgan 写的 *Blame My Brain: The Amazing Teenage Brain Revealed*（2013）一书改写的。作者在原著里谈到了写这本书的意图：

> Your brain is who you are and it is also who you will be. You own your brain and most of the time it is more or less in your control. And understanding more about your brain, as you do now, helps you have control. Only sometimes, when you can't do anything about it, when your brain takes over and biology rules, can you fairly shout,"Don't blame me— blame my brain!" (2013: 193)

显然作者写这本书的意图不是对第一段提出的问题就事论事地给出一个科学答案。他关注的是如何帮助青少年应对在生长期所出现的各种非主观能控制的问题，提升他们的自尊心和自信心。他想告诉青少年有许多行为与生理生长周期或其他不可控因素的负面干扰有关。出现问题不要妄自菲薄，不要责怪自己，因为这些问题都不是自己主观选择的结果。过了这个生理周期，青少年就可以更有效地应对各种问题了：

And if you're around 17, stop worrying, because your brain has reached the point where you can more easily make wise decisions.

从这个角度看，他的生理学解释或者课文的标题 Blame your brain 就有了不同的意义。文章最后一段的建议提示 Blame your brain 只是这篇课文主话题的一部分，blame 并不意味着消极地寻找借口。从下面这段话里我们可以找到主话题的提示：

You can get your dopamine fix in lots of other exciting ways. Roller coasters, skateboarding and surfing will all give you the same "wow" factor.

虽然在这个生理周期有不可控的因素影响我们的行为，但我们还是应该发挥主观能动性，通过各种主动选择去调节自己的生理状况。比对原著，课文把书名里的 my 改成了 your，这个改动有意义吗？

本章推荐书目

［1］Brown, G. and G. Yule. 1983. *Discourse Analysis*. Cambridge: Cambridge University Press.

［2］Chafe, W. 1994. *Discourse, Consciousness, and Time: The flow and displacement of conscious experience in speaking and writing*. Chicago: University of Chicago Press.

［3］Givon, T. 1983. *Topic Continuity in Discourse: A Quantitative Cross-Language Study*. Amsterdam: John Benjamins.

第七章 语篇的词汇关系

导引问题：

- 什么是语篇的词汇关系？
- 分析语篇的词汇关系对理解语篇有什么作用？

本章提要：

　　词汇关系（lexical relations）指的是词语在语篇的具体语境里所形成的特定语义关系。最有影响的词汇关系研究是 Halliday 和 Hasan 的衔接理论和 Hoey 的词汇触发假说。衔接可以分为语法衔接和词汇衔接两大类。语法衔接指的是通过某种语法手段在形式上显示句子间关系。词汇衔接借助词汇实现句子之间的意义关联，分复现和搭配两大类。词汇触发假说有两个关键内容，一是语义联想，即一个词的使用会触发读者相关词汇的联想。另外一个是语义集的触发，即一个词语触发的不是一个相关单词，而是一个语义集，也就是语义场。**语义场**是分析搭配关系最重要的概念。

一、概说

　　语篇的载体是语言，词汇是语言最主要的表意手段。我们这里讨论的词汇关系指的是词语在语篇具体语境里形成的特定语义关系。语篇分析里最有影响的词汇关系研究是 Halliday 和 Hasan（1976）提出的衔接（cohesion）理论和 Hoey 发展的词汇模式（patterns of lexis），尤其是"词汇触发"（lexical priming）[1]假说。

我们这里主要依据的是 Halliday 和 Hasan 的衔接理论。与"连贯"（coherence）不同，"衔接"通过衔接手段（cohesive ties）[2]从形式上标明句子之间的关联：

Maria lost her library card. So John could not borrow books.（衔接）
John lost his library card yesterday. The boy was really careless.（衔接）

例 1 用 so 标明了 Maria 丢失她的借书证和 John 借书之间的语义关联。也就是说，John 是用 Maria 的借书证借书的。例 2 里的 the boy 指的是 John，因而两句也有呼应。Halliday 和 Hasan 把 so 和 the boy 这样的词语称为"衔接手段"，so 是语法衔接，boy 是词汇衔接。

参照 Halliday 和 Hasan（1976）的理论，衔接可以分为语法衔接（grammatical cohesion）和词汇衔接（lexical cohesion）两大类。语法衔接指的是通过某种语法手段在形式上显示句子间关系。语法衔接主要分为四种：① 指代（reference）；② 替代（substitution）；③ 省略（ellipsis）；④ 连接（conjunction）。

1. 指代关系（reference）[3]

指代关系主要指用代词等代指出现的名词。英语的代词通常分为：人称代词（personal）；指示代词（demonstrative）和比较关系代

---

① 也有学者将其翻译成"词汇启动"。
② 也有学者把它翻译成"衔接结"。我们这里采用"衔接手段"主要是因为它似乎更容易理解。
③ 也有学者把 reference 译成"指称关系"。

词（comparative）。

（1）人称代词

<u>John</u> lost his library card. <u>He</u> could not borrow books.

（2）指示代词

Tim has just read "The Road Not Taken". <u>He</u> really likes <u>that</u> poem.

（3）比较关系

Jane was given ten days for the book. John was not given <u>the same</u> amount of time.

2. 替代（substitution）

替代是用非代词词汇替代名词、动词或从句，主要有三种形式：

（1）名词类替代

I don't like the colour of the hat. Please get me a green <u>one</u>.

（2）动词类替代

I did not check the answer. John <u>did</u>.

（3）从句类替代

Has John passed the exam? I hope <u>so</u>.

3. 省略（ellipsis）

虽然 Halliday 和 Hasan 后来将替代和省略合并为一类，但考虑到两者实际上存在的区别，我们还是依据 Halliday 和 Hasan 早年的这段话将它们单列：

The starting point of the discussion of ellipsis can be the familiar notion that it is "something left unsaid." There is no implication here that what is unsaid is not understood; on the contrary, "unsaid implies but understood nevertheless," ... (1976:142)

省略和替代的主要区别就是省略部分没有任何形式标志。省略也分三种：

（1）名词省略

Which phone will you choose? This is the best.

（2）动词省略

Have you read the poem? Yes, I have.

（3）小句省略

A: What were they doing?

B: Playing football.

4. 连接（conjunction）

连接通过副词等衔接手段建立句子之间的关联。和前面三种语法衔接不一样的是，连接并不表示所连接的两个部分有照应关系。它只是标明它们在特定语境里有意义关联。要强调的是，这里的连接仅涉及两个单句的连接。连接分四种：

（1）增补类（additive）

John likes Robert Frost. <u>And</u> he likes William Wordsworth, too.

（2）转折类（adversative）

We have checked all the answers. <u>Still</u> we failed to pass the test.

（3）原因类（causal）

She was bored by the discussion. <u>So</u> she left for home.

（4）时间类（temporal）

John shook his head. <u>Then</u> he stood up and left.

词汇衔接借助词汇实现句子之间的意义关联。Halliday 和 Hason 将词汇衔接分为复现（reiteration）①和搭配（collocation）两大类。复

———————

① 也有学者将 reiteration 译成"重述"。

163

现一般指同一词项（lexical item）等级范围内的词项复现。之所以称之为复现，是因为后一句用了相同或其他词语再次呈现了前句的名词。判断复现的关键是确定两个词语之间的所指关系。复现包括：重复（repetition）、同义词（synonym）、上义词（superordinate）、概括词（general word）等四种。

（1）重复

I enjoy <u>movies</u>. <u>Movies</u> are good ways to pass time.

（2）同义词

He cared a lot about his <u>reputation</u>. <u>Fame</u> was all he was after.

（3）上义词

The <u>dog</u> always barks when strangers pass by. I generally dislike unfriendly <u>animals</u>.

（4）概括词

John invited me to a <u>party</u> but I declined. I don't like <u>these kinds of things</u>.

搭配（collocation）与复现不同。搭配关系的依据并不是来自句子，而是常识、语言知识、语境等。搭配关系是否能建立取决于读者是否能通过联想找到或构建相关词语的共享语义场（semantic field）。与复现不同的是，在搭配里，词语间不存在所指关系，如：

John invited me to a <u>party</u> but I declined. I don't like <u>these kinds of things</u>.

在这句里，party 和 these kinds of things 存在所指关系。我们可以比较下面这句：

I regret paying so much for <u>the old book</u>. <u>Many pages</u> are missing.

book 和 pages 之间并没有所指关系。然而，按照一般的常识，

pages 是 book 的一部分。两者共享的语义场使两句句子之间形成衔接关系。

又如：

I really enjoyed my stay in <u>Florence</u>. <u>Historic sites</u> are neighours with fancy restaurants and high-end shops.

Florence 是意大利的著名古城，古城自然有 historic sites，因此两者有共享的语义场。如果我们把这句改成下面这样，衔接关系就不成立了：

I really enjoyed my stay in <u>Shenzhen</u>. <u>Historic sites</u> are neighours with fancy restaurants and high-end shops.

Shenzhen 是个新兴城市，它和 historic sites 不共享同一语义场。假如做下面的改动，两句句子的衔接关系就没问题了。

I really enjoyed my stay in <u>Shenzhen</u>. <u>Residential areas</u> are neighours with fancy restaurants and high-end shops.

搭配关系的推导主要依据语境。如：

I don't want to talk about yesterday's <u>performance</u>. <u>The fiasco</u> will haunt me for the rest of my life.

performance 和 fiasco 之间并没有直接的语义关联。特定的语境为两者建立起了特定的语义关系。

由于搭配衔接关系主要依据的是语境、认知等非语言因素，具有很大的不确定性，因此搭配衔接关系也是很有争议的概念。Halliday 和 Hasan 在讨论搭配时一开始就没有回避问题：

We now come to the most problematical part of lexical cohesion ...
(1976:284)

他们把不能归类于复现的，都纳入搭配：

... in other words, all lexical cohesion that is not covered by what we have called "reiteration"—and treat it under the general heading of collocation, or collocational cohesion ... (1976:287)

虽然 Halliday 和 Hasan 没有强调语义场的作用，但标明词汇意义关系类别的语义场是分析搭配关系最重要的概念。按照 Lehrer 的定义，语义场的核心内容是概念域（conceptual domain）：

a set of lexemes which cover a certain conceptual domain and which bear certain specifiable relations to one another (1985).

通过对词语所属语义场的分析，我们可以找到识别搭配关系的主要线索。

除了 Halliday 和 Hasan 的理论外，Michael Hoey 的"词汇触发"理论从认知的角度解释了搭配关系运作机制。他提出的"语义启动"（semantic priming）尤其重要：

... the notion of semantic priming is used to discuss the way a "priming" word may provoke a particular "target word." (2005: 8)

按照 Hoey 的假设，词汇触发有两个关键内容，一是语义联想，即一个词的使用会使读者产生相关词汇的联想。另外一个是语义集（semantic set）的触发，即一个词语触发的不是另外一个相关单词，而是一个语义集，也就是语义场。

二、词汇关系与教学

阅读教学从词语开始，帮助学生理解作者是如何通过操控词汇构建语篇是教学的主要任务。我们这里主要讨论的是搭配衔接关系。其他类别虽然为分析语篇的词汇关系提供了很好的分析框架，但对理解本身的帮助却有限。就阅读教学而言，这些类别的衔接对语境依赖程度低，识别难度不高，理解也就相对容易。与以研究为目的的运用不同，语篇分析在教学中的运用主要是为理解复杂而不易识别的词汇现象提供分析框架。

想要理解语篇中的词汇关系，我们就必须细读文本，留意词语在语篇里可能产生与一般意义不同的特定意义。为了培养和提高学生对词汇关系和词义变化的敏感度，我们可以要求学生在阅读中经常考虑这样几个问题：

（1）作者为什么要用这个词？

（2）看到这个词是否会联想到其他词语？

（3）这些词的使用建立了什么样的语义场？

（4）该段落或语篇涉及几个语义场？

（5）我们可以依据这些搭配关系或语义场构建怎样的语言场景？

（6）这些语言场景对语篇的主题理解有什么帮助？

三、词汇关系分析

1. 语法衔接

语法衔接是语篇衔接的显性手段。由于语法衔接显示的是句子间的语法关系，基本不涉及复杂的语境，学生只要掌握相关的语法知识就能够识别，因此语法衔接的识别对理解语篇深层含义的作用并不大。虽然它是学生必须掌握的基本语言知识，但它不应该成为以培养阅读能力为教学目标的阅读课的教学重点。

我们这里仅用 A road less travelled[①] 的前三段稍作分析展示，以了解语法衔接在语篇中的实际运作。

Amy Carter-James is small, blue-eyed and blonde, with a friendly smile. She doesn't look like she could change the lives of thousands of people but, clearly, she has.

It all started when Amy took a gap year in Africa after she finished university. "I spent eight months volunteering in a very poor countryside school in Kenya," she says. "That was the first time I saw poverty. I was so young and so easily inspired and I thought, 'Why can't tourism do the same thing for community development?'"

在第一段里，作者至少用了两个语法衔接连接手段：指代（she）和省略（she has）。第二段除了其他衔接手段以外，还用 it 指代 "she could change the lives of thousands of people"，将第二段和第一段衔接了起来。

这篇课文的第三段向我们展示了作者是如何使用多种衔接手段以避免主语枯燥的重复。

On her return to England, 22-year-old Amy and her boyfriend Neal decided to take "the road less travelled". They（指代 22-year-old Amy and her

---

① 邹为诚. 普通高中教科书　英语　必修第三册［M］. 上海：上海教育出版社，2021：60–61.

boyfriend Neal) drove across <u>Mozambique</u>, one of the poorest countries in Africa, but it wasn't exactly a holiday. <u>Mozambique</u>（重复）had two qualities which appealed to them: great attraction as a travel destination and local people who badly needed help. Once there, <u>the couple</u>（复现 22-year-old Amy and her boyfriend Neal) got off the beaten track and headed for Quirimbas National Park, where <u>they</u>（指代）found a tiny stretch of white sand close to a village. <u>Life</u>（复现。概括词，涵盖后面指的 little clean water 等一系列情况）in the village was hard: there was little clean water and not enough food. Health care was poor and people in the village had a life expectancy of 38 years. <u>Amy and Neal</u>（复现）had no qualifications in tourism or health care but <u>they</u> had common sense, enthusiasm and determination. <u>They</u>（指代）talked to the <u>villagers</u> about their plan to create a small beach resort, which would provide employment for people so that <u>they</u> could have a better life. The response from the <u>villagers</u>（重复）was extremely positive. <u>Their</u>（指代）only question was: "When can you start?"

2. 词汇衔接

语法衔接的认知只是一个识别，也就是解码（decoding）过程，相对机械。虽然词汇衔接的识别主要依据的是词语的语义场等，但词汇衔接常常受到具体语境的制约，不同语境会触发不同的词汇联想关系。搭配关系的认知因而是一个推导（inferential）过程。它相对语法衔接而言，具有不确定性。通过对词汇衔接的分析，我们不仅能了解词汇在语篇中是如何传递意义，而且能发现作者是如何操控词汇关系传递自己的意图。

分析词汇衔接关系的主要做法就是找到词汇的共享语义场，揭示词汇在语篇中形成的词义关系群，通过词义关系群的线索去寻找语篇的主题提示。

理解和分析词汇关系通常有这么几个步骤：

（1）第一步是同类词语关系识别，如名词与名词的共享语义场等；

（2）第二步是跨类关系识别，如名词与形容词之间的关系，名词与动词之间的关系等；

（3）第三步是推导这些关系的含义；

（4）第四步是根据这些关系推导作者选择这些关系想表达的意图。

Robert Frost 的 The rose family 是一首短诗，非常方便词汇关系的详细分析。

The rose family

The rose is a rose,
And was always a rose.
But the theory now goes
That the apple's a rose,
And the pear is, and so's
The plum, I suppose.
The dear only knows
What will next prove a rose.
You, of course, are a rose —
But were always a rose.

如果按语义场对这首诗里的名词性词组和代词进行分类，它们大概可以分成五类：第一类是 I 和 you；第二类是花卉 rose；第三类是水果 apple，pear，plum；第四类是科学 theory；第五类是 the dear。

这里的 the dear 婉转地指 God[1]。

诗人选择 theory 这个词来指科学也意味深长。按照 *Merriam-Webster Dictionary* 的解释，theory 是个可数名词，它的意思是：

a plausible or scientifically acceptable general principle or body of principles offered to explain phenomena[2]

plausible 这个形容词明确表明 theory 并不具有确定性。诗人用 theory 的单数，外加定冠词，似乎 theory 如同 the sun 之类一样，是独一无二的事物，这种感觉又因为 the dear 的出现而进一步得到了加强。"The dear knows" 是个俗语，字面上是 "God knows"，实际的意思是 "Nobody knows"。这很让人产生科学的一家之言肆无忌惮、独霸天下的感觉。诗人说将 rose 和 apple 等划为不同类别，这是传统的做法。按照现在 the theory 的分类，它们都属于蔷薇科植物（rosaceae），传统的界线就不复存在。

这首诗的动词选择也很值得思考。be 动词有现在时和过去时两个不同时态，分别对应科学和传统。suppose 和 prove，即假设和证明应该属于科学类，但 know 这个动词与它们不是一类，因为科学只有假设和证明，没有"知道"一说。go 和 know 一样，属于日常生活类动词。go 在这里既是俗语，又有 the theory 横行霸道的形象暗示。

诗人对词汇关系的驾驭还体现在他通过主语选择挑战了两个不同语义场的界线。suppose 的主语是不相信科学分类的"I"。这就使 "... and so's/The plum, I suppose" 这句话产生了"连我都能做科学假设"的言外之意。科学意义上的 prove 是可预测（predictable）、可

---

① https://idioms.thefreedictionary.com/the+dear+knows.

② https://www.merriam-webster.com/dictionary/theory.

复制的（retrievable），但诗人用"The dear only knows/What will next prove a rose"完全消解了 prove 的科学含义。同样，the theory 是个庄重的正式词语，诗人用 go 这个词来引出科学分类，the theory 的正式程度自然也就有降格的可能。

作者的企图在 rose 一词的用法里体现得非常充分。"The rose is a rose"其实不是同义反复的主张，因为在"The rose is a rose"这个句式里，第一个 rose 前是定冠词，因此两个 rose 之间不是重复，而是复现里的上下义关系。第一个 rose 是指具体花卉的下义词（hyponym），第二个 rose 是表示类别，即蔷薇科植物的上义词（hypernym）。我们可以将这个句式与"A rose is a rose"进行比较。诗人在第二行里用"was always a rose"对这个句式里 rose 的类用法提出了质疑。这句里的 rose 其实是重复（repetition），不表达类概念，暗示现在的分类与过去有差异，包括了太多本来不是 rose 的花卉，因而不再单纯。

诗人在最后两行里的破折号"—"表明 rose 这个词的纯洁已经被 the theory 腐蚀，因而有了说明的必要，他用 but 替换前面的 and，表达了对 the theory 的挑战：

You, of course, are a rose —
But were always a rose.

简单的语义关系分析揭示了这首诗里两个语义集的冲突，更重要的是作者企图用常识和一般词汇去消解科学词义以对抗科学分类。破解这首诗要考虑的是科学分类和常识分类是否有本质的区别。

文章的词汇关系分析一般很难做到像分析短诗那样细致，但基本步骤是相似的。以 Is chocolate the answer?^① 为例，课文的第二段是这样的：

> The latest World Happiness Report says that <u>prosperity</u> is not the main <u>reason</u> for <u>happiness</u>. If you suffer real <u>hardship</u>, you are unlikely to be happy, but once your basic <u>needs</u> are met, <u>money</u> and <u>material things</u> become less of a <u>necessity</u>. <u>Happiness</u> depends more on recognizing <u>the things</u> you have and appreciating them, rather than getting more <u>things</u>. Yes, <u>money</u> can buy you the latest <u>smartphone</u>, <u>tablet</u> or <u>fashion item</u>, and you might get <u>a kick</u> out of owning these <u>material objects</u>, but this <u>enjoyment</u> is usually short-lived.

第一步是同类词语关系识别。我们这里仅考虑名词关系。除去 The latest World Happiness Report 和 you 以外，这段里的下划线名词按语义场可以分为这么几类：

prosperity 指的是物质富有，因此它和 money，material things，things，material objects，smartphone，tablet 和 fashion item 等与物质有关的词语共享一个语义场。

reason 在这里并没有其他词语与之直接呼应，因此只能为它单列一个语义场。

happiness，enjoyment，a kick 属于精神层面。

hardship 虽然也可以指精神层面的问题，但参照 *Longman Dictionary Online* 的解释，它主要还是指物质层面的问题：

---

① 邹为诚.普通高中教科书　英语　选择性必修第一册［M］.上海：上海教育出版社，2021：6-7.其实这篇文章的引言里有提示，请参阅"第八章　体裁：叙事类"。

something that makes your life difficult or unpleasant, especially a lack of money, or the condition of having a difficult life[①]

根据 *Longman Dictionary Online* 的解释，necessity 和 needs 既可以指精神层面的，也可以指物质层面的。

hardship, necessity 和 needs 该如何归类呢？我们可能需要考虑其他类别的词语帮助，如这些名词是否有修饰语？这段里有 real，basic，latest，short-lived 等形容词。basic needs 这个搭配可能会让我们想到 Maslow 有关人类五项需求的假设。在他的理论里，生理需求是最基本的，其次是安全需求。这两项构成了人类的基本需求（basic needs）。其他的三项，即社交、尊重和自我实现都是高一层次的需求。这段里的下面这句话显然提示这里的 basic needs 指的是 Maslow 说的第一需要：

If you suffer <u>real hardship</u>, you are unlikely to be happy, but once your <u>basic needs</u> are met, <u>money</u> and <u>material things</u> become less of a <u>necessity</u>.

如果把 real hardship，basic needs，necessity 等词语和 money and material things 一起用，这就意味着它们属于一个语义场。据此，这段中的名词可能涉及三个语义场：

（1）物质：prosperity, money, material things, things, material objects, smartphone, tablet or fashion item, hardship, needs, necessity

（2）精神：happiness, enjoyment, a kick

（3）原因：reason

如果不考虑解释类的 reason，这段里两个语义群呈对立状：精

---

① https://www.ldoceonline.com/dictionary/hardship.

神 vs. 物质。

下一步我们可以考虑动词的情况。这段里除了系动词 be 和表述因果关系的 depend 外，还有 suffer, recognize, appreciate, have, get 等。suffer, recognize 和 appreciate 更多涉及精神层面，而 have 和 get 在这个语境里更多与物质发生关联。也许我们可以简单地把它们归为两类：感知 vs. 拥有。

这样的分类是否可以为理解 "this enjoyment is usually short-lived" 提供线索呢？

课文第二段剩余部分的词汇延续了第一段的语义场，不过不是简单的延续：

Remember all those <u>presents</u> you <u>got</u> for your <u>birthday</u> when you were little? You were over the moon when you <u>opened</u> them, but not for long. A month later, they were <u>lying</u> abandoned at the <u>bottom of a drawer</u>. And have you <u>forgotten</u> those delicious <u>chocolates</u> that <u>made</u> you <u>feel</u> really happy when you were <u>eating</u> them, but ill after you'd <u>finished</u> them all?

这段主要有四个名词：present，birthday，bottom of a drawer，chocolate。birthday 表示缘由，bottom of a drawer 表示地点，present 和 chocolate 则延续了第一段的物质语义场。不过这两个词与前面表示物质的 money, material things, smartphone 等不一样。present 虽然是物质类，但它是会带来愉悦的物品。作者的这个选择似乎将精神和物质两个不同的语义场合二为一了。作者为什么要单列 chocolate 呢？ chocolate 是否属于可以把精神和物质两个不同语义场合并的物品呢？这也是与理解标题有关的问题。

BBC 有一篇报道告诉我们，chocolate 还真有合二为一的功能。

作者的选择确实不是偶然的:

> A study in 1996 showed that chocolate caused the release of endorphins in the brains of American women, making them feel happy.
>
> Chocolate does contain a number of compounds associated with mood-lifting chemicals in the brain. Often mentioned is phenylethylamine, a natural antidepressant and one of the chemicals your brain produces as you fall in love. Tryptophan, an amino acid present in small quantities in chocolate, is linked to the production of serotonin, a neurotransmitter that produces feelings of happiness.[①]

如果再考虑和这些名词搭配的动词,我们会发现这段的动词几乎也是延续两个对立语义场,与第一段有呼应,但角度不一样:

got, opened, lying, forgotten, made ... feel, eating, finished

虽然 lie,eat 都属于持续性动词,但由于 eating 这里用的是进行体,因此它只表示一时的动作。make feel 出现在 when you were eating 的语境,因此它只是 eating 时获得的感觉。get,forget,open 和 finish 属于瞬间动词,但由于 forget 是以完成体形式出现,强调的是结果,因而它表达的也是持续状态。基于这样的考虑,这段的动词也许可以分为:持续 vs. 瞬间。由此我们可以推导物质带来的 happiness 是短暂的。

这也就是为什么课文的第三段的第一句就是:

---

① https://www.sciencefocus.com/the-human-body/does-chocolate-make-you-happy.

It seems that deep, long-lasting happiness comes from intangible things, rather than things like chocolates and smartphones. One essential factor is human relationships. People who have the support of family members and also have strong friendships are more likely to be happy. Feeling protected and respected and knowing you can trust in the people around you is vital. But happiness means you have to give and take. Performing acts of kindness and generosity on a regular basis, for example, listening to a friend in need or carrying a neighbour's shopping, will make you feel on top of the world. Even a simple smile can work wonders. In fact, they say that one smile makes a person feel as good as eating 2,000 bars of chocolate (not all at once, of course!).

如果观察这段的名词，我们发现这段名词基本属于非物质类，也就是与人有关。作者明确指出了这段里的核心词 relationship。按照 *Longman Dictionary Online* 的解释：

the way in which two people or two groups feel about each other and behave towards each other[①]

几乎所有的名词都来自于 relationship 这个语义场：family members，support，friendship，happiness，friend，smile 等。虽然 shopping 在一般情况下不属于这个语义场，但 neighbour's 这个修饰语将它也纳入了 relationship 的语义场。people 本身未必有 relationship 的意思，但和 shopping 一样，people 先被定语从句、后被介词词组赋予关系内容：people <u>who have the support of family members and also have strong friendships</u>，people <u>around you</u>。代

---

① https://www.ldoceonline.com/dictionary/relationship.

词 you 也一样，都出现在有关系含义的语境：Feeling protected and respected and knowing you can trust in the people around you is vital，you have to give and take。

Longman Dictionary Online 的解释里还用了两个动词：feel 和 behave。feel 属于被动类，behave 则是主动类。这段里出现的动词显然都与这两个动词类别有关：

被动类：have, feel

主动类：give, take, perform, listen to, carry, smile

由于第三段的语义场转向人和人际关系，第四段第一句提到 "health is another key contributor to happiness" 就可以理解了：

It's not surprising that health is another key contributor to happiness. Poor health will certainly make you feel down in the mouth. But being healthy and staying healthy require some effort. A healthy diet is crucial and so is regular exercise. Laziness will not make you happy. Exercising for 20 to 30 minutes a day helps to reduce stress and anxiety and makes you feel more positive and optimistic because it releases endorphins (feel-good chemicals). So, if you've been feeling blue and worrying too much about your exams, get exercising. You'll also find that you sleep better.

Talking of sleep, do you often wake up feeling miserable? If so, it's probably because you haven't had enough of it. Teenagers tend to go to bed too late and have to get up early, so many suffer from a lack of sleep. Tiredness will certainly affect your happiness levels and put you in a bad mood. It also affects your ability to concentrate and may slow your growth. So if you want to be happy and do well at school, try to get at least eight hours of sleep a night. Now that you know the theory, it's time to put it all into practice. Smile, everyone!

这段里的名词和动词基本围绕两个语义场：health 和 exercise。第四段的最后一句提示下一段词汇关系的变化：

You'll also find that you sleep better.

如果分析第三、四、五段的主要动词，我们会发现作者选择的动词与前面有关 happiness 讨论里的动词遥相呼应：

Happiness depends more on recognizing the things you have and appreciating them, rather than getting more things.

recognize 和 appreciate 两个动词除了表示精神层面的活动以外，还表示行为具有主动性，即行为人是实施者（agent of the action），不是被动的接受方。与 recognize 和 appreciate 呼应，作者在讨论 human relationships 这段里的动词有被动 vs. 主动两个不同的语义集，能让我们感受幸福的是主动作为的动词。作者对 health 的讨论也是如此。能让我们保持健康的是主动类动词：

被动类：be, stay

主动类：exercise, get exercising

有关 sleep 的讨论也是如此。睡眠不足会影响幸福。这段里有三类动词，一类是被动，如 have, suffer, have to get up；第二类是主动，如 try to get, put it all into practice。第三类也是主动，但这些动作的实施者不是行为人了，如 tend to, affect。tend to 似乎是主动行为，不过这个词通常用来描写所实施的行为并不是行为人主动选择的结果。affect 的实施者自然不是行为人了。从这个角度去分析，这段的动词也可以分为两类：（人的）施动和被动。

我们这里主要试探性地分析了这篇课文中名词、动词的词汇关系。通过分析，我们可以看到，语篇的词语选择都不是随意的，它们构成的系统词汇衔接关系与语篇的话题和主题有直接的关联。

Hoey 在讨论词汇关系时强调了词汇在语篇认知中的触发作用。作者为了有效表达自己的意图，往往会操控语义触发以影响读者的期待。The story of a T-shirt[①] 就是典型的例子。

T-shirt 是大家非常熟悉的词语。有关 T-shirt 的历史背景能为我们更好地理解这篇课文提供语境。据说 T-shirt 起初只是一件内衣，但演员 Marlon Brando 在 1951 年出演 *A Streetcar Named Desire* 时穿了一件 T-shirt，彻底改变了 T-shirt 的地位：

Until then, the T-shirt was largely considered an undergarment, acceptable at best as an unseen layer under a Navy uniform or a proper shirt. But Brando made it look so good that it inspired capable imitators like James Dean, who wore it under his signature red Harrington jacket in 1955's "Rebel without a cause."

Thus validated, the T-shirt became the world's most ubiquitous garment and a blank canvas for expression. It can be unassuming or provocative, it can come from a five-pack or a couture collection, it can be sexy or ironic, it is at once democratic and elitist. "Luxury is the ease of a T-shirt in a very expensive dress," Karl Lagerfeld once said.[②]

从此，T-shirt 有了非同寻常的含义。2018 年，伦敦专门为 T-shirt

---

① 邹为诚. 普通高中教科书 英语 必修第三册 [M]. 上海：上海教育出版社，2021：24–25.

② https://edition.cnn.com/style/article/t-shirt-cult-culture-subversion-exhibition/index.html.

举办了展览会"T-shirt: Cult，Culure，Subversion"。展览会发布的推广词里有这么一句：

> From men's underclothes to symbol of rock and roll rebellion, through punk and politics to luxury fashion item, T-shirts broadcast who we are and who we want to be.[①]

不过，The story of a T-shirt 的词汇所触发的场景与 "Luxury is the ease of a T-shirt in a very expensive dress" 却大不相同。在这篇课文里，我们几乎找不到与 luxury 有关的靓丽词语。课文第一句里的三个形容词 busy，hot 和 dusty 确定了 T-shirt 购买场景的语义场：

> Lagos, Nigeria—Yaba market is busy, hot and dusty. People are looking around the second-hand shops, picking through piles of old clothes, and they're all searching for deals. The market is flooded with cheap clothes from America and Europe, and they usually sell out fairly quickly. "These clothes make people's dreams come true," says Abeke, a shop owner. "Everyone wears them. When they put them on, you can't tell the difference between the rich and the poor." At the front of Abeke's store is a cotton T-shirt with the words "Get Real". It's picked up by a young guy who looks at it carefully. He tries it on and smiles—it fits him and it looks good. It's a simple T-shirt, but it has a long story.

虽然这段里除了 Nigeria 的地理位置，几乎没有与 hot 有呼应的词语，但 piles of old clothes，flooded with cheap clothes 这些属于描写空间的词语，外加在衣服堆里翻找衣服的人群，会使商店的空间

---

① https://www.ftmlondon.org/ftm-exhibitions/t-shirt-cult-culture-subversion/.

显得逼仄而闷热。dusty 也没有直接的关联词语，second-hand shops 的店铺类型，商品堆放和人们寻找商品的方式都提示 Yaba market 的脏乱情况。busy 有一个相对完整的语义集：looking around shops，picking through piles of clothes，searching for deals，sell out fairly quickly，以及 picked up，tries on 等词语都表明在那里的人忙得不亦乐乎。

尽管场景贫困、落后，与 luxury 不沾边，但 T-shirts 依然是 "a blank canvas for expression"，依然 "broadcast who we are and who we want to be"：

"These clothes make people's dreams come true," says Abeke, a shop owner. "Everyone wears them. When they put them on, you can't tell the difference between the rich and the poor."

作者专门提到了 Abeke 柜台前的一个小伙子。小伙子的一系列动作——looks at it carefully，tries it on，smiles 传递出 T-shirt 所赋予当地人的特殊意义。

课文从第二段到第四段描写了完整的 T-shirt 生产、销售链。这是作者呈现的棉花生产过程：

A few years ago, the T-shirt started life in a cotton field in Uzbekistan. The cotton was watered every day and harmful chemicals were used to kill insects in the field. As the cotton grew, a young woman called Feruza picked it. She sweated in the field for ten to twelve hours every day in temperatures of over 30℃, but she was paid very little. Sometimes the chemicals hurt her eyes.

和 T-shirt 的购买场所一样，这段中用于描写生产链的词语触发的是贫困、落后的语义场，与奢侈或现代化这个语义场也毫无关系。作者选择的棉花产地是 Uzbekistan，用了一系列与现代棉花种植相反的词语：... was watered every day, harmful chemicals, sweated in the field for ten to twelve hours, temperatures of over 30° C, paid very little, the chemicals hurt her eyes 等。

特别要解释一下作者为什么要提 the cotton was watered every day。按照科学的种植方式，棉花是不需要天天浇水的：

That's because cotton is a drought-tolerant crop requiring minimal irrigation. The ability to thrive in dry climates makes it one of the most versatile crops on the planet. Unfortunately, years ago, water was overused. At the time, there was an abundance of water and lack of understanding about efficient use and timing of irrigation.[①]

第三段描写的是 T-shirt 的生产。工厂也不在发达国家。作者选择了 India：

Next, the cotton was flown to India. The T-shirt was made in a tiny factory in the Indian port city of Mumbai. There were 20 adults in it, five children and no air conditioning. The adults made the T-shirts and the children checked them.

这段很短，但名词触发的语义场和第一、第二段一脉相承：a tiny factory, 20 adults, five children, no air conditioning。值得注意的

---

① https://gildancorp.com/en/media/news/promising-path-forward-cotton-and-water/.

是两个数字，作者用了不同的表示法。

第四段写的是销售链，似乎场景有切换：

The finished T-shirt was sent to a huge discount shop in the UK. The people who shopped there didn't know where the clothes came from. They didn't want to spend a lot of money, but they wanted to look good. The T-shirt was cheap and it was bought by 15-year-old Ryan who liked the words on it. It was washed, worn and ironed and, after a few months, Ryan threw it away. His mum took it to a charity shop with some other old clothes, which were sold to an export company. A few weeks later, the T-shirt made its way to Yaba market in Nigeria.

这段提到的场景虽然是发达的英国，但里面的名词却与前面几段的语义场一致，很难触发发达、奢侈等语义集，如 discount shop, charity shop。对人群的描写也同样将他们锁定在相同的语义场："The people who shopped there didn't know where the clothes came from. They didn't want to spend a lot of money, but they wanted to look good." T-shirt 被 cheap 修饰。特别值得一提的是系列动词：washed，worn 和 ironed。这些动词形象地表明了这些店出售的 T-shirt 的状态。threw away 与 made its way 相呼应，告诉读者 Yaba market 的 T-shirt 的来源。

课文第五段又把我们带回了第一段的 Yaba market，继续着第一段里选中印有 Get Real 字样 T-shirt 小伙子的故事：

Back at the market, the young man takes off the T-shirt and looks at the $3 price tag. He hesitates for a moment and then he offers Abeke $1.50 because that's all the cash he's got. Abeke shakes her head. As she hangs

up the T-shirt at the front of the shop, <u>the charity shop's price tag is still on</u>
<u>the back: 25p.</u>

这段虽然描写的是讨价还价（bargaining），但动词选择清楚地
反映出小伙子贫穷的状况。显然来 Yaba 的人更穷。作者的动词选
择生动反映出买主与卖主之间的不平等地位。买主 hesitate，而卖主
shake，hang up，并且连慈善商店的价格标签都懒得撕掉，一点也不
掩饰巨大的利润空间。

作者在这篇课文的最后一段完全切换了词语的语义场：

The journey of a T-shirt tells many stories. Stories about people, countries
and cultures. Stories about farmers and factory workers. Stories about
shopping centres. But for most of all, it's a story about <u>choices</u>, and our
choices can make a difference. Do you really need another T-shirt? Do
you care where it's from? What's the cost to the environment? What's the
human cost? Think about it, because our choices could start a new story.

语义场突然变成了 choice。作者为什么要选择这个语义场呢？
作者提出的四个问题涉及现代消费的主要问题："Do you really need
another T-shirt? Do you care where it's from? What's the cost to the
environment? What's the human cost?"这四个问题直接提示这篇课
文的主题。不过，细想作者前面的系列描写，这些问题有简单的答
案吗？换言之，这篇课文的主题容易确定吗？

本章推荐书目

[1]黄国文.语篇分析概要[M].长沙：湖南教育出版社，1988.

［2］Hoey, M. 2000. *Patterns of Lexis in Text*. 上海：上海外语教育出版社.

［3］Hoey, M. 2005. *Lexical Priming: A New Lexical Theory of Words*. London: Routledge.

［4］Halliday, M. A. K. and R. Hasan. 1976. *Cohesion in English*. London: Longman.

［5］Murphy, M. L. 2003. *Semantic Relations and the Lexicon*. Cambridge：Cambridge University Press.

第八章 体裁：叙事类

导引问题:

- 什么是体裁?
- 叙事类体裁语篇理解的要素是什么?

本章提要:

　　体裁（gentre）通常指语篇的类型。与传统修辞学或文学批评不同的是，语篇分析的体裁分类依据是**社会活动类型**。语篇结构仅是体裁分类的一个维度。语篇分析是有目的的社会认知活动。社会认知活动类型决定了我们对语篇的使用。从认知活动的角度去考虑语篇的体裁问题不仅有助于消除阅读教学中体裁判定过于教条化的倾向，同时也能避免课文理解过程的同型化，阅读体验的同质化。叙事并不是简单地重现发生的事件，它是作者根据自己的目的，选择一定的角度对事件进行重构的结果。叙事受到认知框架、语言呈现、叙事习俗、作者意图等因素的制约。叙事类语篇分为文学和非文学两大类。

一、概说

　　体裁是个古老的话题，通常指语篇的类型。语篇分析的体裁理论与修辞和文学批评等理论有很大的不同。受 Wittgenstein 和

Bakhtin 等理论的影响，语篇分析的体裁分类依据已经不再是语篇结构，而是社会活动类型。语篇结构仅仅是体裁分类的一个维度。Fairclough 的定义非常有代表性：

A genre is a way of using language which corresponds to the nature of social practice that is being engaged in; a job interview, for instance, is associated with the special way of using language we call interview genre. (1995: 76)

语篇分析之所以要从社会活动的角度去解析体裁，主要有两个原因。第一个原因是阅读是有目的的社会认知活动。社会认知活动类型通常决定了我们对语篇的使用，语篇结构本身对认知目的和过程的制约有限。如文学作品可以用于各种社会认知活动。在不同的社会认知活动里，文学作品的阅读目的、用途和认知方式大不相同。

第二个原因是语篇结构的特征并不能作为区分语篇类型的充分依据。如诗歌是体裁特征最明显的，但按照传统诗歌的结构特征，有些诗歌很难被归入诗歌类。我们可以简单考察一下诗歌的传统定义：

A composition, a work of verse, which may be in rhyme or may be blank verse or a combination of the two.①

根据这个定义，诗歌的结构要素是押韵或音步，缺一不可。如

---

① Cuddon, J. A. 1979. *A Dictionary of Literary Terms*. London: Andre Deutsch, 515.

William Wordsworth 创作的 I wandered lonely as a cloud^① 就是完全符合传统定义的诗歌：这首诗押韵 ababcc，也有确定的音步结构，每行四个音步（tetrameter）。

I wandered lonely as a cloud

I wandered lonely as a cloud
That floats on high o'er vales and hills,
When all at once I saw a crowd,
A host of golden daffodils;
Beside the lake, beneath the trees,
Fluttering and dancing in the breeze.

Continuous as the stars that shine
And twinkle on the Milky Way,
They stretched in never-ending line
Along the margin of a bay:
Ten thousand saw I at a glance,
Tossing their heads in sprightly dance.

The waves beside them danced; but they
Out-did the sparkling waves in glee:
A poet could not but be gay,
In such a jocund company:
I gazed—and gazed—but little thought
What wealth the show to me had brought:

For oft, when on my couch I lie
In vacant or in pensive mood,
They flash upon that inward eye

---

① 邹为诚. 普通高中教科书 英语 选择性必修第三册［M］. 上海：上海教育出版社，2022：25.

Which is the bliss of solitude;
And then my heart with pleasure fills,
And dances with the daffodils.

然而，Walt Whitman 的作品就不符合 Cuddon 的定义。他的诗既不押韵，也没有确定的音步，学界只好用 free verse 来描写他的诗歌特征。free verse 除了文字排列，没有其他任何结构特征。如下面这首诗歌：

I hear America singing

I hear America singing, the varied carols I hear,
Those of mechanics, each one singing his as it should be blithe and strong,
The carpenter singing his as he measures his plank or beam,
The mason singing his as he makes ready for work, or leaves off work,
The boatman singing what belongs to him in his boat, the deckhand
    singing on the steamboat deck,
The shoemaker singing as he sits on his bench, the hatter singing as he
    stands,
The wood-cutter's song, the ploughboy's on his way in the morning, or
    at noon intermission or at sundown,
The delicious singing of the mother, or of the young wife at work, or of
    the girl sewing or washing,
Each singing what belongs to him or her and to none else,
The day what belongs to the day—at night the party of young fellows,
    robust, friendly,
Singing with open mouths their strong melodious songs.

对传统诗歌定义挑战最激进的是 e. e. cummings。他不仅抛弃了韵步，甚至还颠覆了基本的语言规范。最有代表性的是下面这首诗：

l(a

le

af

fa

ll

s)

one

l

iness

他在单词 loneliness 中插入句子 a leaf falls，在表达孤独不是独处而是脱离的主题时，将静态的孤独动态化，创造出奇特的形象文字效果。

所谓语篇的内在属性也很难区分文学与非文学体裁的语篇。Cuddon 认为区别文学与非文学语篇的内在属性是想象力。Albert Einstein 不以为然，因为在他看来想象力是任何理解的关键要素：

Imagination is more important than knowledge. For knowledge is limited to all we now know and understand, while imagination embraces the entire world, and all there ever will be to know and understand.[1]

Cuddon 提到想象力是为了强调文学作品的虚构性（fictiveness），把文学与历史、新闻等区别开来。但历史叙事、新闻叙事、传记等非文学类的语篇都涉及想象力的运用。许多栩栩如生的历史语篇，虽然基于一定的证据，但其叙事连贯大多是靠想象力实现的。如很少会有人认为阿房宫的历史叙事是文学，人们一直以为项羽火烧阿房

---

① https://www.psychologytoday.com/us/basics/imagination.

宫是历史事实。然而经中国社会科学院考古所的考证，阿房宫根本就没有建成，有关项羽火烧阿房宫的历史叙事显然是有些历史学家参照各种文献，运用想象力进行虚构的产物。

不仅历史叙事有阿房宫这样极端的例子，新闻界也同样有记者用想象力虚构新闻的事件。19 世纪轰动一时的 Life on the moon 报道就是记者为了推销报纸故意制造的一出闹剧。*The New York Sun* 从 1835 年 8 月 21 日起，以当时名声遐迩的天文学家 Sir John Herschel 之名，声称在月亮上发现了生物，将虚构的怪异生物在系列报道中活灵活现地呈现给了大众：

Of animals, he classified nine species of mammalia, and five of ovipara. Among the former is a small kind of rein-deer, the elk, the moose, the horned bear, and the biped beaver. The last resembles the beaver of the earth in every other respect than in its destitution of a tail, and its invariable habit of walking upon only two feet. It carries its young in its arms like a human being, and moves with an easy gliding motion.[1]

The New York Sun 作假被揭露后，没有人认为这篇完全靠想象力编写的作品是文学作品。

这些极端的例子表明，结构特征或内在属性不足以区分语篇的类型。体裁分析需要参照语篇的使用和社会认知活动类型。

语篇分析有关体裁分析的理论有很多。最有影响的是 Swales 等人的理论。虽然他们的体裁研究（1990，2004）主要分析的是学术类语篇，但他们的理论对其他体裁的分析也有很好的借鉴作用。Swales（1990:45–54）提出体裁有五大特性：

---

① https://www.thesocialhistorian.com/fake-news/.

（1）体裁是交际事件中的一个类别；

（2）同一交际目的是将一系列交际事件归纳为同一体裁的主要标准；

（3）就原型属性（prototypicality）而言，同一体裁的文本在程度上会有差异。文本与体裁原型属性的接近程度会对读者对文本的判断和期待产生影响；

（4）体裁对文本的内容、定位、形式等有制约作用；

（5）话语社团为体裁取的名称是理解该体裁的重要依据。

二、体裁与教学

从社会认知活动类型的角度去分析语篇的体裁，重点考虑目的、习俗和相关方法，不仅有助于消除阅读教学中体裁判定过于教条化和简单化的倾向，而且也有利于培养学生语篇体裁的独立判断能力。体裁判定是阅读教学的一个重要组成部分。教师应该鼓励学生参与体裁分类的讨论，引导他们从认知活动的角度去了解体裁分类的目的，向他们介绍不同体裁语篇的阅读目的、习俗和方法。

在讨论体裁时自然不能无视以结构为基准的体裁划分。不过有如日本学者西原丈人[1]指出的那样，教科书里许多课文的体裁都不太容易归类，很多课文类似随笔，说明文、叙事文、议论文等特性兼而有之。以 Life in a day[2] 为例，文章介绍了纪录片 *Life in a Day*。这

---

[1] https://yomiken.jp/4083/.

[2] 邹为诚 . 普通高中教科书 英语 必修第一册［M］. 上海：上海教育出版社，2020：6-7. 请参阅"第三章 语境"和"第四章 视角"。

篇课文属于哪类体裁呢？一般说来，介绍属于说明文。但这篇课文能简单地划归为说明文吗？作者写这篇文章的目的难道仅仅是为了介绍这部纪录片？又如 Blame your blame[①]，简单将它划为说明文对理解这篇课文有帮助吗？

从认知活动的角度去考虑语篇的体裁问题最大的好处是能避免课文理解过程的同型化，阅读体验的同质化。即便是文学作品，如果我们不按文学活动的习俗去阅读，文学作品的文学性会在我们的教学中丧失殆尽。目前许多教学中强调一个作品只有一个中心思想的做法和把牢记中心思想视为文学阅读目的的教法就完全背离了文学活动的宗旨和习俗。

具体说来，我们应该在教学中把确定体裁的任务交给学生，引导他们考虑以下几个问题：

（1）所阅读的语篇属于哪类体裁？判定的依据是什么？

（2）阅读这类体裁语篇通常的目的是什么？

（3）制约这类体裁语篇理解的习俗是什么？

（4）解读这类体裁语篇要关注什么？

（5）这篇语篇的结构特征符合传统体裁的归类吗？

三、叙事类语篇分析

叙事（narrative）是最常见的语篇类型，Jameson（1981）认为叙事是人类大脑的主要功能（the central function or instance of the

① 邹为诚. 普通高中教科书　英语　必修第二册［M］.上海：上海教育出版社，2020：6-7.请参阅"第六章　语篇结构Ⅱ：话题结构和主题结构"。

human mind）。

　　叙事是一个或系列事件的呈现。不过，叙事并不是事件的简单重现。用 Fischer（2003）的话来说：叙事属于阐释模式（interpretive mode）。它是作者根据自己的目的，选择一定的角度对事件进行重构的结果。叙事叙述的实际上并不是事件本身，而是作者对事件的理解。

　　叙事受到四个因素的制约：① 认知框架。认知框架框定（framing）所叙述的事件的角度；② 语言。语言表达方式的选择决定了事件的呈现；③ 习俗。传统习俗对叙事的构建和理解起着至关重要的作用；④ 意图。任何叙事都会有超越叙事本身的意图。

　　叙事的基本构成要素是：① 视角；② 脉络（逻辑）；③ 人物；④ 情节。语篇分析有许多叙事结构理论。Labov（1997）发展的叙事理论影响最大。他提出叙事通常有六个基本构成成分：

　　（1）点题（abstract）。点题的主要功能是唤醒读者的兴趣。它是故事的引入部分，可以是介绍、小结，也可以是吸引读者兴趣的一两句话；

　　（2）指向（orientation）。指向的作用是为读者理解叙事提供必要的信息。这部分通常会提供如人物、场景、时间等相关的背景信息；

　　（3）进展（complicating actions）。进展是故事发生的事件。它通常由具体的行动或言语组成。在有些叙事里，进展则由一系列思维活动组成；

　　（4）评议（evaluation）。评议是叙事者的主观陈述部分，通常说明讲述事件的原因、目的、对事件或人物的态度、评价等。评议的表达可以分成两种，一种是附加或事件外的（external），另外一种是隐性或内嵌的（embedded）。前者发生在叙事外，而后者则是通过叙事中的人物、事件等间接表达；

（5）结局（resolution）。结局，有时也称为结果（result），是叙事的完结；

（6）结尾（coda）。结尾是个相对复杂的概念，并不是每个叙事都有。它主要谈论叙事与现实或其他非叙事内容的关联。

叙事类语篇分文学和非文学两大类。如前所述，文学和非文学类的区别主要与社会认知活动类型有关。文学活动以体验为主，以想象力作为构建或理解叙事的主要手段，以象征作为叙事深层意义的主要表达方式。非文学类如历史、新闻、哲学等的叙事受到各自认知活动类型习俗的制约，以理性推导为主，想象力通常是辅助性的。读者不是通过解读象征而是通过历史或现实的关联性去寻找叙事的意义。

必须强调的是，在非叙事类的语篇中，如议论文、说明文等，常常也有叙事穿插其中。叙事类与非叙事类语篇的主要区别在于叙事类语篇以事件的发展为主要脉络。非叙事类语篇里的叙事通常被用作作者观点的支撑材料，因而观点而不是事件是语篇的主要脉络。

1. 文学叙事类语篇

文学类叙事虽然常见，但从理论上说清楚"什么是文学"是学界一个悬而未决的古老话题。我们这里的讨论参照 *Britannica* 的解释①，把目的作为主要的区分依据。文学作品的目的是借助想象力传递美学体验（aesthetic experience）。如果我们接受 *Britannica* 的解释，判断文学类体裁有两个主要标准：一是想象力的运用；二是美学体验的传递。构建文学类语篇需要想象力，理解这类语篇同样也需要想

---

① 有关文学的定义太多了。我们这里只是为了讨论方便选择了 *Britannica* 的定义。

象力。没有想象力，阅读文学只能是知性认知，并不是美学体验。

Rosenblatt（1994）在讨论文学阅读时也强调了美学体验在文学阅读中的重要地位。他认为文学阅读的目的是体验（reading for experience），也就是说阅读文学不是为了获取理性的答案。阅读时是否有身心体验，这是文学体裁和非文学体裁最重要的区别。文学形式是美学体验的主要来源（Attridge 2017）。不能触发想象力的阅读很少能获取美学体验，只获取知识而没有体验的阅读不是文学阅读。

阅读文学作品时所产生的感动和体验与读者想象自己亲历其境有关。知性理解可以相同，但想象体验却是因人而异的。想象力运用的依据是读者的生活体验。理解文学作品主题的重要标志是是否能找到叙事的象征意义。象征意义的寻找主要靠的不是理性推导而是读者的想象力。文学作品的象征意义会因为读者不同的生活体验得到不同的联想。

文学类叙事的活动特点要求我们在文学教学活动中关注以下几个重要内容：

（1）由于想象力是个体体验行为，受到个体生活体验的制约，因此文学阅读要强调个体体验。现在有不少文学阅读课在教学时过于倚重专家评论或教师的理解，这显然有悖于文学活动的要点。专家和教师的理解是基于他们的知识和生活体验所得出的结论，极可能与学生的知识和体验不符。要求学生按照他们的理解去阅读作品，这自然改变了为了体验阅读的文学活动性质。这样的阅读无助于激活学生自主想象。

（2）由于文学叙事是由体验触发感悟，体验是文学体裁阅读的关键，简言之，文学阅读过程是最重要的。按照 Attridge 的假设，阅读过程中需要对作品的形式给予充分的关注。任何细小的疏忽或关注都可能导致不同的感悟产生。文学阅读教学要引导学生自己关注作品的形式和细节，并根据自己的知识和生活体验得出自己的结论。

（3）鉴于文学的表意手段主要是象征，因此在文学阅读过程中要鼓励学生根据自己的生活经历，运用想象力去探索作品的象征意义，也就是去发掘作品深层次的含义。在这个过程中要注意的是，想象力运用的线索是作品本身，作品的象征含义虽然有无限开放的可能，但任何象征都需要从作品中寻找依据。

2. 诗歌

理解诗歌，我们通常要考虑这么几个基本问题：

（1）诗歌的话题是什么？

（2）诗歌的话题是如何呈现的？

（3）诗歌的呈现有什么形式特点？

（4）这首诗里有哪些触发象征联想的线索？

（5）诗歌带给我们的美学体验或感性愉悦是什么？

我们可以通过讨论 William Carlos Williams 的一首诗来观察诗歌理解中所涉及的基本问题。

This Is Just To Say

I have eaten

the plums

that were in

the icebox

and which

you were probably

saving

for breakfast

Forgive me
they were delicious
so sweet
and so cold

　　这篇语篇分成几个诗节（stanza），符合传统诗歌的结构特点，且Williams 也是把它作为诗歌发表的，因此它属于诗歌类体裁。这首诗叙述的话题很简单，"我对吃了冰箱里的李子表示歉意"。话题以高度口语化的歉意纸条形式呈现。

　　因为这是一首诗歌，所以我们自然不会满足对诗歌表层的理解。我们期待诗歌有超越表层含义的深层意义。这首诗的深层意义，即主题是什么呢？文学的主题是通过象征表达的。于是要问的问题是：这首诗能触发什么样的象征联想呢？

　　要联想诗歌的象征意义，首先必须寻找象征的线索。这首诗里有一系列名词，如 plums, icebox, breakfast 等。plums 代表什么？icebox 象征什么？ saving for breakfast 又是什么意思？诗人为什么要特别指出 plums were delicious, sweet 和 cold？诗人道歉时为什么要用 delicious, so sweet and so cold 来表示诱惑实在难以抵挡为自己辩解？

　　对于这些问题的解答可能会有助于我们想象这首诗的象征意义。这首诗有多种解释的主要原因就是因为诗歌的这些线索对想象力的运用高度开放。

　　William Wordsworth 的诗 I wandered lonely as a cloud[①] 是一首经典的英语诗歌（见 p.189），这首诗的内容似乎简单，诗人叙述说他现

---

① 邹为诚 . 普通高中教科书　英语　选择性必修第三册［M］. 上海：上海教育出版社，2022：25. 请参阅"第三章　语境"。

在独自一人躺在椅子上时，脑海里会经常闪现那天他一个人独自徘徊看到一簇水仙花的情景。不过，如果细细分析诗歌话题的呈现方式，这首诗还是有许多需要认真揣摩的地方。在第一节中，我们不仅能发现两类信息，还能注意到两个不同且对立的语义场。

> I wandered lonely as a cloud
> That floats on high o'er vales and hills,

诗人是独自一人徘徊，似乎像天上的云彩一样自由自在。但吸引他的却是地上的一簇水仙花：

> When all at once I saw a crowd,
> A host, of golden daffodils;

这里至少涉及三个有强烈反差的对比：① 一朵云与一簇花；② 天上与地上；③ 无羁绊的云与扎根土地的花。花的位置也很有意思：

> Beside the lake, beneath the trees,
> Fluttering and dancing in the breeze.

为什么要在河边和树下？当然这是他和 Dorothy 所看到的真实情景的复现。但诗人为什么要复现花的具体位置呢？ golden daffodils 的随风起舞不难想象，但作者为什么要用 flutter 呢？ flutter 多用来描写有翅膀的动物：

> ... if a bird or insect flutters, or if it flutters its wings, it flies by moving its

wings lightly up and down[1]

daffodils 扎根于土地，显然不能腾空飞起。这和前面提到的
cloud 有对比关系吗？

第二节同样也有两个不同的信息集。一个是喻体（vehicle）
stars，另外一个是本体（tenor）。诗人用 continuous 这个形容词点出
了比喻的喻底（ground）：

Continuous as the stars that shine
And twinkle on the Milky Way,

诗人选择 stars 难道仅仅是为了体现 daffodils 连绵不断地
（continuous）多吗？为什么要提 stars 的 shine 和 twinkle？作者为什
么要选择这个比喻去描写 daffodils？其实这节里有一个似乎自相矛
盾的描述：

They stretched in never-ending line
Along the margin of a bay:
Ten thousand saw I at a glance,
Tossing their heads in sprightly dance.

既然 never-ending，诗人怎么能一眼就确定有 ten thousand 呢？
诗人为什么要说一眼望去（at a glance）并给出具体数字呢？在
第一节里已经提到了它们的舞姿，这里为什么还要更具体地描写
daffodils 的舞姿 tossing their heads in sprightly dance 呢？

---

[1] https://www.ldoceonline.com/dictionary/flutter.

诗人在第三节里变换了信息呈现手法，将比喻改成了对比，将 daffodils 与 waves 进行对比：

The waves beside them danced; but they
Out-did the sparkling waves in glee:

诗人这里用了 out-did 这个词。他为什么要说 daffodils 的舞姿胜过 waves 呢？耐人寻味的是作者这里用了 sparkling 这个词。这个词和前面的 shine 和 twinkle 属于同一个语义场吗？ *Merriam-Webster Dictionary* 的解释也许能给我们一些启示：

sparkle: to give off or reflect bright moving points of light[①]
shine: to emit rays of light[②]
twinkle: to shine with a flickering or sparkling light[③]

在诗人的眼里，waves 是 reflect light，而 stars 是 emit rays of light[④]。一个被动，一个主动，两者的区别似乎是很明显的，可 daffodils 实际上也是随风起舞啊！另外一个问题是为什么 daffodils 是在 glee 方面超过 waves 呢？这些问题有答案吗？或者说去哪里寻找答案？这一节诗人用了四行叙述自己当时的状态：

A poet could not but be gay,
In such a jocund company:

---

① https://www.ldoceonline.com/dictionary/sparkle.
② https://www.ldoceonline.com/dictionary/light.
③ https://www.merriam-webster.com/dictionary/twinkle.
④ 这里分析的是诗人选择词语的区别，与科学解释无关。

I gazed—and gazed—but little thought
What wealth the show to me had brought:

如果我们分析描述诗人状态的词语组合，如 gay, jocund, gaze, little thought 等，不难发现诗人这时完全沉浸在观花的感性喜悦中。我们也只能借想象力去复制诗人的感性体验来寻找问题的答案了。

虽然这首诗的前三节主要描写感性体验，但诗歌的结尾却很有些理性思考的意味：

For oft, when on my couch I lie
In vacant or in pensive mood,
They flash upon that inward eye
Which is the bliss of solitude;
And then my heart with pleasure fills,
And dances with the daffodils.

不过，作者选择的 vacant 和 pensive 这两个词似乎消解了他心理活动的理性色彩。为什么是他 vacant mood 的时候呢？究竟清空了什么呢？ pensive 是个带有伤感的词语。为什么 "They flash upon the inward eye" 时是诗人处于 pensive 的时候呢？为什么是 inward eye？值得注意的是，这时的诗人已经不再 "wander as a cloud"，而是 "lie on a couch"。诗人状态的转换说明什么呢？诗人为什么要说 "the bliss of solitude"？"vacant or pensive mood" 与 solitude 有什么关系？这些和诗人相信的诗歌是 "emotions recollected in tranquility[①]" 有关吗？为什么 daffodils 会使他内心充满快乐？值得注意的是，诗

---

① 这是 Wordsworth 诗歌创作的一个信念。

人当时只是 gaze，而此时却是 "heart dances with the daffodils"。这样的转变究竟传递什么意思？

除了梳理这些细节，我们还要考虑两个问题：① 诗歌带给我们的美学体验或感性愉悦是什么呢？ ② 这首诗的深层意义是什么呢？美学体验取决于我们是否能运用想象力根据诗人的描写细节在自己的脑海里重构生动的画面；深层含义取决于我们对诗歌里出现的 a cloud、daffodils、stars、waves 等象征意义作何联想以及对诗歌最后一段叙述的思考。

许多学者认为这首诗主要表现的是对大自然的热爱以及与大自然进行交流的重要性。这种解释自然有一定的道理，但这种解释似乎忽略了一个重要的情节：在这首诗里，诗人不是与大自然进行对话，他只是与自己的回忆进行对话，而且他仅仅选择了与记忆中的 daffodils 进行对话。作者选择 daffodils 又是出于什么考虑呢？

要回答这些问题，也许我们需要对诗人的思想和其他作品有更多的了解。虽然 Wordsworth 是浪漫主义的著名代表，浪漫主义的基本要素是情感和自然以及两者之间的互动，但 Wordsworth 对自然的态度与其他浪漫主义诗人并不完全一样。他早在 1798 年 7 月 13 日写的另外一首诗 Tintern Abbey（Lines composed on a few miles above Tintern Abby）里的几句话可能对我们理解这些问题有一定的帮助：

These beauteous forms,
Through a long absence, have not been to me
As is a landscape to a blind man's eye:
But oft, in lonely rooms, and 'mid the din
Of towns and cities, I have owed to them,
In hours of weariness, sensations sweet,

Felt in the blood, and felt along the heart;

And passing even into my purer mind

With tranquil restoration: ...①

这一节显然与 I wandered lonely as a cloud 的最后一节有呼应。

3. 小说

小说的叙述更强调情节。虽然小说的情节源于历史事件或生活体验，但历史事件或生活体验只是虚构小说情节的引子。如果我们阅读小说时仅仅考虑小说情节与历史事件或生活体验的关系，或按照历史或生活思路去理解小说的情节，那我们不是在从事文学阅读活动。

小说主要由四个内容板块组成：① 情节；② 人物；③ 情境；④ 会话。有关情节，我们需要厘清小说故事发展的脉络，理解各情节之间的关系。对情节的梳理至少要考虑这么几个问题：

（1）小说有多少情节？

（2）情节之间有何关联？

（3）主情节是什么？

（4）哪个情节是小说的高潮？

小说的人物通常有不同的功能分布（functional distribution），有主要人物和次要人物之分，分析时具体涉及以下几个问题：

（1）小说有几个人物？

（2）人物描写给了我们什么提示？

（2）主要人物是谁？

---

① https://www.poetryfoundation.org/poems/45527/lines-composed-a-few-miles-above-tintern-abbey-on-revisiting-the-banks-of-the-wye-during-a-tour-july-13-1798.

（3）人物之间的关系是什么？

（4）次要人物的作用是什么？

小说的情境描述都有其专门的目的，关联性是理解和分析情境最重要的考量：

（1）小说里有情境描述吗？

（2）这些情境是否涉及小说的大背景？

（3）这些情境描写与情节发展有什么关系？

（4）这些情境与人物有什么关系？

绝大多数小说都有会话。许多小说的情节发展和人物刻画都是通过会话实现的，会话分析也很重要：

（1）会话是由谁发起的？

（2）会话的话题是什么？

（3）有没有话题转换？

（4）会话的话轮转换是如何进行的？

（5）会话与人物或情节的发展有什么关系？

梳理小说的情节和人物关系只是第一步。文学作品都有超越作品本身的象征意义。有关小说的象征意义，我们可以从感情共鸣、代表性、关联性和启发性这几个角度去探讨：

（1）小说打动我们的原因是什么？它触发了我们什么情感？

（2）小说的人物有什么抽象的代表性吗？

（3）小说的故事是否有社会或现实的关联？

（4）小说对我们理解生活有什么启发？

课文 The Last Leaf^① 是根据美国短篇小说家 O. Henry 的短篇小

---

① 邹为诚.普通高中教科书　英语　选择性必修第二册［M］.上海：上海教育出版社，2021：60-61.

说改写的。虽然改写后的课文对原著有很多的删节，但课文还是有相对的完整性：

At the top of a three-storey brick house Sue and Johnsy had their studio. In November Johnsy was struck down by pneumonia. She lay, hardly moving, on her bed looking through the window at the blank side of the next brick house.

One morning the doctor told Sue something privately. "Johnsy has made up her mind that she's not going to get well. I will do all that I can. But unless she changes her mind, chances are 50/50 whether she will pull through or not."

In the room, Johnsy whispered to Sue. "They're falling faster now. Three days ago there were almost a hundred. There goes another one. There are only five left now."

"Five what, dear?"

"Leaves. On the ivy vine. When the last one falls, I must go too. Didn't the doctor tell you?"

"Oh, I never heard of such nonsense," complained Sue. "I don't want you to keep looking at those silly ivy leaves. Try to sleep, dear," said Sue. "I want to draw and I must call Behrman up to be my model. I'll not be gone a minute. Don't try to move till I come back."

Old Behrman was a painter who lived on the ground floor. He was past 60 and was a failure in art. He had been always about to paint a masterpiece, but had never yet begun it. He earned a little by serving as a model to young artists. He regarded himself as a special protector of the two young artists in the studio above.

Sue told Behrman of Johnsy's fancy about the ivy leaves outside her window. Old Behrman was not happy to hear such stupid thoughts.

"What!" he cried. "That's silly. Who in the world dies because leaves drop off from a vine? I have not heard of such a thing. Someday I will paint a masterpiece, and you shall both leave this awful house with the money I give you!"

Johnsy was sleeping when they went upstairs. Sue pulled the shade down, and motioned Behrman into the other room. They peered out the window fearfully at the ivy vine. Then they looked at each other for a moment without speaking. A constant, cold rain was falling, mixed with snow.

When Sue awoke the next morning, she found Johnsy staring at the drawn green shade.

"Pull it up; I want to see," she ordered, in a whisper.

Sue pulled it up. But, lo! After the heavy rain and strong wind, there yet stood out against the brick wall one firm ivy leaf. It was the last on the vine. Still dark green near its stem, it hung bravely from a branch some 20 feet above the ground.

"It is the last one," said Johnsy calmly. "It will fall today, and I shall die at the same time."

The day wore away, and they could see the lone ivy leaf clinging to its stem against the wall. And even the next day, the ivy leaf was still there. Johnsy lay for a long time observing it. And then she called to Sue, who was cooking her chicken soup in the kitchen.

"I've been a bad girl, Sue," said Johnsy. "Something has made that last leaf stay there to show me how bad I was. It is a sin to want to die. You may bring me a little soup now. I will eat it." Sue eagerly did what she said.

The doctor came in the afternoon. He hopefully noted Johnsy's change for the better. The doctor told Sue, "Johnsy is recovering. Now I must see another case downstairs. Behrman, some kind of an artist, I believe. Pneumonia too. He is an old, weak man. There is no hope for him."

Johnsy seemed stronger the next morning. That afternoon Sue came to the bed where Johnsy lay and put one arm around her.

"I have something to tell you," she said. "Mr Behrman died of pneumonia today.

He was ill only two days. The doorkeeper found him sick in his room downstairs. His shoes and clothing were wet through and icy cold.

They couldn't imagine where he had been. And then they found a lantern and a ladder, and some brushes, and green and yellow paint—look out of the window, dear, at the last surviving ivy leaf on the wall. Didn't you wonder why it never moved when the wind blew? It's Behrman's masterpiece—he painted it there the night that the last leaf fell."

　　这篇小说的主要情节并不复杂。Sue 的朋友 Johnsy 得了肺炎，她情绪低落，以为没救了。医生告诉 Sue 除非她改变态度，不然她康复的希望只有百分之五十。绝望中的 Johnsy 告诉 Sue 如果窗外的常春藤叶子落尽，她必死无疑。Sue 把 Johnsy 的想法告诉了 Old Behrman。后者是位画家。他冒着狂风暴雨为 Johnsy 画了最后一片常春藤的叶子。然而他不幸染上肺炎去世了。

　　这篇故事大概可以细分为这么几个情节：

　　（1）医生把 Johnsy 的情况告诉了 Sue。

　　（2）Johnsy 把她对落叶的担忧告诉了 Sue。

　　（3）Sue 把 Johnsy 的担忧告诉了 Old Behrman。

　　（4）Johnsy 发现还有一片叶子没有掉落，燃起生的欲望。

　　（5）医生告诉 Sue，Behrman 得了肺炎，情况很不好。

　　（6）Sue 把 Behrman 死亡的消息和他画那片叶子的事情告诉了 Johnsy。

这些情节之间的时间关联似乎很清楚。虽然时间关联很明显，但情节发展主要是围绕 Johnsy 的担忧展开。究竟哪个情节是故事的高潮？是 Johnsy 看见最后一片叶子没有掉落，还是 Sue 告知 Johnsy 画叶子的消息？这也许取决于对故事主题的推导。

小说的人物不多，有 Sue、Johnsy、Behrman、doctor。这篇小说的主要人物是谁呢？虽然 Sue 出现得最多，但她的作用似乎是串联性的，doctor 的作用也是这样。故事讲的更多的是 Johnsy 和 Old Behrman。他们两位究竟谁更重要呢？如果是 Behrman，Sue 和 Johnsy 的作用是什么呢？如果是 Johnsy，那 Behrman 和 Sue 究竟扮演什么角色呢？故事主要人物的确定对主题的理解非常关键。

小说的情境描写不多：

(1) At the top of a three-storey brick house Sue and Johnsy had their studio. In November Johnsy was struck down by pneumonia.

(2) A constant, cold rain was falling, mixed with snow.

(3) After the heavy rain and strong wind, there yet stood out against the brick wall one firm ivy leaf. It was the last on the vine. Still dark green near its stem, it hung bravely from a branch some 20 feet above the ground.

(4) The day wore away, and they could see the lone ivy leaf clinging to its stem against the wall. And even the next day, the ivy leaf was still there.

这些情境与情节和人物的关联还是比较清楚的。第一个情境不仅交代了时间和地点，更暗示了 Sue 和 Johnsy 的经济状况。小说是 1907 年发表的。美国历史上有 The Panic of 1907① 的说法。原著一

————————
① 1907 年银行危机，也被称为"大恐慌"，是 20 世纪首次全球性的金融危机。

开始有更明确的交代：

In a small part of the city west of Washington Square, the streets have gone wild. They turn in different directions. They are broken into small pieces called "places." One street goes across itself one or two times. A painter once discovered something possible and valuable about this street. Suppose a painter had some painting materials for which he had not paid. Suppose he had no money. Suppose a man came to get the money. The man might walk down that street and suddenly meet himself coming back, without having received a cent!

This part of the city is called Greenwich Village. And to old Greenwich Village the painters soon came. Here they found rooms they like, with good light and at a low cost.[①]

  第二个情境与落叶有关。雨雪交加，常春藤叶子的掉落几乎是不可避免的事情。第三个情境描写的是最后那片没有掉落的叶子。第四个情境是那片叶子奇迹般地继续生存。

  会话是这篇小说情节推进的主要手段。语篇分析有多种会话分析的方法（Liddicoat 2007）。我们这里简单讨论其中两个方法。一是话轮转换（turn-taking）。话轮转换是会话最显著的语篇特点，它指的是说话人和听话人在会话过程中的角色切换，具体涉及会话由谁发起、如何发起、说话人与听话人角色如何切换、角色切换所采用的策略等。二是话题和话题转换，主要讨论会话的话题是什么、话题如何确定、话题如何发展、话题如何发生转换以及话题转换的手段和含义等。话轮与话题的分析对理解会话的内容、会话的作用和会话人之间的关系等有非常重要的意义。

---

① https://americanenglish.state.gov/files/ae/resource_files/the-last-leaf.pdf.

这篇小说一共有这么几段会话：

（1）医生与 Sue 的会话。这段会话是医生发起，其实也只有医生的话，没有 Sue 的回应：

The doctor: Johnsy has made up her mind that she's not going to get well. I will do all that I can. But unless she changes her mind, chances are 50/50 whether she will pull through or not.

（2）Johnsy 和 Sue 的会话。由 Johnsy 发起：

Johnsy: They're falling faster now. Three days ago there were almost a hundred. There goes another one. There are only five left now.
Sue: Five what, dear?
Johnsy: Leaves. On the ivy vine. When the last one falls, I must go too. Didn't the doctor tell you?"
Sue: Oh, I never heard of such nonsense. I don't want you to keep looking at those silly ivy leaves. Try to sleep, dear. I want to draw and I must call Behrman up to be my model. I'll not be gone a minute. Don't try to move till I come back.

（3）Sue 与 Behrman 的会话。值得注意的是，这段会话虽然是由 Sue 发起的，但她的话是作者转述的：

Sue told Behrman of Johnsy's fancy about the ivy leaves outside her window.

Behrman: What! That's silly. Who in the world dies because leaves drop off from a vine? I have not heard of such a thing. Someday I will paint a masterpiece, and you shall both leave this awful house with the money I give you!

（4）Johnsy 和 Sue 的会话，也是由 Johnsy 发起的。不过，Sue 似乎没有接过话轮，这里只有 Johnsy 的话，Sue 只有行动的呼应：

Johnsy: Pull it up; I want to see.
Sue pulled it up. But, lo!
Johnsy: It is the last one. It will fall today, and I shall die at the same time.

这段里的"lo!"应该是呼叫语，意在唤起别人的注意。为什么 O. Henry 没有标明这是谁脱口而出的呼叫呢？或者这呼叫究竟是否脱口而出呢？

（5）还是 Johnsy 与 Sue 的会话，Sue 还是没有接过话轮，依然只是行动呼应：

Johnsy: I've been a bad girl, Sue. Something has made that last leaf stay there to show me how bad I was. It is a sin to want to die. You may bring me a little soup now. I will eat it.

Sue eagerly did what she said.

（6）还是医生与 Sue 的会话，同样也没有 Sue 的回复：

The doctor: Johnsy is recovering. Now I must see another case downstairs. Behrman, some kind of an artist, I believe. Pneumonia too. He is an old, weak man. There is no hope for him.

（7）小说最后一段 Sue 和 Joshnsy 的会话是由 Sue 发起的。与前面不一样，这里只有 Sue 一个人的话，Johnsy 没有回应：

Sue: I have something to tell you. Mr Behrman died of pneumonia today. He was ill only two days. The doorkeeper found him sick in his room downstairs. His shoes and clothing were wet through and icy cold.

They couldn't imagine where he had been. And then they found a lantern and a ladder, and some brushes, and green and yellow paint—look out of the window, dear, at the last surviving ivy leaf on the wall. Didn't you wonder why it never moved when the wind blew? It's Behrman's masterpiece—he painted it there the night that the last leaf fell.

我们可以根据会话话题分布，推测故事人物的角色。医生的话题基本围绕病情以及对病情发展的预测。值得深思的是，连医生对 Johnsy 的前景都不抱乐观情绪：

But unless she changes her mind, chances are 50/50 whether she will pull through or not.

He is an old, weak man. There is no hope for him.

Sue 在会话里主要有两个角色，一是信息接受，二是传播信息。作为信息接受者，她基本是对别人的话题作出回应，如她和 Johnsy 的第一段会话里，她话题转换的目的并不是继续会话而是结束会话。她提出话题时，基本是转述性的。第一次是向 Behrman 转述 Johnsy 的话，第二次转述 the doorkeeper 的话。不过在最后这段话里，她第一次提出了自己的话题。这是为什么？

— look out of the window, dear, at the last surviving ivy leaf on the wall. Didn't you wonder why it never moved when the wind blew? It's Behrman's masterpiece — he painted it there the night that the last leaf fell.

Johnsy 的话题都与是自己的感受有关，病魔占据了她的脑子，使绝望的她变得迷信起来。即便是最后类似忏悔的话，她讲的和考虑的也只是自己。

Behrman 只有一段话，但他这段话与其他人的话题形成截然不同的对比。他不仅对 Johnsy 的迷信想法提出了批评，而且还表达了行动的意愿。Sue 最后的转述表明，他不仅有意愿，而且还将意愿付诸行动。特别需要强调的是，与 Johnsy 不同的是，他的意愿和行动都不是为了自己，而是为了别人。

课文的情节发展基本靠的是会话。从会话角色的分布看，课文中的人物并不是随意的选择。他们都有一定的代表性。不过，将言语付诸行动、将绝望变成希望的也只有 Behrman 一个人。课文的会话角色的分配是不是在暗示小说的主要人物是谁？这个暗示是不是有助于我们理解小说的主题呢？

4. 非文学叙事类语篇

我们平时阅读到的大部分叙事都属于非文学类的。我们对一般叙事的期待不会像文学那么复杂，通常关注的是这么几个问题：

（1）叙事的主要事件是什么？

（2）叙事的视角是什么？

（3）事件的呈现方式是什么？

（4）叙事有会话吗？作用是什么？

（4）叙事里人物之间是什么关系？

（5）作者通过叙事想说明什么问题？

就具体分析而言，我们也许可以考虑这么几个问题：

（1）文章的标题给出了什么提示？

（2）文章为什么这么开始？

（3）为什么要叙述这些细节？

（4）为什么要选择以这样的方式叙述细节？

（5）为什么要选择以这样的方式描写人物？

课文 A road less travelled[①] 是一篇非文学类的叙事。我们可以通过分析这篇叙事来了解非文学类叙事的一些特点。

Amy Carter-James is small, blue-eyed and blonde, with a friendly smile. She doesn't look like she could change the lives of thousands of people but, clearly, she has.

It all started when Amy took a gap year in Africa after she finished university. "I spent eight months volunteering in a very poor countryside school in Kenya," she says. "That was the first time I saw poverty. I was so young and so easily inspired and I thought, 'Why can't tourism do the same thing for community development?'"

On her return to England, 22-year-old Amy and her boyfriend Neal decided to take "the road less travelled". They drove across Mozambique, one of the poorest countries in Africa, but it wasn't exactly a holiday. Mozambique had two qualities which appealed to them: great attraction as a travel destination and local people who badly needed help. Once there, the couple got off the beaten track and headed for Quirimbas National Park, where they found a tiny stretch of white sand close to a village. Life in the village was hard: there was little clean water and not enough food. Health

---

① 邹为诚.普通高中教科书　英语　必修第三册［M］.上海：上海教育出版社，2021：60-61.

care was poor and people in the village had a life expectancy of 38 years. Amy and Neal had no qualifications in tourism or health care but they had common sense, enthusiasm and determination. They talked to the villagers about their plan to create a small beach resort, which would provide employment for people so that they could have a better life. The response from the villagers was extremely positive. Their only question was: "When can you start?"

The couple set to work on a beach lodge, building beach huts from local materials and employing people from the area. Once the lodge was complete, they set up a charitable foundation called NEMA, which received 5% of the money made. This money was used to create clean water points, fund health care projects, build two primary schools and support conservation projects—it helped to improve the lives of thousands of people. "We wanted to show the world the power of tourism, that it could be a vehicle for change," says Amy.

It isn't easy to get to this village. It's not a typical package holiday with airport pick-ups and drop-offs. There's no public transport, either. The nearest city is about 260 kilometres away and once there, you have to take a boat or go on a three-hour car journey along badly maintained roads. But the village lodge is worth the effort. Today the lodge has nine beach huts, with beautiful sea views. There are no overpriced gift shops and other tourist traps. It's the perfect place to take time out, escape the crowds and soak up the sun. Visitors can see the sights— explore the island nearby with a tour guide, go scuba-diving or observe African wildlife. But the highlight for many is getting to know people in the village, taking part in festivals and learning about NEMA's work. "People who stay with us often come for the diving or the beach," says Amy, "but it's the communities that really blow them away."

Amy and Neal are not alone: all over the world, similar community-based tourism projects are being set up. This new concept is changing tourism and recreation, one lodge at a time.

课文的标题 A road less travelled 让我们想到了 Robert Frost 的诗歌 The Road Not Taken。less travelled 是课文叙述的主要视角。几乎课文的每一段都体现了这个视角。

课文以描述 Amy 的外貌开始：

Amy Carter-James is small, blue-eyed and blonde, with a friendly smile.

在西方社会，small，尤其是 blue-eyed and blonde 通常会触发某种固化女性形象（stereotype）。这从作者紧接着的话里可以看出，不过作者用的 but 表明她不属于固化类型：

She doesn't look like she could change the lives of thousands of people but, clearly, she has.

课文的第二段叙述了事件的起因。Amy 在她大学毕业找工作前的一年里去了肯尼亚（Kenya）。在那里她第一次目睹了贫困，由此她立下志愿要改变当地的状况。她提出的问题表明她是从不同角度思考旅游业的作用：

Why can't tourism do the same thing for community development?

课文的第三段是 Amy 和她的男朋友 Neal 进行的可行性探索。他们的目标和常规做旅游的不完全相同。他们选择莫桑比克（Mozambique）不仅仅是因为它有旅游资源，更重要的是当地人很贫困，非常需要他们的帮助。他们选择旅游度假地的思路另辟蹊径：

Once there, the couple got off the beaten track and headed for Quirimbas National Park, where they found a tiny stretch of white sand close to a village.

一片白色的沙滩符合旅游资源的要求，但村庄的状况应该不会吸引常规旅游投资者：

Life in the village was hard: there was little clean water and not enough food. Health care was poor and people in the village had a life expectancy of 38 years.

作者在这段里特别提到了 Amy 和 Neal 并没有相关的资质：

Amy and Neal had no qualifications in tourism or health care but they had common sense, enthusiasm and determination.

这话暗示的是他们的视野和思路不会受到相关专业训练的限制。他们与当地人谈话的角度也与许多在非洲的外国投资人大相径庭。他们的重点不是图回报而是改善当地人的生活：

They talked to the villagers about their plan to create a small beach resort, which would provide employment for people so that they could have a better life.

他们选址完后立刻开始了旅游景点的建设。他们的做法也独树一帜。他们不仅选用当地的材料，雇佣当地的居民，而且还成立了基金会以改善当地的水质，建立医疗保健，创办学校等。

第四段描写了他们所选择的地点并不像大多数旅游景点那样有

便捷的交通。和一般非洲旅游不同的是，他们的项目最激动人心的内容是了解当地人的生活。在这个景点游客不仅能体验潜水或海滩的乐趣，更重要的是他们能与当地居民有近距离沟通：

"People who stay with us often come for the diving or the beach," says Amy, "but it's the communities that really blow them away."

最后一段的第一句话 "Amy and Neal are not alone" 又让我们想起了 Frost 的 The Road Not Taken：

Two roads diverged in a yellow wood,
And sorry I could not travel both
And be one traveler, long I stood
And looked down one as far as I could
To where it bent in the undergrowth;

所不同的是，Amy 和 Neal 不是孤单的探索者。作者为什么要这么说呢？课文最后的这段话提示 Amy 和 Neal 的所作所为具有社会公益精神，比诗歌里孤独的探寻者有更积极的社会意义，因而会得到更多人的响应。受益于他们的选择的不仅是他们个人，更是整个社会：

... all over the world, similar community-based tourism projects are being set up. This new concept is changing tourism and recreation, one lodge at a time.

本章推荐书目

［1］Montgomery, A., A. Durant, N. Fabb, T., Furniss and S. Mills. 1992. *Ways of Reading: Advanced Reading Skills for Students of English Literature*. London: Routledge.

［2］Rosenblatt, L. M. 1994. *The Reader, the Text, the Poem: The Transactional Theory of the Literary Work*. Carbondale and Edwardsville: Southern Illinois University Press.

［3］Swales, J. M. 1990. *Genre Analysis: English in Academic and Research Settings*. Cambridge: Cambridge University Press.

［4］Todorov, T. 1990. *Genres in Discourse*. Tr. C. Porter. Cambridge: Cambridge University Press.

第九章　体裁：非叙事类

?

导引问题：
- 理解说明文的依据是什么？
- 理解议论文的依据是什么？

本章提要：

　　说明文的目的是就某个议题提供解释性信息，关注的是 how/why。说明文的解释依据是作者所选择的**知识场域**。说明文所提供的信息一般涉及"如何做"和"如何理解"两个类别。许多学者将说明文分为程序、因果、对比、解决问题、描述、分类等六大类。议论文的目的不在解释 how 或 why，而在于说服读者接受作者的主张。议论文以理服人，因而强调论证。理解议论文的关键是识别作者的**主张**，了解作者对主张里核心词的界定以及根据作者的界定去判断议论文论证和论据的关联性和充分性。我们一方面要根据作者提供的认知框架去理解议论文，另一方面也要注意作者认知框架的局限，从而不被作者设定的认知框架左右。

一、概说

　　说明类（exposition）体裁与叙事类相对容易区分。说明文的目的是就某个议题提供解释性信息。现在有许多学者[1]把说明文称作"信息文"（informational texts）。叙事类[2]则不同，记叙文的目的是讲述事件，或者通过叙事传递信息。也许我们可以用两个简单的问题来区别这两种体裁：说明文是有关 how/why，而叙事类则是有关 what：

（1）How/Why does it happen this way?（说明文）

（2）What has happened?（记叙文）

虽然有些说明文内也会出现叙事片段，但这些叙事片段只是用于示例，目的是为了让解释更具体或更容易理解。

说明文和议论文（argumentation）的区别相对复杂，因为议论文也关注 how 或 why。社会认知活动的分类方便两者的区分。议论文的目的不在解释 how 或 why，而在证明作者的主张。说明文关注的是议题本身，其目的是提供解释而不是证明哪个解释更合理。议论文考虑更多的是如何说服读者，因而强调论证。说明文侧重的则是如何让读者理解，因而注重解释。

说明文所提供的信息一般涉及两个类别。第一个类别是"如何做"（how to do it）。这个类别的说明文主要是为操作提供指导。一般的产品说明书就属于这一类，如：

How to buy a ticket[3]
Step 1. Tap "Buy Tickets"

---

[1] Roehling, J. V., M. Hebert, J. R. Nelson and J. J. Bohaty. 2017. Text Structure Strategies for Improving Expository Reading Comprehension. *The Reading Teacher*. 71(1): 71–82.

[2] 请参阅"第八章　体裁：叙事类"。

[3] https://metrolinktrains.com/ticketsOverview/where-to-buy/ticket-machines/.

Step 2. Choose your ticket type

The ticket machines still offer the same ticket types you enjoy.

Step 3. Choose your destination

Enter or select your destination station with just one tap.

Step 4. Select your departure date and ticket quantity

Step 5. Pay for your ticket

The machines accept Visa, MasterCard, American Express, Discover, Diners Club, JCB, debit cards, Corporate Quick Cards, promotional codes, and cash in $1, $2, $5, $10, $20, $50, $100 bills. The ticket machines also accept touchless payment options using Apple Pay, Samsung Pay and Google Pay. Additionally, the Metrolink ticket machine voucher is an accepted payment form for your convenience.

第二个类别是"如何理解"（how to understand it）。这类说明文的重点是提供解释以方便读者理解问题，如：

A ticketing kiosk is an electronic, self-service ticketing solution that handles ticket sales and dispensing via an automated system rather than through a live agent. The purpose of the ticket kiosk is to allow a customer to purchase what he or she needs without having to wait in line to speak with an employee, thus freeing up staff for more pertinent tasks.[①]

一般说来，第一类的说明文与议论文不会混淆。第二类的技术性说明文也很少会被视作议论文。但第二类非技术性的说明文有时与议论文之间的区分界线就不太容易确立。我们可以比较以下两个段落：

---

① https://redyref.com/what-is-a-ticketing-kiosk/.

Self-service kiosks are an essential part of many businesses as they can be quite cost-efficient. Automation allows for better allocation of human resources, such as customer service agents. This frees up staff to handle more complex or time-sensitive tasks. Second, with kiosks functioning as another form of brand marketing, automated kiosks present a great opportunity for businesses to market themselves in a much more visible, interactive way than traditional advertisements.

这篇介绍自动售票机好处的段落出现在 *Ticket Kiosk Guide 2020*。不仅这个语境，而且技术性很强的解释都提示它是说明文。下面这个段落也是讨论自动售票机的好处：

Service windows are great, <u>but</u> they need to be staffed. Nowadays, automated fare collection systems can remove the necessity to have more than one or two service windows for a whole town, and these are mainly used for top-ups by people who are still not tech-savvy enough to use web-based portals or mobile applications. <u>But</u> since all riders need to have access to options to purchase tickets easily and quickly, TVMs fill the gap for people who cannot or simply do not want to use technology or service windows. This includes unbanked people and those who ride infrequently.[①]

这个段落出现的语境完全不同，它来源于一个讨论 ticket vending machines 的利弊的网站。这个语境表明它的写作目的不是为了解释而是为了说服，因而语境提示它应该属于议论文。这个段落的技术含量相对较低，第一句中的 but 更使这个段落有了对话和论辩的意味。

① https://www.modeshift.com/pros-cons-ticket-vending-machines/.

不过，即便是说明文，作者也会表达一定的立场 [1]，说明文的作者希望他们的解释能被读者接受，因而也难说说明文没有说服的目的。这些原因使有些说明文和议论文之间的界线很不清楚。

二、说明文

由于说明文的主要目的是提供解释性信息，它会受到知识场域（field）的制约。针对不同的目的和对象，说明文的知识场域可以分成一般和专业。一般指的是常识，专业主要指的是专业知识。专业知识场域既可以按知识体系划分，如文学、法学、物理学等，也可以按社会活动类型划分，如经济、政治、外交、教育等。知识场域决定了说明文的解释框架和视角。

由于说明文的意图主要是向所针对的人群提供解释性信息，作者在选择解释框架时会有两个考虑。第一是读者对解释体系的了解程度。说明文的知识技术含量会因读者人群不同而不同。人群越专业，知识的技术含量就越高。说明文的技术含量高低在语言层面有很清楚的反映。高技术含量的说明文会有较高密度的术语。术语除了表明说明文的专业程度以外，它们也是识别说明文知识场域的主要提示。

第二，读者对解释体系的态度。知识场域是一个宽泛的概念。在同一场域里会存在各种不同的解释体系，有些体系相互对立。作者选择的解释体系如果不为读者认可，说明文的效率会大打折扣。

自从 Meyer（1975）提出了文本结构（text structure）知识影响

---

[1] 请参阅"第十章　立场"。

阅读理解，尤其是说明文的理解之后，说明文的结构特征不仅是学者分析说明文的一个重要内容，而且也成为说明文教学的一个重点。学界的基本共识是，说明文不同的结构体现的是说明文不同的解释路径。了解这些路径有利于理解说明文的运作机制。目前较流行的是将说明文的结构分成六类，分类的标准是作者的意图：

（1）程序性（procedural）：作者的意图是指导我们如何操作；

（2）因果（cause/effect）：作者的意图是说明为什么会出现这样的结果；

（3）对比（comparative/contrastive）：作者的意图是比较两者的异同；

（4）解决问题（problem/solution）：作者的意图是提供解决问题的思路；

（5）描述（descriptive）：作者的意图是解释概念、人物、物体等；

（6）分类（classification）：作者的意图是告知如何分类。

三、说明文的教学

说明文教学主要关注的是三个基本问题：① 文章解释的议题是什么？ ② 文章的解释依据是什么？ ③ 文章是如何解释的？

理解说明文首先要了解说明文的议题。了解议题主要是了解议题所涉及的问题以及该议题解释的必要性。有些议题似乎简单，如课文 Journalists on the job[1] 的议题是择业。对择业涉及哪些问题或择

---

[1] 邹为诚.普通高中教科书　英语　必修第三册［M］.上海：上海教育出版社，2021：6-7.

业讨论必要性的了解会对理解说明文有很大的影响。又如 A question of taste[①]。味觉大家都有，但大家对味觉的机制是否了解呢？

其次是要了解说明文的解释依据，也就是所选择的知识场域。掌握相关知识是理解说明文的关键。据此，教学中首先要考虑学生是否拥有足够的知识以识别说明文所选择的知识场域，理解说明文的解释。

最后，了解说明文的解释途径对理解说明文至关重要。说明文的结构分析能帮助我们理解说明文的关注点和解释步骤。

具体说来，我们在教学中应考虑这么几个问题：

（1）说明文要解释的是什么问题？

（2）对这个问题你有了解吗？

（3）说明文依据的是哪个知识场域的知识？

（4）对这个场域的知识你有了解吗？

（5）说明文属于哪个结构类别？

（6）就这个类别而言，说明文是否提供了清晰的解释？

四、说明文的分析

A question of taste 这篇课文是很有代表性的因果类说明文：

They're often green, they can be crunchy, soft, cooked or raw and food experts insist they're highly beneficial to your health. What are they?

---

① 邹为诚．普通高中教科书　英语　选择性必修第一册［M］．上海：上海教育出版社，2021：60-61.

Vegetables. If you're not entirely convinced by what they say, don't worry. There's a good reason for this: according to scientists, young people's taste buds, the small points on your tongue that detect the taste of food, are not ready for the bitter taste of some vegetables. Our taste buds develop as we get older, meaning that we might view cabbage or onions more favourably, but until then young people's mouths prefer sweet food. In fact, it's not just young people that like sweet-tasting food. Most of us do, just like our prehistoric ancestors. They ate a lot of sweet, ripe fruit because it was widely available and easy to notice on trees, and it was a good source of energy. They also realized that they had to be exceptionally careful with plants that had a bitter taste, since they were often poisonous.

So, apart from bitter and sweet, what other tastes can we detect? You might be surprised to learn that our taste buds can only distinguish three more: salty, sour and umami. When we reach our early teens, we start to prefer sour things to sweet things. However, recent studies have shown that girls and boys experience taste in different ways. Girls have more sensitive taste buds and can differentiate flavours more easily, especially sweet and sour, while boys prefer stronger, more extreme flavours.

For everyone, though, food has to be wet for it to be tasty. When we smell food, our mouths produce saliva and when we eat it, the saliva transports its taste to our taste buds. Without saliva, some food would have no taste at all. If you dry your tongue and then put some food on it, you'll find it fairly tasteless. Fortunately, our mouths produce enough saliva every year to fill a bath, so it's unlikely this will ever happen!

We don't just taste with our mouths, we also use our noses! Our nose can detect 10,000 different smells and when food is cooked, it produces aromas that make us hungry. When we put food in our mouths, our taste buds and noses work together to decide what flavour the food has. Have you ever noticed that food which has been cooked doesn't taste as good when it goes cold? When the cooking smells disappear, so does some of the taste. You can do a simple experiment to test this. Close your eyes and pinch your nose between your fingers. Then ask someone to put a small piece of food in your mouth and try to identify it. Without any smell to help you, it's somewhat difficult!

Finally, the texture of food on our tongue is also important in our perception of its taste. Some people consider thick or creamy foods extremely unpleasant, however it tastes. This is because our brain perceives the look or feel of something and sends a message to our tongue telling it not to like that food.

So, if you really don't have any appetite for those vegetables on your plate, you can now claim that there is a generally accepted scientific explanation for this. However, don't tell your parents everything that you have read in this article because they might tell you to hold your nose and dry your tongue before serving you a big plate of vegetables!

这篇课文要解释什么问题？标题 A question of taste 很笼统。我们需要从课文的第一段里去寻找具体议题：

They're often <u>green</u>, they can be <u>crunchy</u>, <u>soft</u>, <u>cooked</u> or <u>raw</u> and food experts insist they're highly beneficial to your health. What are they? Vegetables. If you're not entirely convinced by <u>what they say</u>, don't worry. <u>There's a good reason for this: according to scientists, young people's taste buds, the small points on your tongue that detect the taste of food, are not ready for the bitter taste of some vegetables.</u>

课文第一句明确告诉我们课文要解释的现象涉及蔬菜。作者精心挑选 5 个形容词划定所涉及蔬菜的种类。五个形容词分三个语义场。green 单列，提示所涉及蔬菜的范围，即绿叶蔬菜。onion 属于

allium（葱属类）植物，因此包括在 green 这个范围内，而 tomato、carrot 等则不在讨论范围内；crunchy 和 soft 这两个形容词属于味觉；cooked 和 raw 属于蔬菜的加工方式。

课文的第四句提示了要解释的现象，即年轻人（第五句在解释 young people's taste buds 时确定了 you 的所指）不相信蔬菜对健康的好处。值得注意的是这句里 they 的用法。第一个 they 出现在第二句中，是后照应（cataphroic reference），指代后面的 vegetables。what they say 里的 they 是前照应（anaphoric reference），指代 food experts。有意思的是，作者似乎没有把 food experts 划归为 scientists。作者在第五句提出了课文的解释依据：according to scientists。他同时也给出了结论：

> ... young people's taste buds, the small points on your tongue that detect the taste of food, are not ready for the bitter taste of some vegetables.

至此，作者将课文要解释的议题比较清楚地呈现出来。课文要解释的不是为什么年轻人不喜欢吃蔬菜，而是为什么年轻人不喜欢吃带有苦味的蔬菜？

随着作者的解释在这段后半部分展开，我们可能会注意到两个问题：一是作者的分析框架并不完全是生理学的。作者还指出了历史的原因：

> In fact, it's not just young people that like sweet-tasting food. Most of us do, just like our prehistoric ancestors. They ate a lot of sweet, ripe fruit <u>because it was widely available</u> and easy to notice on trees, and <u>it was a good source of energy. They also realized that they had to be exceptionally</u>

careful with plants that had a bitter taste, since they were often poisonous.

作者为什么要指出历史原因呢？这是我们在阅读时要思考的问题。

从课文的解释路径看，这是一篇典型的因果类（cause/effect）说明文。因果类说明文的基本路径是：用一般的"因"（cause）去解释具体的"果"（effect）。在课文第一段提出了具体要解释的议题（effect）之后，课文的第二段到第五段是味觉的基本知识（cause）介绍，以方便读者理解因果关系。第二段主要介绍了三个内容。一是味觉的种类：

You might be surprised to learn that our taste buds can only distinguish three more: salty, sour and umami.

二是味觉发展的顺序：

When we reach our early teens, we start to prefer sour things to sweet things.

三是男女味觉的差异：

Girls have more sensitive taste buds and can differentiate flavours more easily, especially sweet and sour, while boys prefer stronger, more extreme flavours.

第三段介绍的是味觉产生的先决条件：

For everyone, though, food has to be wet for it to be tasty ... Without saliva, some food would have no taste at all.

第四段是味觉体验的原理：

... our taste buds and noses work together to decide what flavour the food has.

第五段介绍的是食物的质地（texture）对味觉体验的影响：

Finally, the texture of food on our tongue is also important in our perception of its taste.

在这段里，作者同时谈到了大脑在味觉体验中的决定性作用：

This is because our brain perceives the look or feel of something and sends a message to our tongue telling it not to like that food.

大脑的运作涉及记忆等各种认知机制，因而大脑的介入表明味觉并不完全是生理的本能反应。这个解释使非生理的其他因素介入味觉判断变得可能，也与第一段提到的历史原因有呼应。

课文最后一段是总结，即确定所讨论的现象可以用味觉产生和运作的原理解释：

... you can now claim that there is a generally accepted scientific explanation for this.

最后需要指出的是，这篇课文的对象是一般的年轻读者。这个判断主要有三个依据。一是课文第一段中的 you。二是课文的专业术语并不多，主要是 taste buds 这个术语。作者解释这个术语用的也是日常语言：

... the small points on your tongue that detect the taste of food

我们可以对比一下专业的解释：

Taste buds are tiny sensory organs that allow you to experience taste. They're located inside the tiny bumps covering your tongue called papillae. Taste buds let you know what you're eating and drinking and whether it tastes "good" or "bad."[①]

三是课文的语体。作者似乎在和年轻人进行对话，除了第五段，其他段落都是如此：

What are they? Vegetables. If you're not entirely convinced by what they say, don't worry.

You might be surprised to learn ...

If you dry your tongue and then put some food on it, you'll find it fairly tasteless.

Have you ever noticed that food which has been cooked doesn't taste as good when it goes cold?

最后一段更是像在和年轻人直接对话：

---

① https://my.clevelandclinic.org/health/body/24684-taste-buds.

So, if you really don't have any appetite for those vegetables on your plate, you can now claim that there is a generally accepted scientific explanation for this. However, don't tell your parents everything that you have read in this article because they might tell you to hold your nose and dry your tongue before serving you a big plate of vegetables!

对比下面这篇解释同样议题的短文，我们就可以体会出两篇说明文在语体上的差别了。

Why can't children and vegetables live together in peace?

Vegetables are usually at a disadvantage compared to other foods. First of all, they are relatively low in calories and therefore have fewer perceptible physiological effects, such as satiety. Next, most vegetables are not very sweet, and some also have compounds with a slightly bitter or sulfurous taste (spinach, fennel, cauliflower, Brussels sprouts, etc.). The sensitivity of children to these molecules depends on their perception of bitterness.

Finally, kids' rejection of vegetables is also often linked to a lack of diversity. Just because a child rejects grated carrots does not mean that she won't enjoy cooked carrots or raw tomatoes. That is why it is important to encourage children, who are in the middle of developing their dietary preferences, to eat a variety of vegetables repeatedly.[1]

对比（comparative/contrastive）也是很常见的说明文类型。对比类的说明文有两个基本类型。一是 A vs. B 对比。这类对比分别列举 A 和 B 两个对比项的特征以显示两者的异同。如：

---

[1] https://www.fondation-louisbonduelle.org/en/getting-kids-to-like-vegetables/why-children-dont-like-vegetables/.

Japanese food vs. Chinese: everything you need to know[①]

Japanese cuisine has a long and storied history, dating back to the Yayoi period (300 BC – 300 AD). It is characterized by its emphasis on fresh, seasonal ingredients, simple cooking techniques, and delicate flavors. Japanese cuisine has been influenced by various cultures throughout history, including Chinese, Korean, and Western cuisines.

Chinese cuisine is an amalgamation of diverse regional cuisines, each with its own unique characteristics. Its roots can be traced back to ancient China, where different regions developed distinct culinary styles based on local ingredients, cooking methods, and cultural influences. Chinese cuisine is known for its bold flavors, extensive use of spices, and variety of cooking techniques.

Both Japanese and Chinese cuisines emphasize the use of fresh, high-quality ingredients. This focus on freshness ensures that dishes are packed with flavor and nutrients.

Rice is a staple food in both Japanese and Chinese cuisines. It is served with almost every meal and is often used as an ingredient in various dishes.

Seafood and vegetables play a significant role in both culinary traditions. Japanese cuisine often features raw fish, such as sushi and sashimi, while Chinese cuisine incorporates a wider variety of seafood and vegetables into stir-fries, soups, and stews.

One of the key differences between Japanese and Chinese cuisine lies in their flavor profiles. Japanese cuisine is generally known for its subtle, delicate flavors, while Chinese cuisine is characterized by its bold, robust flavors.

Japanese cuisine often employs simple cooking techniques that highlight the natural flavors of the ingredients. Steaming, grilling, and simmering

---

① https://cooknight.net/japanese-food-vs-chinese/. 引用时有改动。

236

are common methods. Chinese cuisine, on the other hand, utilizes a wider range of cooking techniques, including stir-frying, deep-frying, and braising, which result in more complex flavors.

Japanese cuisine is known for its emphasis on umami, a savory flavor that is often derived from ingredients like seaweed, mushrooms, and fermented soybeans. Chinese cuisine, on the other hand, is known for its extensive use of spices, such as chili peppers, cumin, and Sichuan peppercorns, which add heat and complexity to dishes.

二是 A against B 对比。在这类说明文里，B 是对比的参照系数，也就是解释框架。与因果类说明文最大的不同是，因果类说明文的解释途径是根据一般原理解释个案，而 A against B 的说明文则通过 A 与 B 的对比，用异同解释 A。The influencers[1] 是很典型的例子。

Imagine this: you are in a café when you hear a young man talking about a new computer game. He's explaining its amazing features to a girl, who then asks where she can buy it. Nothing unusual, you might say, until after 15 minutes, they move to another café and have an identical conversation. On your way home, a "tourist" in the street asks you to take a photo with their camera. You do and, afterwards, they tell you how they bought the camera recently and how it's on special offer. Welcome to the world of stealth marketing. You may say you haven't met a stealth marketer yet, but that's the point. Contrary to what you might expect, this practice is quite common.

Stealth or "word of mouth" marketing isn't like normal advertising. We can recognize advertisements on billboards or in fashion magazines, but it's

---

[1] 邹为诚. 普通高中教科书 英语 选择性必修第一册 [M]. 上海：上海教育出版社，2021：42-43.

difficult to spot stealth marketing—it just tricks us. Studies have shown that people are more likely to trust a person on the street, who they think is giving free advice, rather than an advertisement. In fact, in a recent survey of young adults, only 5% believed advertisements, compared with 52% who trusted their friends.

More than $500 billion a year is spent on advertising worldwide, but compared with conventional advertising campaigns, stealth marketing is cheap and effective. So how does it work? Well, let's look at company X. Company X wants to launch a new product for 20–25-year-olds. They need their product to look "cool" and interesting, so they decide to pay young people to talk about it. These young marketers are carefully selected—company X researches social media and targets the most popular people or "trendsetters". These people sign contracts where they agree to promote the company's products, for instance by talking favourably about its products on social media. Twenty-year-old Tanya Fulham is one of them.

Tanya Fulham is beautiful, sporty and clever. She's interested in fashion, loves shopping, and listens to the latest pop music. She has more than 15,000 followers on social media and she often influences their choices and opinions. She's been hired by an undercover marketing agency to promote brands in blogs and on social media. "Products which are fashionable or have a strong brand image are easy to sell," explains Tanya. "I can usually get people to buy everything from make-up to luxury goods, like designer jeans." Other young marketers upload videos of themselves, which describe recent shopping trips and display their latest purchases. They show people how a product works or what it looks like up close.

"It's great to get free samples of cool, new products that my friends haven't heard about," adds Tanya. "It makes me feel important because I have insider knowledge." But do her friends know that she is paid to promote them? "No, they don't," she admits. "But I don't think it's dishonest. If I find something I like, I talk about it. It doesn't make any difference whether I'm paid or not."

Perhaps Tanya is right. Anyhow, lots of people tell others about the new book they're reading, a new place they've discovered or a cool gadget they've just bought. We're also a 24/7 generation and see more than 3,000 ads a day, so what difference does it make? However, other people are worried. "You think a person is being helpful," says a psychologist, "but that's very different from someone telling us something because they are getting paid for it. You don't know who to trust or who to listen to anymore." Sometimes it's hard to tell the difference between free advice and paid advertisements. We have already met the stealth marketers and they are just like us.

首先要明确的是这篇课文要解释的是什么问题。这篇课文的标题是 The influencers，不过 influencer 的意思有点宽。我们需要借助课文的第一段来明确这篇课文的具体议题：

Imagine this: you are in a café when you hear a young man talking about a new computer game. He's explaining its amazing features to a girl, who then asks where she can buy it. Nothing unusual, you might say, until after 15 minutes, they move to another café and have an identical conversation. On your way home, a "tourist" in the street asks you to take a photo with their camera. You do and, afterwards, they tell you how they bought the camera recently and how it's on special offer. <u>Welcome to the world of stealth marketing</u>. You may say you haven't met a stealth marketer yet, but that's the point. Contrary to what you might expect, this practice is quite common.

第一段里的两个例子已告诉我们课文要讨论的现象与正常的销售不一样。这段里的 Welcome to the world of stealth marketing 则点出了课文的议题。

第二段的第一句就提示课文的说明文类型，即 stealth marketing against normal advertising：

Stealth or "word of mouth" marketing isn't like normal advertising.

作者在这段里对比了 stealth marketing 和 normal advertising 的主要区别：

(1) We can recognize advertisements on billboards or in fashion magazines, but it's difficult to spot stealth marketing — it just tricks us.

(2) Studies have shown that people are more likely to trust a person on the street, who they think is giving free advice, rather than an advertisement.

(3) ... only 5% believed advertisements, compared with 52% who trusted their friends.

之所以说 normal advertising 是对比参数，主要是因为在接下来的讨论里，课文主要介绍的是 stealth marketing 与 normal advertising 的不同之处。在第三段讨论 "How does it work?" 里，作者一字不提 normal advertising，把它作为读者的已知信息。

第四段主要叙述 Tanya Fulham。虽然这里也没有提 normal advertising，但作者在这里的用词所突出的 casual, personal 等因素，与期刊、电视等媒体里的 normal advertising 形成强烈反差。

第五段指出了 stealth marketing 和 normal advertising 最关键的区别。stealth marketing 的推销对象是朋友，而且这些朋友并没有意识到这是 marketing，这段是对 stealth 一个很好的注脚。

课文的最后一段引用心理学家的担忧，指出了 stealth marketing 带来的问题比 normal advertising 更严重：

You don't know who to trust or who to listen to anymore.

如果我们了解 advertising 的运作机制，也许我们对作者的担忧会有更好的理解。Vance Packard 早在 1957 年出版的 *The Hidden Persuaders*[①] 一书中指出，advertising 是在潜意识层面影响我们：

Typically these efforts take place beneath our level of awareness; so that the appeals which move us are often, in a sense, "hidden." The result is that many of us are being influenced and manipulated, far more than we realize, in the patterns of our everyday lives. (1980: 31)

stealth marketing 则是利用我们对朋友或熟人的信任。信任是社会和谐的基石，因而它造成的伤害就会更大。

这篇说明文的话题结构特征非常明显：第一段是议题；第二段是对比框架；第三段至第五段是具体的对比参数：运作方式、运作人员、运作原理；最后一段是对 stealth marketing 的评价。五个段落分成三个层级：

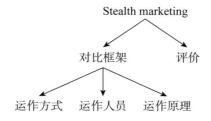

---

① Packard, V. 1957/1980. *The Hidden Persuaders*. New York: Ig Publishing.

stealth marketing 和 normal advertising 两者的差异不仅体现在运作模式上，作者用的语言也凸显两者的不同。如第二段里作者选择 "trick" 来描述 stealth marketing。提到 normal advertising 时的语体相对正式，提到 stealth marketing 时则随意很多，如 recognize、spot 等。特别值得一提的是 "normal" 这个词的使用。根据语义学的原型（prototype）假设，我们对词语的语义理解都是建立在典型意义的基础之上。典型意义自然就是 normal。因而提 advertising 时，normal 这个词根本没有必要。作者的用意显然不在 advertising，而是在 stealth marketing。他用 normal 凸显鲜明的反差。虽然作者没有明确表态，但课文的结束语似乎提示 stealth marketing 其实是一种 abnormal advertising：

Sometimes it's hard to tell the difference between free advice and paid advertisements. We have already met the stealth marketers and they are just like us.

为了凸显 stealth marketing 的特征，课文在介绍 stealth marketing 时所用的语言口语色彩很浓，几乎没有什么其他术语。作者的语体选择冲淡了 stealth marketing 这个术语的知识技术含量。我们可以对比下面这篇介绍 stealth marketing 说明文的开头：

There is an indirect way to marketing items, which is known as stealth marketing to concentrate on generating buzz between the customers without letting everyone realize that items are marketed to them. It can be performed in many ways, like forming a buzz in social media platforms where people can jump into comments, discussions, and tags regarding items, live audience interactions on boosting events, and many more. As a result, customers can go with the flow, then developing a keen interest in commodities by default. Also, the environment where marketing is created has a vital role in seeding people's curiosity about specific products.[1]

这段的语体要正式得多，术语也相对多：marketing items, stealth marketing, social media platform 等。

五、议论文

议论文的目的是要说服读者，大多数议论文会开门见山地提出所要证明的主张（claim），因此识别议论文的主张并不难。相对复杂的是确定该主张所需要证明的内容。确定内容的关键是找出议论文主张里的核心词语和作者对这些核心词语的界定。了解核心词语的界定不仅能方便我们读懂主张所要证明的内容和理解作者议论的视角和认知框架，还能帮助我们判断议论文的论据是否有充分的关联[2]。

一般说来，为了方便读者理解或者说为了使读者按照作者所选择的认知框架去理解议论文的主张，作者会对核心词语，尤其是那些有多种理解可能的常见词语进行定义。作者在定义时通常会考虑四个问题：① 如何确定核心词语在具体语境里的词义，以排除一般理解的干扰；② 如何使核心词语的定义既服从于议论文的目的，又被读者认可；③ 如何通过定义在核心词语之间建立清晰的逻辑关系；④ 如何避免核心词语的定义太抽象或与支撑论据脱节。

如在讨论"What makes a good teacher?"时，我们必须注意的是

---

① https://avada.io/resources/stealth-marketing.html.
② 详细讨论可参阅曲卫国（2021）。

核心词语 good teacher 是由 good 和 teacher 两个词组成。good 的定义其实是由 teacher 决定的。也许我们可以把 teacher 理解为微观语境提示语。下面这位作者在定义时完全参照了 teacher 这个语境：

> A teacher is someone who helps students learn and grow. They play a vital role in shaping the minds of young people and preparing them for the future. Good teachers are passionate about their subjects and are always looking for new ways to make learning fun and engaging. They are patient, understanding, and supportive, and they always put the needs of their students first.[①]

作者在定义 good teacher 时，首先定义 teacher，然后根据 teacher 的作用选定判断 good teacher 的标准。第一条是 "passionate about their subjects"。教师都了解自己的教课内容，但好教师不仅了解，而且必须对教课内容充满激情。第二条是 "are always looking for new ways to make learning fun and engaging"。教师的任务是教学，好教师的教学必须能充分吸引学生，使他们能身心投入。第三条是 "patient, understanding, and supportive"。这三个形容词是好教师在与学生打交道时必须有的品质。第四条是 "always put the needs of their students first"。好教师必须始终坚持学生需求至上的原则。

由于这个定义所依据的标准是教师特有的作用，它不仅能使读者清楚地了解议论文主张的内容，告知读者作者所选择的认知框架，而且由于这四条标准与教师的作用密切相关，基于这些标准的论据也会有高度的关联性。

---

① https://aspiringyouths.com/essay/what-makes-a-good-teacher.

六、议论文的教学

虽然大多数议论文会开宗明义，一开始就提出主张，但也有不少议论文开始只是提出问题，将作者的主张放到文章的末尾。据此，在议论文教学中，首先要区分议论的话题和作者的主张。

其次，要重视议论文主张里核心词语是否有定义以及作者是如何定义这些核心词语的。尽管大多数议论文一开始就会直接给出定义，但也有部分议论文，尤其是随笔性的议论文，它们的定义是在讨论中间接给出的。在阅读这类议论文时，我们需要从作者给出的论据里去梳理出作者的定义。

判断议论文论据关联性的主要依据是作者的主张，而不是读者自己对议题的理解。在议论文教学中如何排除自身观点的干扰，依据作者对核心词语的定义及其认知框架对论证过程和论据进行判断非常重要。

作者对核心词语的定义不仅会告诉我们如何理解文章的主张，更会提示作者议论的认知框架。在教学中，我们一方面要提示学生根据作者提供的认知框架去理解议论文，另一方面也要提醒学生注意该认知框架的局限，从而使他们不轻易被左右。这对培养学生的独立和批判思维有很大的帮助。

议论文是以理服人的说服活动。然而，由于议论文常常涉及一些敏感问题，不仅作者的议论，读者的阅读也容易受到个人情绪的干扰。如何防止正面或负面情绪对议论文理解的干扰是教学中特别需要注意的问题。被唤起的情绪会严重影响我们的理性推导，以至于我们会完全按照自己的身份或观点去曲解议论文。

在分析议论文时，我们通常会提请学生关注以下具体问题：

（1）议论文的主张是什么？

（2）该主张里的核心词语是哪些？

（3）作者对核心词语是否有直接的界定？

（4）作者的界定是否有含混的地方？

（5）主张里的核心词语之间是否有重叠或冲突？

（6）议论文提出的论据与主张是否有关联？

（7）议论文提出的论据是否充分？

（8）议论文的论证过程是否受到作者情绪的干扰？

（9）我们在阅读过程中是否受到自己的身份和观点的影响？

七、议论文的分析

Andrew Buhrmann 在 Euthanasia and intrinsic value of life[①] 一文里，有选择地对一系列词语进行了定义。这些定义不仅使读者很好地理解核心词语的特定含义，方便读者了解文章的认知框架，而且在核心词语之间所建立的逻辑关系也使他的论证也更严谨、深入。

Life in itself has no specific value to us, other than as the way we can have experiences, and these experiences are what we find to be valuable. Humans do not put the value of life into the physical state of mere aliveness, but give it value through its ability to allow for experiences. Life, as a set of experiences that are good, is what has value, and our capacity to have them is the intrinsic value of life.

---

① https://www.csueastbay.edu/philosophy/reflections/2008/contents/andrew-buhr. html.

Our values of life come from our environment. The heaviest influences are our contacts in our daily life and the culture and society we live within. We as humans also have a certain sense of human community, and with few exceptions, put human life above and separate from all other life. This separation gives our common definition of life an intrinsic value, but it is only from being able to feel alive and enjoy experiences that we have come to give human life any additional value. The value of life, therefore, is one that is not derived from our ability to exist physically, but to exist in the human experience and be a part of experiences that are themselves considered desirable or good.

Life gains its intrinsic value from the ability to experience, and this value is not reducible to the physical, but the physical contains the potential for these experiences. The term physical is particularly broad here, because it would be false and discriminatory to try to contain physical capability as any standard, or to even estimate how experiences can come from it, because the possibilities here are endless. When the physical sense is tied to the notion of quality of life, it disregards what has been found to be valuable in experience. The quality of life as used to describe a person's physical status is an attempt to place value on a person's physical being. When value is attempted to be placed on something other than what we find valuable, it is not likely productive. The intrinsic value of a life is then exclusively linked to experiences.

Apply the idea of life's intrinsic value to euthanasia; it would seem that the potential for life that comes from a working body, which for now will consist of, at a minimum, a brain that functions enough to pump blood or even a body mostly sustained by machines but has a pulse. The working definition here should be considered broad enough to include those in persistent vegetative states, severely retarded, suicidal or in need of machines to support biological function.

When a person is in a persistent vegetative state, has a body that functions only based on lower brain function, and is potentially in poor physical shape, his quality of life will likely come into question. What quality of life means here is that he is potentially in pain, has minimal body functions (he may in fact has no cognitive, vascular, pulmonary or digestive functions at all) and very little chance of recovery. The quality of life argument appeals to our strong emotional attachment to the definition of life as experience. By definition of being alive, this person has at least some brain function and can continue to show basic vital signs, and is therefore a living being. The push to terminate this life comes from our perception that the conditions of this person's state of being do not measure up to what others believe a life should be. If a good quality of life includes having loved ones, being financially stable, and having the basic human needs met (e.g. food, shelter), then does this require us to consider the termination of a diamond miner, who works hard all day and does not have adequate food, clothing, water and shelter and may not have any family at all? No one would argue that, but there are no efforts made to improve his life's quality. If this person is not living at the level considered desirable, then why is he less of a candidate? He has a certain potential to have the good set of experiences because he has a working body, but also no real opportunity to get to these valued experiences. He may have the potential to live a better quality level, but he is also not likely to. This means that our normal quality of life definition is not universal enough to be considered a standard.

Likely the appeal to our emotions that occurs from looking at the quality of a person's life is similar to our use of life's intrinsic value. Our reaction to each point of view comes from two general responses; one tells us a human life is valuable, and also that there is a certain standard at which life is considered to be of a good quality. This conflict is at the heart of mercy killing; robbing potential could produce as bad of a situation as a poor quality of existence. The level of quality cannot be made into a universal standard, nor is it succinct enough to be a measuring point. The ways in which a person can have experiences are endless and should be, so we cannot define, constrict, and confine them to a specific quality standard, which is commonly used in the quality of life argument. As an argument, the quality of life position cannot hold that a person must have a certain specific quality of life. Of course, one can reduce this to an example where the patient has many years of comatose existence, has no real chance of recovery, and even if recovery occurs, may have become too physically deteriorated to continue physically, therefore having a poor quality of life and being a candidate for euthanasia. This is refuted because we allow any level of physical being to dictate what our perception of this life's value might be. It comes forward only because we have an ability to see and have a sense of the physical matters here, which then in effect obscure our vision of the experiential side. If this were used, then it would go against our definition that a life is valuable based on experience, not physical status.

So it follows now that life does not derive value from the physical being, but physical being is used as a standard where evidence of life can be found. Because we can show life through physical means, it becomes our measuring point. We could use this as a basis to say "yes" or "no" when it comes to mercy killing, but that would ignore the experience of the patient. The argument against euthanasia from evidence of physical life has a strong appeal because we have a sense of it, but it does not follow in our understanding of what is valuable.

Showing evidence of experience and mental states is much more difficult, however, regardless of how much or how little knowledge we can have of it, the experiences are the valued set here. This offers then, the protection of a life, which is defined here as a set of experiences, which are occurring beyond any physical existence. This protection is based on the potential for experience without the direct knowledge of experience, that is that our limited knowledge only prevents us from being able to evidence mental experience as easily as physical status, but does not mean our value of experience is diminished any amount.

Our value of life and how it develops into the intrinsic value we assign to human life comes from how we value experiences. Positive experience is held as desirable and is separate from our physical being. Because we have a separation and have assigned that value to the experiential side, physical status is not an acceptable point for determining euthanasia. To do so goes against our inclination that value is derived from the experiences of life.

作者没有选择定义 euthanasia 这个专业词语，因为该词的语义单一明确，不会引起误解。the value of life 是个相当常见、有各种不同理解的词语。如果要使读者接受文章的主张，作者就必须对 the value of life 进行明确的定义。作者首先选择对 life 在这个特定语境里的意义做了专门的限定：

Life, as a set of experiences that are good, is what has value, and our capacity to have them is the intrinsic value of life.

由于 experience 是 life 定义里的核心词，且 experience 又是一个可能会产生各种理解的词语，作者在第二段的一开始就对 experience 进行了解释，用 contact 这个词明确 experience 在这篇文章中的意义：

Our values of life come from our environment. The heaviest influences are our contacts in our daily life and the culture and society we live within.

根据 life 的定义，他从 experience 的角度去界定 the value of life：

The value of life, therefore, is one that is not derived from our ability to exist physically, but to exist in the human experience and be a part of experiences that are themselves considered desirable or good.

作者为了帮助读者更好地理解他对 life 的定义，强调 the value of life is not reducible to the physical，他在文章里还专门讨论了 physical 的含义：

... the physical contains the potential for these experiences.

将 being alive 和 life 做了区分：

By definition of being alive, this person has at least some brain function and can continue to show basic vital signs, and is therefore a living being.

基于这一系列的定义，作者提出了他对实施 euthanasia 的观点：

Because we have a separation and have assigned that value to the experiential side, physical status is not an acceptable point for determining euthanasia.

Capital Punishment Is Wrong! [1] 的作者在文章的标题里就明确提

---

[1] https://k12.thoughtfullearning.com/assessmentmodels/capital-punishment-wrong.

出了自己的主张，他不仅在第一段界定了 capital punishment 这个概念，而且还对 wrong 这个词进行了界定：

Capital punishment results in death by execution. It is legal in many states as a punishment for serious crimes, but that does not make it right. Capital punishment should be stopped <u>because it is morally wrong, expensive, and such a slow process.</u>

不过，capital punishment 是非常专业的词语，语义单一，一般不会引起误解，但值得注意的是，morally wrong, expensive 和 slow process 三个核心词语触发的是三个不同的认知框架：morally wrong 是道德的，expensive 是经济的，而 slow process 是效率的。这三个认知框架之间会有冲突吗？

文章的第二段主要是从 moral 的角度论证作者的主张：

First of all, there is no moral basis for it. When we use the death penalty, we are following the criminals' example by doing something equally as bad ourselves. We are taking one life for another life. There is also a chance that a mistake will be made, and the wrong person will be put to death. Is this type of revenge worth such a risk?

作者指出，如果实行 capital punishment，我们犯了和罪犯一样剥夺他人性命的罪行。作者这里依据的是 "do not kill under any circumstances" 这个绝对的道德原则。不过，该段落的第四句话里提到的 a chance 却与这个绝对原则有冲突，因为按照这个原则，是否会误杀是不相干的。提到误杀的可能就会产生这样的推测：如果没有误判，capital punishment 是可以实施的。这显然背离了绝对道德原则。

第三段对接主张里的第二个词 expensive：

Another problem with capital punishment is the high cost. For example, the special prison housing is expensive to staff and keep up. States with the death penalty use taxes to pay these expenses. Over the past 13 years, Florida has spent $57 million to carry out 18 executions. If you divide this dollar amount by the number of executions, you come up with a cost of $3.2 million for each execution. That is a great deal of money.

从经济角度去考虑 capital punishment 无可厚非，问题是如果我们能证明 capital punishment 是 cost-effective，我们是否可以无视绝对的道德原则实施 capital punishment 呢？从作者的描述看，capital punishment 确实耗费了不少经费，但如果仅仅从 high cost 的角度看问题，这里涉及的不是 capital punishment 本身的问题，而是实施方法问题。如果采用更快、更简单的行刑方法，大大降低实施成本，capital punishment 是否比 life sentence（无期徒刑）更省钱呢？

第四段讨论的是主张里的第三个核心词 slow process，也就是效率问题：

In addition, using the death penalty is a very slow process. At least 97 percent of all death-row prisoners are not executed on time. As a result, the waiting list for executions grows year after year. If the U.S. legal system executed one inmate every day, it would still take 30 years to empty all of the cells on death row. A process this slow does not make sense.

与经济角度一样，效率问题涉及的也是 capital punishment 的实施问题，而不是 capital punishment 本身的问题。从这个角度看，假如能提高效率，capital punishment 似乎可以实施。如果是这样，绝对的道德原则是否要遵守呢？

作者在结尾更是凸显了主张里后两个核心词语与第一个核心词的冲突：

> In conclusion, capital punishment should be dropped from our legal system. People should see that it is morally wrong. If not, then common sense should tell them that it doesn't work well since it is so expensive and such a slow process.

许多议论文的标题并没有直接提出议论文的主张，如 Is chocolate the answer?[①]。这个标题似乎告诉我们课文要论证的是"Whether chocolate is the answer"。要确认这篇文章的主张，我们必须要搞清楚究竟巧克力是什么问题的答案：

> **Have you ever wondered what makes people happy? Why are some people on cloud nine while others are always down in the dumps? What's the secret? Is it pots of money, good health, loving relationships, owning the latest gadget or simply chocolate?**[②]
>
> The latest World Happiness Report says that prosperity is not the main reason for happiness. If you suffer real hardship, you are unlikely to be happy, but once your basic needs are met, money and material things become less of a necessity. Happiness depends more on recognizing the things you have and appreciating them, rather than getting more things. Yes, money can buy you the latest smartphone, tablet or fashion item, and you might

---

① 邹为诚. 普通高中教科书　英语　选择性必修第一册［M］. 上海：上海教育出版社，2021：6-7. 请参阅"第七章　语篇的词汇关系"。
② 课文第一段黑体字是提示语，并不是正文的开始。

get a kick out of owning these material objects, but this enjoyment is usually short-lived. Remember all those presents you got for your birthday when you were little? You were over the moon when you opened them, but not for long. A month later, they were lying abandoned at the bottom of a drawer. And have you forgotten those delicious chocolates that made you feel really happy when you were eating them, but ill after you'd finished them all?

It seems that deep, long-lasting happiness comes from intangible things, rather than things like chocolates and smartphones. One essential factor is human relationships. People who have the support of family members and also have strong friendships are more likely to be happy. Feeling protected and respected and knowing you can trust in the people around you is vital. But happiness means you have to give and take. Performing acts of kindness and generosity on a regular basis, for example, listening to a friend in need or carrying a neighbour's shopping, will make you feel on top of the world. Even a simple smile can work wonders. In fact, they say that one smile makes a person feel as good as eating 2,000 bars of chocolate (not all at once, of course!).

It's not surprising that health is another key contributor to happiness. Poor health will certainly make you feel down in the mouth. But being healthy and staying healthy require some effort. A healthy diet is crucial and so is regular exercise. Laziness will not make you happy. Exercising for 20 to 30 minutes a day helps to reduce stress and anxiety and makes you feel more positive and optimistic because it releases endorphins (feel-good chemicals). So, if you've been feeling blue and worrying too much about your exams, get exercising. You'll also find that you sleep better.

Talking of sleep, do you often wake up feeling miserable? If so, it's probably because you haven't had enough of it. Teenagers tend to go to bed too late and have to get up early, so many suffer from a lack of sleep. Tiredness will certainly affect your happiness levels and put you in a bad mood. It also affects your ability to concentrate and may slow your growth. So if you want to be happy and do well at school, try to get at least eight hours of sleep a night. Now that you know the theory, it's time to put it all into practice. Smile, everyone!

课文的第一句就提到了 happiness 与 prosperity 的关系：

The latest World Happiness Report says that prosperity is not the main reason for happiness.

这句话也提示课文要论证的具体问题，即"Whether chocolate is the answer to happiness"。

作者在这篇课文里并没有直接给出 happiness 的定义。在这句之后，作者给出了 happiness 的前提条件。只有当生活基本需求满足时，我们才可能感受幸福：

If you suffer real hardship, you are unlikely to be happy, but once your basic needs are met, money and material things become less of a necessity.

为了更好地理解课文，我们需要考虑 happiness 的定义。按照 *Britannica* 的定义，happiness 是一种主观感受：

Happiness, in psychology, a state of emotional well-being that a person experiences either in a narrow sense, when good things happen in a specific moment, or more broadly, as a positive evaluation of one's life and accomplishments overall—that is, subjective well-being.[1]

---

① https://www.britannica.com/topic/happiness.

作者的思路与 *Britannica* 的定义应该是基本一致的：

Happiness depends more on recognizing the things you have and appreciating them, rather than getting more things.

recognizing 和 appreciating 就是精神或情感的体验。作者接着对这句话做了简单的解释：

Yes, money can buy you the latest smartphone, tablet or fashion item, and you might <u>get a kick out of</u> owning these material objects, but <u>this enjoyment</u> is usually <u>short-lived</u>.

作者用 a kick 表示物质带来的快感（pleasure）主要是感性的。值得注意的是，作者在这句里用的是 enjoyment，不是 happiness。虽然有关快乐（pleausre）和幸福（happiness）的区别有各种假说，但基本共识是快乐主要是感官表层的，外界刺激停止后，快感也就随之消失了：

Pleasure is when you feel good and enjoy what you are doing. External stimuli usually cause pleasure and often involve the five senses. ... Pleasure often only lasts for a while since the attention moves to other matters soon ...[1]

幸福是内心深层的情感，超越感官的控制：

---

[1] https://www.successconsciousness.com/blog/happiness-fun/pleasure-and-happiness/.

Happiness is different. It is an inner sensation that does not depend on the five senses.[①]

课文的第一段中，作者对物质和幸福的关系进行了论证，以证明物质带来的快感是短暂的：

You were over the moon when you opened them, but not for long.

作者在这段里提到了出现在标题里的 chocolate：

And have you forgotten those delicious chocolates that made you feel really happy when you were eating them, but ill after you'd finished them all?

与提到其他物质名词时不同的是，作者这里将 chocoloate 与 happy 联系在一起。不过，值得注意的是作者在时间状语里用了进行体 were eating，对幸福的持续时间进行了暗示。进行体的选择表明在作者看来幸福只是发生在 eating 的时候。作者接着指出了 chocolate 的负作用："ill after you'd finished them all"。这显然在进一步提示 chocolate 的物质属性。

既然如此，那作者为什么要提 chocolate？为什么要论证它是否能作为幸福的答案呢？ chocolate 与 smartphone 等其他物质有区别吗？如果我们根据课文的宏观语境，调动有关 chocolate 的知识资源，我们会发现作者的选择是有深意的：

① https://www.successconsciousness.com/blog/happiness-fun/pleasure-and-happiness/.

The brain often releases chemicals known as neurotransmitters to control how neurons communicate with each other in the body. The chemicals are known as endorphins.

Endorphins interact with brain receptors to trigger positive emotions or feelings in your body, and reduce the perception of pain. The neurotransmitters can affect your feelings and actions directly depending on the circumstance ...

Cocoa (the primary ingredient used to make chocolates), according to various studies, triggers the brain to release endorphins, the "feel good" hormones. ...[1]

根据科学的解释，含有特殊成分的 chocolate 确实能给我们带来 feelings of happiness。既然 chocolate 能带来 happiness，那为什么 "Chocolate is not the answer" 呢？

作者在第二段展开了为什么 "Chocolate is not the answer" 的论证。作者首先指出，他 / 她所讲的 happiness 是源于 "intangible things" 的 "deep, long-lasting happiness"。作者用 intangible 这个词是有重要考虑的。tangible 是物质的，intangible 则是非物质的。如作者前面所描述的那样，chocolate 虽然能给我们带来幸福感，但这种幸福还是源于物质刺激。但凡物质触发的感觉都会很快消亡的。要想让幸福感长久，幸福就必须源于非物质的事物。

intangible things 究竟指的是什么呢？作者选择了三个内容：human relationships, health and sleep。

作者讨论这三个内容时所选择的角度与讨论 happiness 用的 recognize and appreciate 有呼应。这两个动词都预设主动行为。有关

---

[1] https://acadofchoc.com/why-endorphins-is-linked-to-chocolates/.

human relationship，作者这样写道：

People who have the support of family members and also have strong friendships are more likely to be happy. Feeling protected and respected and knowing you can trust in the people around you is vital.

如何能做到这些呢？作者提出要实现这种可能，还需要我们有主动的作为：

But happiness means you have to give and take. Performing acts of kindness and generosity on a regular basis, ...

作者在这段末尾提出：

Even a simple smile can work wonders. In fact, they say that one smile makes a person feel as good as eating 2,000 bars of chocolate (not all at once, of course!).

作者讨论 health 的时候也强调了主动性：

But being healthy and staying healthy require some effort.

因为锻炼不仅能使身体好，而且也能刺激体内 endorphins 的释放：

Exercising for 20 to 30 minutes a day helps to reduce stress and anxiety and makes you feel more positive and optimistic because it releases endorphins (feel-good chemicals).

作者最后提出了睡眠的重要性，因为睡眠不足，也会影响幸福度：

Tiredness will certainly affect your happiness levels and put you in a bad mood.

这也不难理解。疲惫容易造成 disabling，导致 anxiety, depression 或 disorders[①]。和讨论 health 一样，作者的角度也是我们应该主动去改善睡眠：

... try to get at least eight hours of sleep a night. Now that you know the theory, it's time to put it all into practice. Smile, everyone!

写到这里，也许 chocolate 不能作为答案的原因似乎有点清晰了。幸福感只能是通过对非物质内容的主动追求才有实现的可能。虽然 chocolate 含有让人兴奋的物质成分，但它只是让人被动地感受快感。

这篇课文的目的显然不是解释为什么"Chocolate is not the answer to happiness"，而是说服我们接受作者有关幸福来源于非物质主动追求的主张。文章虽然很短，但作者的论证过程却有较强的科学依据。

本章推荐书目

[1] 曲卫国. 思辨与明理——高中英语议论文写作教学指导 [M]. 上海：上海教育出版社，2021.
[2] Meyer, B. J. F. and M. N. Ray. 2011. Structure strategy

---

① https://www.ncbi.nlm.nih.gov/pmc/articles/PMC1124000/.

interventions: Increasing reading comprehension of expository text. *International Electronic Journal of Elementary Education*. 4(1): 127–152.

[3] Roehling, J. V., M. Hebert, J. R. Nelson and J. J. Bohaty. 2017. Text Structure Strategies for Improving Expository Reading Comprehension. *The Reading Teacher*. 71(1):71–82.

[4] Rottenberg, A. and D. H. Winchell. 2017. *Elements of Argument: A Text and Reader*. 12th Edition. Boston: Bedford/ St. Martin's.

第十章　立场

导引问题：

- 为什么要了解语篇里作者的立场？
- 作者的立场表达有哪几种方式？

本章提要：

　　立场（Stance）是作者在语篇中表达的**主观倾向**，是态度的上位词。作者的立场不仅决定语篇传递什么样的信息，还决定了信息结构的构成。识别作者的立场是语篇理解的重要内容，是培养独立思考和批判性思维能力不可缺少的重要一环。语篇的立场表达分为显性和隐性。所谓显性，指的是作者直白、不加掩饰地明示自己的立场。隐性表达则指作者出于某种考虑，隐晦地暗示自己的立场。立场表达是通过**语言**、**信息**、**结构**、**语体**、**视角**等各个层面的语篇策略实现的。

一、概说

　　语篇理解至少有三个维度：① 语篇的话题，即作者在说些什么；② 语篇的主题，即作者想通过语篇传递什么样的信息；③ 作者的立场，即作者为什么要传递这样的信息。

　　传统的阅读教学通常重视的是前两个问题，对第三个问题关注不够充分。然而，任何语篇，哪怕是科学报告都会受到作者立场的影响。作者的立场不仅决定语篇传递什么样的信息，还决定了信息结构以及信息用于什么目的。识别作者的立场是语篇理解的重要内容，是培养独立思考和批判性思维能力不可缺少的重要一环。

　　"立场"指的是作者在语篇中表达的主观倾向。与"立场"有密切关联的是"态度"（attitude）。一般认为，立场是态度的上位词。Biber 等学者在他们对立场的定义里除了态度，还提到了情感、价值判断等内容：

> In addition to communicating propositional content, speakers and writers commonly express personal feelings, attitudes, value judgments, or assessments; that is, they express 'a stance.' (1999: 966)

　　语篇的立场表达分为显性和隐性。所谓显性，指的是作者直白、不加掩饰地明示自己的立场。显性表达通常有明确的语言提示：

> I really <u>enjoyed</u> this show because the teacher had such a positive effect on the students.
>
> I <u>prefer</u> to think that, as our population grows, we can celebrate not the similarities but the wonderful differences of the human race.

　　在显性表达立场的语篇里，作者的立场常常是主题的一部分。理解主题的同时也了解了作者的立场。

　　隐性表达则指作者出于某种考虑，隐晦地暗示自己的立场。在这类语篇中，由于作者故意掩饰自己的主观倾向，主题的破解并不一定能昭示作者的立场。隐性表达一般会通过语言进行暗示：

An experiment in education[①]

这个标题虽然没有明示作者的立场，但作者选择 experiment 这个词就暗含现有的教育有改善的余地。作者选择这个科学色彩较强的词也提示作者赞成这样的尝试。

句式有时也可以用来提示立场，如：

Is chocolate the answer?[②]

作者选择疑问句式暗示他 / 她可能不认可 "Chocolate is the answer" 这种主张。不过，问题句式的立场提示受到语境的严重制约。有些语篇的标题似乎很中立，基本没有给出任何立场的提示，如：

A day in the life of a digital human[③]

这篇语篇作者的立场需要阅读正文才可能了解。

有许多因素制约作者立场表达方式的选择。我们这里主要强调语篇的体裁类型和读者定位（positioning）。议论文类体裁显性表达立场的通常比较多，因为议论文的目的是说服读者，所以作者通常

① 邹为诚.普通高中教科书 英语 必修第二册［M］.上海：上海教育出版社，2020：24-25.请参阅"第四章 视角"。
② 邹为诚.普通高中教科书 英语 选择性必修第一册［M］.上海：上海教育出版社，2021：6-7.请参阅"第九章 体裁：非叙事类"。
③ 邹为诚.普通高中教科书 英语 选择性必修第二册［M］.上海：上海教育出版社，2021：24-25.具体分析请参阅下面的讨论。

不会闪烁立场。说明文则不一样。说明文的目的是提供解释性信息，因而作者通常不会彰显自己的立场，会努力使说明文显得客观、中立。当然，解释框架选择本身就提示了作者的立场。叙事类体裁的语篇则比较复杂。文学作品作者的立场一般通过作品的主题表达，但新闻类的叙事语篇则未必如此。由于客观报道是读者对新闻的基本期待，作者的立场常常通过事件报道的视角、信息、信息源选择等方面表现出来[①]。

读者是作者选择立场表达方式的另外一个重要考量因素。作者会根据语篇所针对的不同读者选择显性或隐性立场表达。显性表达立场的好处是旗帜鲜明，方便说服与作者立场一致的读者，但也容易与持有不同立场的读者产生对立。过激的表达更可能与立场不确定的读者之间产生隔阂。由于隐性表达立场貌似客观，它争取各类读者认可的可能性更大。采用隐性立场的语篇涉及更多、更细的操控。

学界有许多立场分析的方法，我们这里主要介绍 Biber 等人的研究[②]。他们主要分析副词或其他语法手段在立场表达中的作用。他们的分析对识别显性立场表达有非常大的帮助：

(1) Stance adverbials

Unfortunately, we cannot do anything about it.

He is kind of talked himself into it.

(2) Stance complement clauses

I just hope that I've plugged it in properly.

It's amazing that judges can get away with outrageous

---

① 请参阅"第五章 语篇结构Ⅰ：信息结构"。

② 本书这里的介绍较为简单，详细内容请参阅 Biber 等（1999）。这里的例子选自于 Biber 等（1999）。

statements.

(3) Modals and semi-modals

I <u>might be</u> up before you go.

She <u>has to go</u> to a special school.

(4) Stance noun + prepositional phrase

They deny <u>the possibility of a death wish</u> lurking amidst the gardens of lust.

(5) Premodifying stance adverb

I am <u>so</u> happy for you. Honestly, I'm <u>really</u> happy for you.[①]

有必要强调的是，立场表达是通过语言、信息、结构、语体、视角等各个层面的语篇策略操控实现的。除了副词和特定的语法结构，作者的词语、视角、信息选择等是立场分析的主要内容。

二、立场与教学

传统阅读教学通常关注的是语篇的内容和主题，对作者的立场分析相对较少。随着 Biber 等学者理论在外语教学界的引介，语篇的立场开始得到关注。然而，受他们分析方法的影响，目前大多数讨论聚焦的是语篇立场的显性表达，对隐性立场表达重视得不够。

分析立场的前提是对语篇提示的识别。即便是隐性的立场表达，作者还是会给出提示的，因为作者的根本意图是让读者从他们的立场去看问题。显性与隐性表达的主要区别是明说与暗示，两者的差别只是度的问题。立场识别重点要考虑以下三个基本问题：

---

① Biber (1999): 967–8.

（1）作者为什么说这些？

（2）作者为什么这么说？

（3）如果换个立场，作者的所说是否成立？

我们这里主要讨论立场表达的两种策略：视角提示和信息提示，即作者是如何通过视角和信息选择提示立场的。要强调的是，作者的立场表达是全方位的，涉及所有层面的策略。

三、立场分析

1. 视角提示[①]

由于视角是语篇叙述或议论的切入点，切入点的选择自然与作者的立场关系密切，因此语篇的视角常常会提示作者的立场。显性视角的提示通常选用明确表达立场的词语，如：

Blame your brain[②]

这个标题的祈使句句式和 blame 这个动词在明确告知读者语篇视角的同时也提示了作者的立场。

隐性视角提示则相对隐晦，作者一般会选择相对中性的词语暗示自己的立场，如：

Making school meaningful[③]

---

① 请参阅"第四章　视角"。

② 邹为诚．普通高中教科书　英语　必修第二册［M］．上海：上海教育出版社，2020：6-7. 请参阅"第六章　语篇结构Ⅱ：话题结构和主题结构"。

③ 邹为诚．普通高中教科书　英语　选择性必修第三册［M］．上海：上海教育出版社，2022：6-7.

这篇课文的标题通过 make ... meaningful 暗示现实中的 school①
存在问题，这个词语的选择提示作者对现实教育的批判立场。

作者在课文里并没有直接陈述他／她的批判立场。课文的第一
段给出的信息间接提示作者的批判是从哪个群体的角度展开的：

Wagner Iworrigan, a 17-year-old high school senior on St Lawrence
Island in Alaska, knows a lot about biology and maths. He's an expert at
telling whether a walrus is too sick to eat, if the weather is likely to turn
dangerous, and the best angle for throwing a spear at a whale.

这段的第一句给出了三个信息。首先是人物：Wagner Iworrigan
的名字表明了他原住民的身份归属。其次是地点：St Lawrence
Island in Alaska。这是一个以原住民为主的尚未"开发"的岛屿：

St. Lawrence Island is largely undeveloped and is home to about 1,400
people who live in the villages of Gampbell and Savoonga on the northern
coast. Residents are 95.5 percent Alaska Native or part Alaska Native. The
isolation of the island has helped maintain their traditional St Lawrence
Yupik culture, their language, and a subsistence lifestyle based on marine
mammals.②

人物和地点的选择表明作者是从非主流文化的视角去审视现实
教育。第三个信息是"Wagner knows a lot about biology and maths"。
这个信息非常重要。这个信息进一步明确了他的锋芒所指。他质疑
的不是 Wagner 是否有能力学习学制教育的科目，或这些科目教育

---

① school 在这里的意思是学制教育，指 schooling, formal schooling。
② https://www.travelalaska.com/Destinations/Cities-Towns/St-Lawrence-Island.

本身有什么问题。

这段的第二句提示了 Wagner 的兴趣之所在。里面提到的 walrus, weather 和 whale 与原住民的生活息息相关，但它们不在学制教育的范围之内。虽然作者没有明说，但兴趣不在学制教育范围之内，这还是给出了具体的提示。

课文第二段的第一句就明确点出了这个问题：

Wagner might make a good scientist, but he's not planning on going to college.

虽然 Wagner 可能有做一个优秀科学家的潜质，但他却不打算进高校深造，因为他需要照顾兄弟姐妹，大学离他家太远。也许更重要的是他不太清楚高校的学习科目和他的生活有什么关联：

He's also unclear about what he would do with a degree: "We don't have a lot of jobs here," he says.

作者在第三段借学生之口对学制教育的关联性提出了质疑。学制教育的内容与当地生活方式大相径庭，因而对选择继续居住在岛屿上的年轻人没有什么帮助：

The benefits of a degree are not obvious to people who live on this remote island.

学制教育之所以不能使在岛上生活的年轻人受益，一个重要原因是学制教育内容并不能有效地帮助这些年轻人应对生活中的挑战：

"We want our children to achieve academically, but we need to be able to design programs that deal with the challenges they face day-to-day."

不仅不能应对挑战，由于学制教育的科目与岛屿的生活方式和文化没有关联，接受这样的教育会危及岛屿文化的生存：

Families also worry that sending children away to study in higher education could endanger the Yupik language and culture. ... Respect for the old ways and knowledge of traditions are disappearing.

课文的第六、第七段描写的是 The Yupik 原住民所面临的多方面的严峻挑战。许多年轻人已经放弃了传统的生活方式。学制教育在其中也起了推波助澜的作用。作者最后借助一位原住民的话指出，教育之所以出现这样的问题，是因为人们混淆了学制教育（school）与教育（education）的本质区别：

There's a distinction between education and school. Education is what Native people have been doing for their children since the beginning of time. School has been what has been imposed on people from outside.

作者在通篇课文里始终没有明确表达自己的立场，但他 / 她从原住民的视角去审视学制教育带来的问题，这毫无疑问地披露了作者的立场。作者选择用 Making school meaningful 这个相对宽泛的标题不正是表明 St. Lawrence Island 所面临的教育问题有普遍的意义吗？

The stuff in our lives[①] 这篇课文的立场表达也是很微妙的。首先，

_____

① 邹为诚.普通高中教科书　英语　选择性必修第三册［M］.上海：上海教育出版社，2022：30-31.

参照 *Longman Dictionary Online* 的解释，标题里的 stuff 应该有某种态度提示：

> informal, used when you are talking about things such as substances, materials, or groups of objects when you do not know what they are called, or it is not important to say exactly what they are.[1]

显然，对于珍视的东西，我们一般不会用 stuff。其次，标题里的 our 究竟是泛指还是特指？这也是需要思考的问题。

课文第一段明确课文是从 Elaine 和 Susie Hall 的视角去看她们母亲的囤积（hoarding）习惯：

> Elaine and Susie Hall live in a large house in a typical New Jersey suburb. They appear to be normal American teenagers, although appearances can be deceptive. The truth is that everyday life for the sisters is far from normal: things which we might take for granted, like cooking a meal or picking out a dress in front of the mirror, are incredibly difficult for the girls. Why? Because their mum, Sharon, is a compulsive hoarder. "We spend most of our time in a small area in the living room, just in front of the TV," complains Susie. "Mum's stuff has spread out everywhere. It's taken over our lives—it's total chaos!"

第一、第二句话的主语是 Elaine and Susie Hall。第三句的主语是 the truth，但 for the sisters 这个词组表明这话的角度也是这对姐妹的。虽然 because 这句的主语似乎是 Sharon，但其实 Sharon 是 their mum 的同位语，主语是 their mum。their 这个词也表明这句话的视

---

[1] https://www.ldoceonline.com/dictionary/stuff.

角还是这对姐妹的 [①]。这段最后以 Susie 的话结束,更是进一步表明了她们对视角的主宰。我们要考虑的问题是,这样的视角提示,或者说这对姐妹的立场与作者的立场有关系吗?

> In Sharon's house, every room is filled with piles of jazz records and CDs, mountains of clothes and stacks of magazines. The kitchen is impossible to use, so meals are cooked in a microwave in the garage and dishes are washed in the shower. Even making a cup of tea is next to impossible: the water kettle is hidden beneath a pile of clothes on top of an empty fish tank. All this stuff spread out at random around the house makes daily life a nightmare.

虽然第二段一开始有 Sharon's house,这似乎让人感觉是视角有可能切换到 Sharon 的角度,但由于这一段是紧接着 Susie 的埋怨 "Mum's stuff has spread out everywhere" 对 Sharon's house 所做的描述,且这段里的主语都是物体,这段顺着 Elaine 和 Susie Hall 视角的迹象非常明显。有两个地方特别值得一提,一个是 to use 这个不定式的主语没有标注,另一个是 making a cup of tea 这个动名词结构的主语也被隐去。把这些结构的主语理解为母亲或这对姐妹都可以。但第一段结束时 Susie 所说的 "Mum's stuff has spread out everywhere. It's taken over our lives—it's total chaos!" 与这段末尾的 "All this stuff spread out at random around the house makes daily life a nightmare." 相呼应,这很难让读者觉得这视角不是这对姐妹的。

更值得玩味的是,Susie 前面用的是 Mum's stuff,而作者这段一开始用的是 Sharon's house,由物体到房间的转换,自然会让读者产

---

① 请参阅"第四章 视角"。

生联想：由于母亲的 hoarding 习惯，她彻底霸占和统治了原本是属于三个人的房子。

标题和开始两段所设定的视角使读者只能选择从女儿的角度去看待母亲的行为。这对姐妹所看到的情景以及母亲 hoarding 习惯对她们生活的负面影响必然会触发读者的负面态度。作者并没有对此做任何消解，因此这个视角的选择应该是暴露了他／她的立场。

作者在第三段一开始明确了自己看问题的角度，他用的是 compulsive hoarding 这个术语。

Compulsive hoarding can be an extreme condition and this family has run out of space. But while it's true that most of us would never hoard to this extent, the fact is that many of us buy more things than we need and, once we have them, we're reluctant to throw them away.

compulsive hoarding 是心理学术语，专门用于描述 hoarding disorder：

Compulsive or pathological hoarding is a problematic behavior characterized by:

(1) acquiring and failing to throw out a large number of items that would appear to have little or no value to others, such as old magazines, containers, clothes, books, junk mail, receipts, notes, or lists

(2) severe cluttering of the person's home so that the home is no longer able to function as a viable living space

(3) significant distress or impairment in work or social life[1]

---

① https://www.verywellmind.com/hoarding-treatment-2510619.

作者的选择表明他把这种情况看成是病态行为。虽然作者在这段指出 hoarding 是普遍现象，我们或多或少都有这个习惯，而她只不过是程度上过于严重而已，表露出对 Sharon 情况的宽容和理解，但一旦将其归结为极端行为，compulsive hoarding 也就没有丝毫正面或积极价值可言。

作者对 hoarding 历史的简单追溯似乎想解释 hoarding 这种现象的历史原因，但作者在追溯历史时并没有区分 hoarding 和 compulsive hoarding，这更强化了对 hoarding 的负面认知：

> According to social scientists, people have been collecting stuff for centuries. About 15,000 years ago, primitive communities began to lose their nomadic ways and rely on stored food, resulting in a change in our material culture. Permanent homes were built as people acquired more objects, and these things soon became impossible to carry around. The loss of nomadic ways was not just thanks to agriculture, but also to the number of possessions people had.

作者接着尝试从现代消费文化理念去探讨原因。有意思的是，这段讨论的开始是 Sharon 的物品对 Elaine 正常学习的妨碍。junk 可以看作是 Elaine 的用语，但 the untidy living environment 这句评论显然是作者的直接介入。作者用 "unfortunately"（stance adverbial）更清晰地表明了立场：

> Back in New Jersey, Elaine is feeling increasingly annoyed by her mother's junk as she searches for a place to do her homework. The untidy living environment is a constant source of friction. In the end, she uses a heap of clothes as a temporary desk. "After a while you just put up with it," she

says. "You start thinking it's normal." In some ways it is normal, because <u>unfortunately</u> our modern consumer culture actively encourages us to own things. Advertisements convince us that we can't live without certain products and imply that these things can change our lives. It's very difficult to resist this culture, to opt out and buy less.

不过值得思考的是，作者引入现代消费文化理念似乎有两个问题。一是如果这种现象是现代消费文化造成的，那染上这种现象的应该是年轻人。而这篇课文却正好相反。二是现代消费文化的核心不是 hoarding，而是 consumption。consumption 意味着不断更新。广告在说服我们一定得拥有某些物品的同时，也不断地催促我们进行物品的更新换代。从这个角度看，现代消费文化与 compulsive hoarding 未必一定有关联。如果作者说的 "It's very difficult to resist this culture, to opt out and buy less." 成立，那为什么 Elaine 和 Susie 能抵制这种习惯呢？我们要问的问题是，作者为什么要选择这个框架去解释这种现象呢？

作者接着又提出了心理学的解释：

So why is it so difficult to get rid of things? One explanation is that people are naturally resistant to change and prefer things the way they are; the end result is loads of clutter, taking up valuable space. Psychologists also talk about the "endowment effect", or the way we attach more value to things once we own them. For example, you might not use your old MP3 player, but it still has "value" because it belongs to you. Ownership is as important as usefulness. But as Elaine says, "Mum needs to ask herself: if I didn't have it, would I go out and buy it? If the answer is 'no', then she should bin it."

按照心理学 endowment effect 的解释，物品的拥有者会因为物品对他们有某种情感或象征意义而不愿意丢弃它们。endowment effect 预设 "Ownership is as important as usefulness."。从这个角度看，Sharon 的 hoarding 就有了正当性。作者用 "as Elaine says" 这个结构表示他 / 她同意 Elaine 的质疑："if I didn't have it, would I go out and buy it? If the answer is 'no', then she should bin it."。不过，Elaine 的质疑是否合理呢？ endowment effect 产生于拥有之后。也就是说正是因为有了，才会觉得有价值。

作者在下面一段用 sentimental value 和 emotional currency 两个术语对 hoarding 的原因做了进一步的解释：

"Sentimental value" is another reason for not <u>junking things</u>. Many of the objects we keep have connections to a place, an event or a person in our past, such as birthday cards from a grandparent or an old football shirt from an important match. These objects, like Sharon's record collection, have emotional currency, which is why we never throw them out.

作者这里说的 emotional currency 自然指的不是 money，而是指这些物品具有 Levinson 在她那本 *Emotional Currency* 书里所说的情结："emotionally charged; deeply personal and culturally complex[①]"。既然如此，母亲的 hoarding 还是有充分理由的。然而，作者在这里再次用了 junk 这个词语，而且这次他用的是动词 junking things。这又是为什么？

文章的最后一段作者用 stance adverbial "luckily" 再次明确自己

---

① Levinson, K. 2011. *Emotional Currency: A Woman's Guide to Building Healthy Relationship with Money.* New York: Celestial Arts.

立场。作者这里说的 a happy ending 完全是从 Elaine 和 Susie 的角度出发：

> Luckily, Elaine and Susie's story has a happy ending. Sharon has finally got help with her hoarding and has slowly started to clear out their home. "She had to," says Elaine, "or our family would have fallen apart." It's been a few months, but the girls are helping out and things are gradually getting better.

这段的第二句里用了 their home 而不是第二段的 Sharon's house。这意味着房子不再由母亲独霸，house 也换成了 home。*Longman Dictionary Online* 词典对两个单词的区别很好地揭示了名词切换的含义：

> **house:** a building that someone lives in, especially one that has more than one level and is intended to be used by one family[1]
>
> **home:** the place where you came from or where you usually live, especially when this is the place where you feel happy and comfortable[2]

Sharon 虽然在第二句担任主语，但谓语是 has finally got help，她其实是被动的接受方。Elaine 说得很清楚："She had to"。与课文的第一段遥相呼应，这段的主语是 Elaine 和 Susie。"Elaine and Susie's story ..., says Elaine, ... the girls are helping out ..."。最后的 "things are gradually getting better" 自然也是由这对姐妹判断的。

作者立场主导的视角自然影响了我们对 Sharon 的 hoarding 习

---

① https://www.ldoceonline.com/dictionary/house.

② https://www.ldoceonline.com/dictionary/home.

惯的判断。不过,我们读完课文后也许可以换个角度问问题:姑娘们是高兴了,但她们的母亲呢?

2. 信息提示 [①]

前面提到的 Making school meaningful 和 The stuff in our lives 的标题都有视角提示,这些提示提供了处理语篇信息的角度,帮助我们理解作者在处理这些信息时的立场。但也有许多语篇,标题里的视角提示很微妙,作者的立场需要结合语篇提供的信息内容才可能破解。当然还有不少语篇不仅在标题,甚至在开始段落里都没有明确的视角提示。分析信息选择和信息排列是揭示作者在这类语篇暗设立场的有效途径。

课文 A day in the life of a digital human [②] 的标题非常微妙地提示了作者的视角,但对这微妙的破解需要结合考虑这篇课文的信息选择和排列。之所以说这篇课文的标题很微妙,因为乍一看,A day in the life of a digital human 似乎没有给出任何视角提示。与 Making school meaningful 和 The stuff in our lives 不同的是,这个标题里的词语似乎都属于中性。但如果我们结合课文提供的信息看,便会发现作者实际上提供了确切的视角,也就是说作者在标题里暗示了他的立场。

标题里暗示视角的词语是 a digital human。a digital human 是:

an avatar that can produce a whole range of human body language. [③]

---

① 参阅"第五章 语篇结构Ⅰ:信息结构"。

② 邹为诚. 普通高中教科书 英语 选择性必修第二册 [M]. 上海:上海教育出版社,2021:24–25.

③ https://www2.deloitte.com/nl/nl/pages/customer-and-marketing/articles/digital-human.html.

所谓的 avatar，指的是 an electronic image 或者说 human-like virtual being。按照这个界定，这篇课文应该讨论的是电子虚拟人生活中的一天。其实不然。这篇课文第一段就明确说了文章的主角是真人——teenager Song Lili，不是 avatar：

> As part of our week on digital humans, we asked teenager Song Lili to keep a digital diary. Psychologist Mia Graham analysed the results.

既然课文记录和讨论的是有名有姓真人的一天的生活，作者为什么要用 a digital human 这个词语呢？这个词语的选择难道不是在暗示作者的立场吗？

作者选择了与 Song Lili 一天五个时间点有关的信息。第一个时间点是 7:30 a.m.：

> I'm usually on social media first thing and today was no different. I actually logged in while I was still in bed, just to see what my friends had posted the night before and to catch up with the gossip. Over breakfast, I did a status update and within 30 minutes, I had a dozen likes and two comments. Nothing special about that—it was just another ordinary day. I bet everyone does the same thing.

作者在这个时间点上又选择了两个时间点的信息：起床前和吃早饭。我们可以从这些信息里了解到，Song 的一天是从社交媒体开始的。她还没起床就已经上网了：

> I actually logged in while I was still in bed ...

作者给出的信息非常具体：within 30 minutes。

Over breakfast, I did a status update and within 30 minutes, I had a dozen likes and two comments.

我们可以想象一下，对于一个上学的学生来说，一顿早饭通常会花多少时间呢？特别值得一提的是作者提到了"it was just another ordinary day"。这个信息显然在提醒读者，Song 的日记内容反映的是她一贯的生活方式。另外一句 "I bet everyone does the same thing." 表明，Song 认为，她所记录的生活是有典型性和代表性的。

第二个时间点是 8:45 a.m.。在这个时间点上，作者选择的是上学路上：

As I was walking to school, I noticed that I'd been tagged in a picture. I looked absolutely awful, so I clicked "untag". It's stressed me out, so I'm currently checking the latest updates again. I pray that no one will recognize me in the picture.

耐人寻味的是作者提供的 Song 在社交媒体上关注的内容，以及由此引起的焦虑：

I noticed that I'd been tagged in a picture.

其实，我们在社交媒体上会看到五花八门的内容。作者为什么要选 picture 这个内容呢？

第三个时间点是 12:30 p.m.：

At lunchtime, a friend posted quite a nasty comment about another friend on my profile. The two girls recently had a row, but they need to get over it and make up with each other. I deleted the comment because I don't want to get involved.

这是 Song 午饭时间在社交媒体上关心的内容。她的一位朋友在她的个人空间对另外一位朋友发布不友好的评论。这两位女孩子发生了争吵，Song 不想让自己受到牵连，因而删除了这条评论。这条信息又传递什么样的观点呢？

第四个时间点是 5:30 p.m.。为什么选择 5:30 呢？这可能是晚饭前 Song 可以自主支配的时间。她还是在网上。她发布了一条有关她喜欢男孩的帖子：

At home, I wrote a post about a boy I quite like. He left his mobile in class today and I found it. It was nice to talk to him. He was friendly and we have a lot in common—we really hit it off!

Song 用这段帖子记录她对那位男孩一拍即合、一见如故的感觉。作者把她发这样的帖子挑出来又是出于什么目的呢？

文章最后记录的时间点是 11：00 p.m.。11 点应该是 Song 做完作业准备睡觉的空闲时间。她在这段有限的时间里又干了什么呢？

I updated my status before I went to bed and I had two friend requests, which I accepted. I didn't know one of them, but that's why social media is so exciting. You can chat with people who you possibly wouldn't run into in your everyday life and you can contact people who you haven't seen for years ...

　　她还是在网上，关注社交媒体的事情。这次是关于素不相识的人要求加入她社交空间的事情。虽然 Song 不认识他们，但她还是马上接受了。作者专门提到与陌生人或许久不见的朋友在虚拟世界建立联系是 Song 喜欢网络世界的一个重要原因。

　　作者这五个时间点的选择是偶然的吗？串联这五个时间点的逻辑是什么呢？这些信息与 a digital human 有什么关联呢？这些都是需要我们好好考虑的问题。特别需要注意的是，这些都是 Song 可以自主支配的时间点。换言之，Song 除了学校生活和睡觉以外，从她在这些时间点上的所作所想看，她生活的自主时间部分基本被网络占据了。作者对这些自主时间点的选择可能是有深意的。自主时间最能反映一个人的内心生活。如果一个人的内心生活只有虚拟网络世界，我们可以毫不夸张地说这个人被网络控制了。从 Song 绝大多数的社交活动看，她确实是以 avatar 的身份和形象出现的。也许在这个意义上，她还真成了一个 digital human。

　　有血有肉的人成为 digital human 有什么问题吗？作者通过 Mia 的评论表达了自己的立场。Mia 对第一个时间点的评论是：

It's natural for humans to share experiences and open up to people. Lili enjoys being part of a community. She likes it when people from this community comment on her status.

　　Mia 的评论角度很有意思。她认为 "share experiences and open up to people" 是人的自然需要。如果查阅 Song 的日记，我们会发现她的这个自然需求竟然是用非自然、虚拟方式实现的。

　　Mia 对第二个时间点的评论是：

On social media, Lili is always on display and she is under intense pressure to consistently "look good". In a recent survey, 41% of teens said their online image was extremely important; consequently, they made more of an effort to look good at all times. However, friends can compromise this image by tagging you in photos, saying where you've been or what you've said. You might not like it, but you can't stop friends sharing information about you.

Mia 的评论提到了两个问题，一是 consistent pressure to "look good"，另外一个是虚拟世界对自己形象的不可控性。这意味着人在虚拟世界里丧失了独立和自主。

Mia 对第三个时间点的评论是：

It's easy to pick on people in the digital world. Cyberbullies can post an ugly picture or a nasty comment and reach a wide audience. And in an online world, you can't see people break down and weep. As a result, you're less sympathetic and less likely to stick up for them. Lili did the right thing when she deleted the comment.

Mia 指出人在数字世界里不仅脆弱，易受攻击，而且由于虚拟世界没有真人接触，人会变得缺乏同情心，不会挺身而出帮助他人。意味深长的是，Mia 对 Song 明哲保身的做法给予了肯定。这似乎意味着在虚拟世界，不轻易表达感情的自我保护是最佳的策略。

Mia 对第四个时间点的评论是：

Like so many of us, Lili shares personal details of her life online. The problem is that these details stay on the web forever and are easy to dig up again. In a recent survey, 40% of teens said they were concerned about who could view their online activities.

They also worried about how these activities might eventually be perceived by parents, teachers, future employers or their peers. They are right to be concerned about who is watching. The Internet never forgets, so Lili needs to think before she posts. The exposure of personal information online may be dangerous: it is easy to become a victim of cybercrime.

在 Mia 看来，由于虚拟世界参与人群的无限制和不固定，个人的情感极可能遭到别人的滥用和亵渎。Song 在虚拟世界分享自己内心情感的方式不仅无法保护自己的隐私，而且会使自己成为网络犯罪的受害者。

Mia 对最后一个时间点的评论是：

Lili's right—it's good to talk, but she needs to be extremely careful about who she talks to. The average teen has 237 social media friends; however, they have talked to only a fraction of these people in real life. Essentially, it's a question of trust, so before you accept a friend request, consider this: who is this person and do I really want them to read my posts? Don't forget there are people behind the machines.

Mia 的评论告诉我们，对人类交往而言，最重要的不是机器，而是真人。然而，现在青少年虽然可以倾诉的朋友似乎很多，但这些朋友都是虚拟存在，他们在现实生活中真正的朋友很少。虚拟世界的交往因而会动摇 trust 这个人类沟通的基石。

作者是从两个互相关联的角度选择信息的：一是数字人。随着数字网络技术的发展，虚拟世界替代了人的现实世界，虚拟的交际代替了自然沟通。结果人被数字化，成为了数字人。另外一个角度是 Mia 的评论，即从人性和自然需求的角度去看待虚拟世界对人产生的负面影响。作者确实是按照自然时间排列信息，好像没有刻意选择的故意，其实未必。自然时间被虚拟内容排满，这含义是不言而喻的。

如果说 A day in the life of a digital human 在标题里对视角有隐晦的提示，在 From here to eternity① 这篇课文的标题里，我们找不到任何提示。课文的第一段也没有提示。我们需要了解课文提供的大部分或全部信息后才能做出判断。

课文的第一段介绍了 Tyler 有规律的日常生活。值得注意的是作者选择的几个细节，要考虑的问题是为什么选择这几个细节？它们有什么代表性？

Tyler Jamieson has a strict daily routine. He goes jogging every morning at 6:00 a.m., reads the newspapers, then sets off to work an 18-hour day. Tyler is the CEO of a huge corporation and works in a pressured and stressful environment. But despite this—and the fact that he is nearly 100 years old—he has no serious health problems. In fact, Tyler expects to live for many centuries more. His original body "died" several years ago, but his brain lives on in a robot.

第一个细节：goes jogging every morning at 6:00 a.m.

第二个细节：reads the newspapers,

第三个细节：sets off to work an 18-hour day

第四个细节：the CEO of a huge corporation

① 邹为诚.普通高中教科书　英语　选择性必修第四册［M］.上海：上海教育出版社，2022：32-33.

第五个细节：works in a pressured and stressful environment

第六个细节：100 years old

第七个细节：no serious health problems

第八个细节：expects to live for many centuries more

第九个细节：body "died" several years ago, but his brain lives on in a robot

作者在第二段提出了课文讨论的核心议论：

This may sound like an idea from a science fiction film script, but it actually comes from a serious business proposal at the very frontier of scientific knowledge. Some years ago, a media entrepreneur called Dmitry Itskov sent a letter to billionaires offering them a new lease of life. Itskov had 30 scientists working on an immortality project whose aim was to transplant a human mind into a robot body in the near future. "Our research has the potential to free you, as well as the majority of all people on our planet, from disease, old age and even death," claimed Itskov in his letter.

作者在第三段、第四段、第五段和第六段讨论的是一旦这个项目成功后的后果。注意作者选择有关这个项目正面和负面后果的观点以及相关观点的呈现方式。作者在第三段的提问方式似乎是中立的：

Such research may fundamentally transform our lives. Most people's shelf life is a mere 85 to 89 years, so it's hardly surprising that we want to put off the inevitable. Even one of the world's oldest men, 116-year-old Jiroemon Kimura, insisted that although he was tired, he didn't want to die. But is eternal life as attractive as it sounds? What would be the consequences of immortality?

之所以说似乎，因为作者看似不带任何情绪地陈述一个人人都想长寿的渴望，但如果长寿是大家都期待的，而长寿必然有吸引力。那作者提出"is eternal life as attractive as it sounds"这样的问题，难道不是对这个期待提出质疑？

从正负面信息量和分布看，作者接下来的信息安排是顺着质疑展开的。作者先讨论长寿带来的问题，第四、第五两段是有关负面后果。第四段聚焦的是长生不老对个人生活的负面影响：

From a purely practical point of view, immortality poses quite a few problems. The most obvious is the increase in overpopulation, putting more pressure on our planet's already limited resources. Immortality would also cause a number of almost unimaginable problems in society. Crime rates would rise because criminals would no longer be put off by a few years in prison, and how could the state afford "life sentences"? Another big change would be in the length of our working life. People could spend thousands of years in the same job, resulting in severe depression. There would be fewer career opportunities for younger, less experienced generations too.

首先，作者声称选择呈现信息的视角是 purely practical。purely 似乎是中性的副词，但在这个具体语境里还是有立场暗示的。作者的言外之意是，如果这些不带个人清晰色彩的讨论成立，那长寿的负面后果就成立。不过 problem 这个词暴露了他/她的立场。*Longman Dictionary Online* 的释义基本是负面的：

a. a situation that causes difficulties;
b. something wrong with your health or with part of your body

Longman Dictionary Online 特别提出了建议：

In writing, people sometimes prefer to use the word issue rather than problem, as it sounds more neutral and less negative.[1]

Longman Dictionary Online 明确告诉我们，problem 涉及判断，不是一个中性词。与 problem 呼应，作者提供了以下几个方面的信息：

a. overpopulation vs. limited resources

b. rise of the crime rates

c. the length of our working life

d. fewer career opportunities for younger, less experienced generations

这些问题基本涵盖了个人生活的主要方面：资源、安全、休闲和机会。我们要问的是：这些问题难道是永远长寿造成的？在还没有实现永远长寿的今天，我们难道没有苦于应对这些问题？如果人类能找到长寿的办法，难道就没有可能找到解决这些问题的途径？

让我们继续看作者在第五段提供的负面信息。作者在这一段主要提供与社会有关的信息：

Immortality would also influence how society develops and progresses. As the population grew older, there would be more resistance to progress, and societies would become less dynamic. Imagine if everyone from the 18th century were still alive today. Chances are that racial segregation would still exist, gender discrimination would still be common and women wouldn't have any rights. Older generations need to die in order to let the

---

[1] https://www.ldoceonline.com/dictionary/problem.

younger generation breathe life into new concepts and allow society to progress; in a brave new "immortal" world, older people could continue to fend off innovation in favour of the status quo. "A new scientific truth does not succeed by convincing its opponents and making them see the light," said Nobel physicist Max Planck, the father of quantum mechanics, "but rather because its opponents eventually die and a new generation grows up that is familiar with the idea from the beginning."

长寿对发展和进步的影响自然是大问题。作者提出了两点：resistance to progress 和 less dynamic。他提供的信息能支撑这两个观点吗？

作者提出，如果人长生不老，会产生两个社会问题：①racial segregation would still exist；②gender discrimination would still be common，因为老年人因循守旧，冥顽不化。然而，racial segregation 和 gender discrimination 是老人造成的问题吗？或者说这些问题会因为怀有种族隔离和性别歧视的人死了以后自然消失吗？为了证明自己的观点，作者引用了 Nobel physicist Max Planck 的话：

"A new scientific truth does not succeed by convincing its opponents and making them see the light, but rather because its opponents eventually die and a new generation grows up that is familiar with the idea from the beginning."

Planck 的这段话现在被称为是 "Planck's Principle"。我们在理解这段话的时候要考虑具体语境。如果查阅科学发展史，尤其是 20 世纪和 21 世纪科学日新月异的飞速发展状况，科学的发展真的是因为老一代人死后才实现的吗？

作者在第六段提供了正面信息。特别要注意两点：① 有关长寿的正面信息是否对负面信息有回应？ ② 作者呈现的负面信息大多属于事实主张（factual claim）。作者的正面信息是否也属于事实陈述呢？

> Yet those in favour of immortality projects argue that <u>it's unethical to condemn</u> everyone to death when the possibility of indefinite life exists. Modern medicine cures diseases and keeps people in the prime of life for as long as possible; surely, they argue, immortality is the next logical step? People <u>could</u> explore endless possibilities, witness how the human race evolves and dedicate themselves to doing good. Supporters don't believe that the novelty of life <u>might</u> one day wear off. They don't consider that once we have passed all the milestones in life and crossed everything off our bucket lists, we could be condemned to a terrible fate: an eternity of boredom.

不难发现，这里的信息与负面信息并没有形成对应关系，而且作者这里提出的只是价值主张（value claim）——"it's unethical to ..."。价值主张的依据不是事实，而是观点。对负面事实不否定，而采用价值判断，这意味着对负面事实的默认。could 和 might 这两个具有不确定意味的情态动词也暗示了作者的立场。

负面后果的陈述基本没有陈述主体，给人以一般事实陈述的印象。不同的是，这一段几乎所有的陈述都有陈述主体。作者的用词暗示了这些主体的局限性：

Those in favour of ...

Surely, they argue ...

Supporters don't believe ...

They don't consider ...

以部分人的观点去挑战前面似乎是普通接受的事实主张，孰优孰劣自然毋庸多言了。另外，几个否定句式也耐人寻味，很是有这些人拒绝思考的含义。

在课文的最后一段，作者终于亮出了自己的观点：

Today, it is not only Dmitry Itskov who is promising the gift of immortality to his clients; scientific research is also uncovering nature's secrets of longevity. Living forever really is a matter of life and death and the problems it creates cannot be easily shrugged off. Ultimately, by accepting that life is limited and cannot be sustained indefinitely, we're able to give more value to the time we have, and to think carefully about how we are using it and what we hope to achieve, because we might not get another chance. As a wise man once said, "The bad news is, time flies. The good news is, you're the pilot."

作者在这段的第一句话强调了科学介入所造成的威胁。作者在陈述自己观点的时候把假设中的问题当成既成事实：

Living forever really is a matter of life and death and the problems it creates cannot be easily shrugged off.

他给出的忠告是，如果生命是有限的，我们会对生命倍加珍惜：

Ultimately, by accepting that life is limited and cannot be sustained indefinitely, we're able to give more value to the time we have, and to think carefully about how we are using it and what we hope to achieve, because we might not get another chance.

　　且不说历史和现实残酷地告诉我们，有限的生命并不能使前面列举的负面问题消失。假如作者的逻辑成立，这是否意味着生命越有限我们就越珍惜，生活的问题就越少呢？现代医学是否有必要进一步发展呢？

　　作者最后用 Michael Altshuler 的一句名言结束课文。Michael Altshuler 不仅是励志演讲人，也是 The Believe & Achieve Tour 网站的缔造者①。耐人寻味的是，作者在提信息源时没有给出 Altshuler 名字，却用了 a wise man 这个词语。这个词语一方面表明作者对引言的肯定，另一方面它也赋予 Altshuler 泛化了的权威，这对读者的影响自然也不同：

"The bad news is, time flies. The good news is, you're the pilot."

　　然而，如果 Michael Altshuler 这句话成立，那长生不老的人为什么就不可以是时间的驾驶员呢？

本章推荐书目

[1] Biber, D., Johansson, S., Leech, G., Conrad, S. and Finegan, E. 1999. *Longman Grammar of Spoken and Written English*. London: Longman.

[2] Englebretson, R. (Ed.). 2007. *Stancetaking in Discourse: Subjectivity, Evaluation, Interaction*. Amsterdam: John Benjamins.

[3] Jaffe, A. (Ed.). 2009. *Stance: Sociolinguistic Perspective*. Oxford: Oxford University Press.

① http://www.believeandachievetour.org/michael-altshuler-bio.html.

参考文献

［1］黄国文.语篇分析概要［M］.长沙：湖南教育出版社，1988.

［2］廖秋忠.廖秋忠文集［M］.北京：北京语言学院出版社，1992.

［3］曲卫国.话语文体学导论：文本分析的方法［M］.上海：复旦大学出版社，2009.

［4］曲卫国.思辨与明理——高中英语议论文写作教学指导［M］.上海：上海教育出版社，2021.

［5］Attridge, D. 2017. *The Singularity of Literature*. London: Routledge.

［6］Baker, P. and S. Ellece. 2011. *Key Terms in Discourse Analysis*. London: Continuum.

［7］Biancarosa, G. and C. Snow. 2006. *Reading Next — A Vision for Action and Research in Middle and High School Literacy: A report to Carnegie Corporation of New York*. 2nd Edition. Washington DC: Alliance for Excellent Education.

［8］Biber, D., Johansson, S., Leech, G., Conrad, S. and Finegan, E. 1999. *Longman Grammar of Spoken and Written English*. London: Longman.

［9］Bluestein, N. A. 2010. Unlocking Text Features for Determining Importance in Expository Text: A Strategy for Struggling Readers. *The Reading Teacher*. 63(7): 597–600.

［10］Brown, A. L. 1980. Metacognitive Development and Reading. In. R. J. Spiro, B. C. Bruce and W. F. Brewer. (Eds.). *Theoretical Issues in Reading Comprehension*. Hillsdale, NJ: Lawrence Erlbaum.

［11］Brown, G. and G. Yule. 1983. *Discourse Analysis*. Cambridge: Cambridge University Press.

［12］Chafe, W. 1994. *Discourse, Consciousness, and Time: The flow and displacement of conscious experience in speaking and writing*. Chicago: University of Chicago Press.

［13］Clark, H. H. and T. B. Carlson. 1981. Context for Comprehension. In. J. Long and A. Baddeley. (Eds.). *Attention and Performance IX*. Hillsdale, NJ: Lawrence Erlbaum.

［14］De Certeau, M. 1984. *The Practice of Everyday Life*. Berkeley: University of California Press.

［15］Duffy, G. G. 2009. *Explaining Reading: A Resource for Teaching Concepts, Skills, and Strategies*. 2nd Edition. New York: The Guilford Press.

［16］Duranti, A. and C. Goodwin. (Eds.). 1992. *Rethinking Context: Language as an Interactive Phenomenon*. Cambridge: Cambridge University Press.

［17］Durkin, D. 1978−1979. What Classroom Observations Reveal about Reading Comprehension Instruction. *Reading Research Quarterly*. 14 (4)：481−533.

［18］Eco, U. 1990. *The Limits of Interpretation*. Bloomington and Indianapolis: Indiana University Press.

［19］Englebretson, R. (Ed.). 2007. *Stancetaking in Discourse: Subjectivity, Evaluation, Interaction*. Amsterdam: John Benjamins.

［20］Fairclough, N. 1995. *Media Discourse*. London: Bloomsbury Academic.

［21］Fischer, F. 2003. *Reframing Public Policy: Discursive Politics and Deliberative Practices*. New York: Oxford University Press.

［22］Goffman, E. 1981. *Forms of Talk*. Oxford: Blackwell.

［23］Gumperz, J. J. 1982. *Discourse Strategies*. Cambridge: Cambridge University Press.

［24］Hall, S. 1999. Encoding/Decoding. In. S. During. (Ed.). *The Cultural Studies Reader*. London: Routledge, 507−517.

［25］Halliday, M. A. K. 1967. Notes on Transitivity and Theme in English. *Journal of Linguistics*. 3: 37−81.

［26］Halliday, M.A.K. and R. Hasan. 1976. *Cohesion in English*. London: Longman.

［27］Harvey, S. and A. Goudvis. 2017. *Strategies That Work: Teaching Comprehension for Engagement, Understanding, and Building*

Knowledge, Grades K-8. 3rd Edition. London: Routledge.

［28］ Hoey, M. 2000. *Patterns of Lexis in Text.* 上海：上海外语教育出版社.

［29］ Hoey, M. 2005. *Lexical Priming: A New Theory of Words and Language*. London: Routledge.

［30］ Hymes, D. 1964. Introduction: Toward Ethnographies of Communication. *American Anthropologist*. 66(6): 1–34.

［31］ Irvine, J. T. 2009. Stance in a Colonial Encounter: How Mr. Taylor Lost His Footing. In. A. Jaffe. (Ed.). *Stance: Sociolinguistic Perspective*. Oxford: Oxford University Press, 53–71.

［32］ Jaffe, A. (Ed.). 2009. *Stance: Sociolinguistic Perspective*. Oxford: Oxford University Press.

［33］ Jameson, F. 1981. *The Political Unconscious: Narrative as a Socially Symbolic Act*. Ithaca, NY: Cornell University Press.

［34］ Krifka, M. 2000. Focus. In. R. A. Wilson and F. C. Keil. (Eds.). *The MIT Encyclopedia of Cognitive Sciences*. 上海：上海外语教育出版社，315–317.

［35］ Kuno, S. 1976. The Speaker's Empathy and Its Effect on Syntax: A Reexamination of Yura and Kureru in Japanese. *The Journal of the Association of Teachers of Japanese*. 11(2/3): 249–271.

［36］ Labov, W. 1997. Some Further Steps in Narrative Analysis. *Journal of Narrative and Life History*. 7 (1–4): 395–415.

［37］ Liddicoat, A. J. 2007. *An Introduction to Conversation Analysis*. London: Continuum.

［38］ McCarthy, M. and R. Carter. 1994. *Language as Discourse: Perspectives for Language Teaching*. London: Longman.

［39］ Meyer, B. J. F. 1975. *The Organization of Prose and Its Effects on Memory*. New York: North-Holland.

［40］ Meyer, B. J. F. and M. N. Ray. 2011. Structure strategy interventions: Increasing reading comprehension of expository text. *International Electronic Journal of Elementary Education*. 4(1):127–152.

［41］ Montgomery, A., A. Durant, N. Fabb, T. Furniss and S. Mills. 1992. *Ways*

of Reading: Advanced Reading Skills for Students of English Literature.
London: Routledge.

[42] Moreillon, J. 2007. *Collaborative Strategies for Teaching Reading
Comprehension: Maximizing Your Impact.* Chicago: American Library
Association.

[43] Morgan, N. 2013. *Blame My Brain: The Amazing Teenage Brain
Revealed.* London: Walker Books.

[44] Murphy, M. L. 2003. *Semantic Relations and the Lexicon.* Cambridge:
Cambridge University Press.

[45] Nuttall, C. 1996. *Teaching Reading Skills in a Foreign Language.*
Oxford: Heinemann.

[46] Paltridge, B. 2012. *Discourse Analysis: An Introduction.* London:
Bloomsbury.

[47] Porter, J. E. 1986. Intertextuality and the Discourse Community. *Rhetoric
Review.* 5(1): 34–47.

[48] Ricoeur, P. 1976. *Interpretation Theory: Discourse and the Surplus of
Meaning.* Fort Worth, Texas: Texas Christian University Press.

[49] Roehling, J. V., M. Herbert, J. R. Nelson and J. J. Bohaty. 2017. Text
Structure Strategies for Improving Expository Reading Comprehension.
The Reading Teacher. 71(1): 71–82.

[50] Rosenblatt, L. M. 1994. *The Reader, the Text, the Poem: The
Transactional Theory of the Literary Work.* Carbondale and Edwardsville:
Southern Illinois University Press.

[51] Rottenberg, A. and D. H. Winchell. 2017. *Elements of Argument: A Text
and Reader.* 12th Edition. Boston: Bedford/St. Martin's.

[52] Simpson, P. 1993. *Language, Ideology and Point of View.* London:
Routledge.

[53] Smith, B. D. 1995. *Breaking through: College Reading.* 4th Edition. New
York: Harper Collins.

[54] Smith, F. 2004. *Understanding Reading: A Psycholinguistic Analysis
of Reading and Learning to Read.* 6th Edition. Mahwah, NJ: Lawrence

Erlbaum.

[55] Snow, C. 2002. *Reading for Understanding: Toward an R & D Program in Reading Comprehension*. Santa Monica: RAND Education.

[56] Snow, C. E., Burns, M. S. and P. Griffin. (Eds.). 1998. *Preventing Reading Difficulties in Young Children*. Washington, DC: National Academy Press.

[57] Sperber, D. and D. Wilson. 1995. *Relevance: Communication and Cognition*. Oxford: Blackwell.

[58] Swales, J. M. 1990. *Genre Analysis: English in Academic and Research Settings*. Cambridge: Cambridge University Press.

[59] Swales, J. M. 2004. *Research Genres: Explorations and Applications*. Cambridge: Cambridge University Press.

[60] Todorov, T. 1990. *Genres in Discourse*. Tr. C. Porter. Cambridge: Cambridge University Press.

[61] Vacca, R. T. , Mraz, M. and J. A. L. Vacca. 2021. *Content Area Reading: Literacy and Learning Across the Curriculum*. 13th Edition. Hobken, NJ: Pearson.

[62] Van Dijk, T. 2008. *Discourse and Context: A sociocognitive approach*. Cambridge: Cambridge University Press.

[63] Van Dijk, T. 1977. *Text and Context: Explorations in the Semantics and Pragmatics of Discourse*. London: Longman.

附录 1：沪教版高中《英语》Reading 目录及引用章节

《普通高中教科书　英语　必修第一册》

Unit 1　Life in a day（第二章　阅读与阅读教学；第三章　语境；第四章　视角）

Unit 2　Where history comes alive（第五章　语篇结构Ⅰ：信息结构）

Unit 3　The good, the bad and the really ugly（第三章　语境）

Unit 4　The 1940s house（第三章　语境）

《普通高中教科书　英语　必修第二册》

Unit 1　Blame your brain（第三章　语境；第四章　视角；第六章　语篇结构Ⅱ：话题结构和主题结构）

Unit 2　An experiment in education（第四章　视角）

Unit 3　Going global（第三章　语境）

Unit 4　An excerpt from *The Old Man and the Sea*（第三章　语境；第六章　语篇结构Ⅱ：话题结构和主题结构）

《普通高中教科书　英语　必修第三册》

Unit 1　Journalists on the job（第四章　视角）

Unit 2　The story of a T-shirt（第四章　视角；第七章　语篇的词汇关系）

Unit 3　Ideal beauty（第五章　语篇结构Ⅰ：信息结构）

Unit 4　A road less travelled（第七章　语篇的词汇关系；第八章　体裁：叙事类）

《普通高中教科书　英语　选择性必修第一册》

Unit 1　Is chocolate the answer?（第四章　视角；第七章　语篇的词汇关系）

Unit 2　Island story（第六章　语篇结构Ⅱ：话题结构和主题结构）

Unit 3　The influencers（第四章　视角；第九章　体裁：非叙事类）

Unit 4   A question of taste（第六章   语篇结构Ⅱ：话题结构和主题结构；第九章   体裁：非叙事类）

《普通高中教科书   英语   选择性必修第二册》
Unit 1   Finding one's true vocation（第四章   视角）
Unit 2   A day in the life of a digital human（第十章   立场）
Unit 3   The stories behind the names
Unit 4   The Last Leaf（第八章   体裁：叙事类）

《普通高中教科书   英语   选择性必修第三册》
Unit 1   Making school meaningful（第十章   立场）
Unit 2   The stuff in our lives（第十章   立场）
Unit 3   Searching for balance in life
Unit 4   Words, words, words.（第四章   视角）

《普通高中教科书   英语   选择性必修第四册》
Unit 1   Now in the news
Unit 2   From here to eternity（第十章   立场）
Unit 3   Would you eat it?
Unit 4   The next big thing

附录 2：各章引用的材料

第二章　阅读与阅读教学

Life in a day

A healthy mind in a healthy body

A new way of eating: online food delivery services

The rose family

第三章　语境

I wandered lonely as a cloud

An excerpt from *The Old Man and the Sea*

Life in a day

The 1940s house

Going global

The good, the bad and the really ugly

An excerpt from *A Walk in the Woods*

第四章　视角

The confusing way Mexicans tell time

Finding one's true vocation

The influencers

Blame your brain

The story of a T-shirt

The Road Not Taken

Journalists on the job

Life in a day

An experiment in education

第五章　语篇结构Ⅰ：信息结构

Where history comes alive

Ideal beauty

An excerpt from *A Walk in the Woods*

第六章　语篇结构Ⅱ：话题结构和主题结构

A word is dead

A kiss

An excerpt from *The Old Man and the Sea*

Island story

Blame your brain

第七章　语篇的词汇关系

A road less travelled

The rose family

Is chocolate the answer?

The story of a T-shirt

第八章　体裁：叙事类

This is just to say

I wandered lonely as a cloud

The Last Leaf

A road less travelled

第九章　体裁：非叙事类

A question of taste

The influencers

Is chocolate the answer?

第十章　立场

Making school meaningful

The stuff in our lives

A day in the life of a digital human

From here to eternity